Economic Policy, Exchange Rates, and the International System

Economic Policy, Exchange Rates, and the International System

W. MAX CORDEN

OXFORD UNIVERSITY PRESS

1994

Oxford University Press, Walton Street, Oxford OX2 6DP

Oxford is a trade mark of Oxford University Press

Published in the United States by The University of Chicago Press,
Chicago 60637

This book is a revision of *Inflation, Exchange Rates, and the
World Economy*, Third Edition

British Library Cataloguing in Publication Data
Data available

Library of Congress Cataloging in Publication Data
Corden, W. M. (Warner Max)
Economic policy, exchange rates, and the international economy /
W. Max Corden.
p. cm.
Includes bibliographical references.
1. International finance. 2. Foreign exchange rates.
3. Economic policy. I. Title.
HG3881.G6738 1994 332'.042—dc20 94–20621
ISBN 0–19–877408–7
ISBN 0–19–877409–5 (Pbk)

Set by Hope Services (Abingdon) Ltd.
Printed in Great Britain
on acid-free paper by
Biddles Ltd.
Guildford & King's Lynn

PREFACE

THIS book originated in a plan to write a fourth edition of *Inflation, Exchange Rates, and the World Economy*, the third edition of which appeared in 1985. But I ended up writing a new and bigger book, so that it has a new title. I have maintained the rather personal style of the earlier book, but added many more appendices with diagrams.

Chapters 2 and 3 are rewritten and improved versions of two chapters in the earlier book, since these have been very popular. Chapter 11 is also an expanded version of a chapter of that book. Otherwise the book is essentially new, though three chapters (8, 10, 13) deal with topics that also had a chapter each in the earlier book, and little bits of the earlier book (including the main theme of Chapter 10) appear here and there. I have not dealt with two topics that some might expect to find here, namely, the developing country debt crisis and the economics of transition from socialism. These seemed to me too big to deal with adequately in a book that aimed to be fairly brief. On the other hand, I have let myself go on the European Monetary System and proposals for monetary integration.

I am greatly indebted to John Black, Vijay Joshi, and Jim Riedel for their helpful comments on drafts of various chapters. I owe a particular debt to Flora Paoli for patiently correcting and expertly editing the products of my word processor. For four years I have taught a course at the Paul H. Nitze School of Advanced International Studies (SAIS) where I have used the earlier book, along with much else, and the reactions and interests of my students have influenced this book. For a year I test-marketed Chapter 11 with them.

This book was written at SAIS and at Merton College, Oxford. I had the privilege of holding a Visiting Research Fellowship at Merton College during Trinity Term 1993. The book made fantastic progress in the beautiful environment of this College, and I am most grateful to the Warden and Fellows of Merton.

Washington DC W.M.C.
December 1993

CONTENTS

LIST OF FIGURES

LIST OF TABLES

ABBREVIATIONS

BIS	Bank for International Settlements
CAP	Common Agricultural Policy
DM	Deutschmark
ECB	European Central Bank
ECU	European Currency Unit
EMS	European Monetary System
EMU	European Monetary Union
ERM	Exchange Rate Mechanism
GATT	General Agreement on Tariffs and Trade
GDP	Gross Domestic Product
G-3	United States, Germany, Japan
G-7	The major industrial countries: United States, Germany, Japan, Canada, France, Italy, United Kingdom
IMF	International Monetary Fund
LDC	Less Developed Country
OECD	Organization for Economic Cooperation and Development
ROW	Rest of the World

1

Introduction

THIS book deals with central issues in international macroeconomics. The topics are chosen on the basis of their importance for policy, not their theoretical complexity, though occasional complexity could not be avoided. Chapters 2 and 10 are quite basic to the book, but other chapters can be read selectively as independent essays, even though common themes recur. The appendices, with their diagrams, give more rigorous expositions of some topics dealt with purely verbally in the main text.

I. AN OVERVIEW

The first six chapters look at exchange rate policy, the current account, the external effects of fiscal policy, and related matters from the point of view of an individual country. This is often called open economy macroeconomics. Much of the analysis in this part of the book makes the "small country assumption" which can be reasonably applied to all countries other than the United States, Germany, and Japan (the G-3). But this approach also provides the foundation for large country analysis, which is taken up mostly in Chapter 11. The key chapter—which expounds the classic concepts of absorption and switching in terms of the dependent economy model—is Chapter 2. I focus on domestic distributional effects of various policies and shocks in Chapter 3 and pay particular attention—as also elsewhere in this book—to the degree of nominal and real wage rigidity. Many of the issues discussed arise continuously in developing countries. This concerns, above all, the discussion of inflation in Chapter 5. Chapter 6 examines whether a current account deficit is necessarily a problem for a country.

Europe has provided the most adventurous developments and proposals in the international monetary system since the breakdown of Bretton Woods in 1973. Hence, Chapters 7, 8, and 9 discuss the European Monetary System, the theory of monetary integration, and the European proposals to move to monetary union.

Chapters 10 to 13 deal with the post-Bretton Woods managed-floating, high-capital-mobility international system where the United States is at the center. The key chapter here is Chapter 10, where I give my interpretation of the essential *laissez-faire* nature of the system. Chapter 11 expounds in detail how a fiscal or a monetary disturbance in one large country is transmitted to other countries when the exchange rate floats. This is the most taxonomic and rigorous chapter in the book. Chapter 12—on the reasons why floating exchange rates move the way they do—and Chapter 13—on the coordination of macroeconomic policies—deal with topics where there is a vast academic literature. I have sought to summarize and clarify here, as well as suggesting new approaches in Chapter 13.

Chapters 14 and 15 deal with topics that are not usually included in international monetary economics. Chapter 14 outlines the relationship between protection and macroeconomic variables, especially the exchange rate. Chapter 15 deals with the popular and often muddled concept of competitiveness. I show that there are three possible interpretations of the concept, and also examine the possible effects of foreign growth on a country's competitiveness.

Finally, Chapter 16 discusses the future of the international monetary system, and especially exchange rate arrangements. It looks critically at various reform proposals. The main conclusion is that high and still-growing international capital mobility will make the maintenance of fixed-but-adjustable exchange rate arrangements less and less practical.

II. SOME BASIC FACTS

This book is primarily analytical, and does not profess to present in any detail, if at all, the main facts about the issues discussed here, nor the results of econometric research. But some basic facts are required as background. These can be described as six stylized facts applying to the thirteen years from 1980 to 1993.

(1) *Increasing Capital Market Integration*

The single most important development has been the increasing integration of the world capital market. This is explained by financial liberalization in all the major industrial and some other countries; by the removal of exchange controls on capital account transactions—controls which, in any case, had become more and more difficult to enforce; by decreases in the costs of telecommunications, information-gathering, and processing; by the institutionalization of savings; and by a whole range of improvements that have made markets more liquid and more internationally minded. International portfolio investment has increased. For example, there has been a striking increase between 1986 and 1991 in cross-border ownership of equities and of tradable securities.

The growth of the international capital market—which goes back to the 1960s—made possible the transfer of the surplus funds of some oil exporters to middle-income developing countries in the 1970s and large borrowings by other oil-exporting countries, notably Mexico and Venezuela, after the second oil shock, both of which led to the developing country debt crisis. The international capital market also made possible the large current account imbalances among developed countries in the 1980s, which I note below.

On the other hand, world capital market integration has a long way to go yet, as there is still a strong home bias in allocation of funds. For example, the 300 largest pension funds in the world have only about seven per cent of their assets denominated in foreign currency instruments. US investors hold about 94 per cent of their equity holdings in US securities. Exchange controls remain in many developing countries.

Integration is very high for short-term liquid financial instruments traded in the major financial centers. There is a huge pool of liquid internationally mobile capital. These funds move around in the light of interest rate differentials and exchange rate expectations and—as I shall discuss in several later chapters—make it difficult, if not impossible, for monetary authorities in developed (industrial) countries to maintain fixed-but-adjustable exchange rate regimes. International capital mobility plays a role right through this book, but I shall discuss it more specifically in Chapters 12 and 16. One question is whether it would be possible or desirable to re-introduce exchange controls on international capital movements in the industrial countries.

I shall make use of the concept of "perfect capital mobility", an extreme case useful for simple models. This does not mean that the international capital market is assumed to be fully integrated, but rather, that there are enough liquid funds free to move around to ensure uncovered interest rate parity, that is, that any excess of the domestic over the foreign short-term interest rate is equal to the expected rate of depreciation of the domestic currency on an annual basis.

(2) *The Up-and-Down of the Dollar*

Fig. 1.1 shows how the real exchange rate of the dollar moved from 1979 to 1993. It rose by 50 per cent from 1979 to February 1985, this increase being explained by a somewhat similar appreciation of the trade-weighted nominal exchange rate. By 1987 it was back where it had been in 1979 and after that, up to 1993, it fell another 20 per cent or so, though more gradually. This remarkable up-and-down of the dollar relative to other major currencies, especially the yen and the DM, is discussed in detail in Chapter 12. The experience of the dollar underlies numerous proposals for macroeconomic policy coordination and for stabilizing exchange rates discussed in Chapters 13 and 16.

(3) *Big Current Account Imbalances*

The United States developed a large current account deficit, beginning in 1983 and reaching a peak of $167 billion in 1987. The deficit practically disappeared in the recession year of 1991, but was back to over $100 billion in 1993. The United States had experienced deficits before, for example in 1977 and 1978, but never of this magnitude relative to US GDP. The second column of Table 1.1 shows average imbalances for the eight years from 1983 to 1990. The two countries with large surpluses were Japan and Germany, while significant deficits were also run by Canada, France, Italy, and Britain, the four other members of the Group of Seven (G-7)—the world's seven largest economies at the time.

To put the figures in Table 1.1 in perspective, the average US current account deficit of over $100 billion during the period 1983 to 1990 was about 2.5 per cent of US GDP. It can also be

Fig. 1.1. Real Effective Exchange Rate of US Dollar
"Effective" means trade-weighted.
Source: Bank for International Settlements, *Annual Report* 1993.

TABLE 1.1. Current Account Balances
($US billion annual averages)

	1980–82	1983–90
United States	0	− 102.6
Japan	0	+ 56.3
Germany	− 4.1	+ 34.0
Other G-7[a]	− 7.8	− 29.2
LDC fuel exporters[b]	+ 37.7	− 13.6
LDC non-fuel exporters	− 72.6	− 9.7
World		
(statistical discrepancy)	− 67.2	− 84.3

[a] Canada, France, Italy, United Kingdom.

[b] Developing countries where the value of fuel (mostly oil) exports exceeded 50% of total exports 1984–6.

Source: International Monetary Fund, *World Economic Outlook*, 1988, 1991, 1993.

seen from Table 1.1 that from 1980 to 1982—that is, after the second oil shock in 1979—the big current account imbalances were within the developing world. Oil exporters ran surpluses and many others ran deficits. Japan was in deficit in 1980 but back to surpluses in 1981 and 1982. Germany went into deficit from 1991, owing to the costs of German reunification.

The last line of Table 1.1 shows that apparently the world was in large current account deficit. This reflects a statistical discrepancy, which is huge in aggregate, and about 3 per cent of world exports of goods and service. It is explained by the difficulty of measuring current accounts. Thus the statistics overstate the various deficits and understate the surpluses. Hence one should treat all these current account figures with some reserve. The discrepancy is to be found mainly in service and transfer transactions, especially portfolio income, and not in trade statistics. It seems that debtor countries are more likely to recognize payments they make than creditors are to recognize and report receipts. There is also a problem with shipping data.

(4) *Declining Inflation and Two Recessions*

During the thirteen years there have been two recessions. The first column of Table 1.2 shows average annual growth rates of all industrial (developed) countries. Looking at the whole group, there was only one year of real recession, namely 1982, though 1980, 1981, 1991, and 1992 were years of "growth recessions" when growth rates were low relative to the moderately good years 1983 to 1990. The years of negative growth for the United States were 1980, 1982, and 1991, for Germany 1982 and 1993, and for Japan 1993. Britain had four negative growth years, France one (1993), and Italy none. The recession of 1980 to 1982 could be readily explained by tight monetary policies, while the recession of the early 1990s is a more complex story. Broadly speaking, in the United States and Canada, it was caused by a decline in private sector aggregate demand, rather than by a monetary contraction.

The main implication of these recurring recessions is that, at least in the short run, output does depend to some extent on variations in nominal demand. In general, I assume in this book that Keynesian expansionist or contractionist policies can have significant short-term effects.

TABLE 1.2. Growth Rates and Inflation
(%)

	Industrial countries		Developing countries
	Growth rate	Inflation	Growth rate
1970–9 (average)	3.3	8.1	5.6
1980	1.3	9.4	3.4
1981	1.5	8.8	1.6
1982	− 0.3	7.2	1.6
1983–90 (average)	3.4	4.1	4.4
1991	0.5	4.4	4.5
1992	1.7	3.1	5.8
1993 (estimated)	1.1	2.6	6.1

Source: International Monetary Fund, *World Economic Outlook*, 1988, 1991, 1993.

The second column of Table 1.2 shows that inflation in industrial countries had dropped drastically by 1993 compared with the years up to 1982. This was undoubtedly the result of anti-inflation oriented monetary policies and, in the case of France and Italy, a commitment to the exchange rate arrangement of the European Monetary System. In the United States the decline began in 1982. Right through the period policy-makers in the G-7 countries other than the United States were preoccupied either with a fear that earlier high inflation rates would recur or with efforts to get inflation down further.

(5) *The Debt Crisis and Adjustment by Developing Countries*

The developing country debt crisis, affecting mainly a group of middle-income developing countries, resulted from excessive borrowing from 1975 to 1981 and developed suddenly in 1982. For many countries the whole of the 1980s was dominated by the painful process of adjustment. I do not deal with it in this book, nor with various proposals for debt reduction. This subject is a big one on its own. But the first five chapters of this book, especially Chapters 2 and 3, are all about the adjustment process for a small price-taking economy. These chapters could be regarded as an introduction to open economy macroeconomics for developing countries.

Table 1.1 shows that the average current account deficit of non-oil less developed countries (LDCs) fell from nearly $70 billion a year in the three years 1980 to 1982, to about $10 billion a year in the eight years 1983 to 1990. This gives some indication of the adjustments they had to make. In Table 1.2 the relatively high growth rates of developing countries as a whole were very much influenced by high growth rates in east and south-east Asia. The average growth rate of Western Hemisphere developing countries was less than 2 per cent from 1983 to 1990, while 1982 was a year of 1 per cent negative growth. Per capita growth figures were even less, and about zero on average from 1983 to 1990. For countries defined by the IMF as "countries with recent debt servicing difficulties", the ratio of external debt to GDP fell from 57 per cent in 1988 to 43 per cent in 1993, and for Western Hemisphere countries, from 51 per cent to 37.5 per cent.

Table 1.2 does not give inflation rates for developing countries since aggregate figures would be meaningless when there are vast differences between countries. Inflation was a major issue in many Latin American countries, and Latin American experiences have influenced the content of Chapter 5, which deals with inflation.

A feature of 1990 to 1993 was substantial private capital inflow, in the form of direct and portfolio investment, into some developing countries. This went not only to Asian countries, but also to several Latin American countries that had gone through the debt crisis, notably Mexico and Argentina. Capital inflow was associated with real appreciations of their currencies and a return of current account deficits, explained this time not by fiscal deficits but by private sector spending booms. Episodes of this kind raise important issues—the "real appreciation problem" and the significance of current account deficits—discussed at length in Chapters 4 and 6.

(6) *Rise and Fall of the European Monetary System*

Finally, the European Monetary System (EMS) has been embodied within the world-wide floating exchange rate non-system. It operated from 1979 and suffered two major crises, one in September 1992 and the other in August 1993. Chapter 7 describes the system and its history in some detail.

REFERENCES

Detailed up-to-date information and statistics on developments in the world economy can be found in the *World Economic Outlook* of the International Monetary Fund (IMF), the *Economic Outlook* of the Organization for Economic Cooperation and Development (OECD), both published biennially, and the *Annual Report* of the Bank for International Settlements (BIS). These publications include thorough analyses of many of the issues discussed in this book.

Almost all figures cited throughout this book come from the *World Economic Outlook* of the IMF, mostly the October 1993 issue.

On the growing integration of world capital markets and problems of measuring the degree of integration, see Goldstein and Mussa (1994), and also Frankel (1993, Ch. 2) and Obstfeld (1994). Developments in international capital markets are regularly described and analyzed in the annual *International Capital Markets* publication of the IMF and in the *Annual Reports* of the BIS. Facts given in the text come from Goldstein and Mussa (1994) and the IMF.

The current account discrepancy has been carefully analyzed by an IMF working party. See International Monetary Fund (1987a). A summary of the results is in International Monetary Fund (1987b).

Open Economy Macroeconomics

2

A Model of Balance-of-Payments Policy

THIS chapter presents the most basic model of balance-of-payments policy. It is inevitably oversimplified, but provides the foundation for much that follows later. Indeed, for all its limitations, it is an essential tool in the economic policy field. It is further developed in the next chapter, where various limitations are discussed.

It has to be said right from the beginning that the model is basically Keynesian in construction since it assumes that a nominal policy instrument can have real effects, at least for a limited period. It is a model for a single country; it is not a world model. It ignores the international repercussions of one country's policies so that it can be applied more directly to countries that are small in the world economy than to the three large economies—the United States, Germany, and Japan—though it provides a foundation for the more elaborate analysis that is appropriate for these three that is expounded in Chapter 11.

I. ABSORPTION AND SWITCHING[1]

Let us suppose, to start with, that the country concerned is running a deficit in the current account of its balance of payments. Its exchange rate is fixed, though adjustable. The deficit may be financed by running down its foreign exchange reserves, the government or central bank may be borrowing abroad to finance it, or it may be financed by net private capital inflow. For one reason or another, the deficit has to be reduced. Possibly new foreign capital has ceased to be available, or is getting very expensive, or the reserves are getting too low. Thus, the situation can be described as one of external imbalance. This does not mean that the deficit ought to be zero but only that it is higher

[1] Appendix 2.1 represents geometrically the main arguments of this passage.

than what, in the existing situation, is a target or external balance level.

At the same time, let us suppose that there is internal balance. This represents a particular level of demand for domestic factors of production—labor and capital—which can be described as full employment demand and which is thought of as a policy target here. At this level of demand, increased output of some industries can only be brought about by reducing the resources available to some other industries, and this resource shift will require some change in relative prices. Internal balance will be interpreted slightly differently in later chapters of the book, but I shall not anticipate here.

An important tool of analysis is the conceptual division of industries into those producing tradables and those producing non-tradables. Tradables consist of exportables and importables. Exportables, in turn, consist not only of actual exports but also of close substitutes for exports that are sold domestically, like beef sold to Argentineans or Toyotas sold to Japanese. Importables consist of imports as well as of goods produced domestically and sold domestically that are close substitutes for imports, that is, import-competing goods. These tradables have their domestic prices determined broadly by the world market, subject only to tariffs, export subsidies, international transport costs, and, of course, the exchange rate. Tradables include both visibles and invisibles. Finally, non-tradables consist of all those goods and services the prices of which are determined by supply and demand domestically. This category generally consists mainly of services. In practice the line between the two categories cannot be clearly drawn, since there are plenty of borderline goods and services the tradability of which depends on transport costs and is a matter of degree. But the conceptual distinction is useful.

Strictly, it is only valid to aggregate exportables and importables into a composite commodity—tradables—if their relative prices do not change. But this presents no problem here. I shall be assuming such a constant price ratio between exportables and importables until later in this chapter, and again in the next chapter. Thus the terms of trade facing the country are assumed to be unaffected by its various policies. This is the small-country assumption.

To return to the main argument, the domestic excess supply of exportables is equal to actual exports, while the domestic excess demand for importables is actual imports. Combining these two, the current account balance is zero if domestic excess demand for tradables is zero, and there is a current account deficit if the net excess demand is positive. We start in our present story with domestic excess demand for tradables.

At the same time I am assuming that there is initially equilibrium in the market for non-tradables, so that demand for non-tradables equals supply. Furthermore, total output and employment are at the internal balance levels. Combining tradables and non-tradables, there is aggregate excess demand. Demand is generated by expenditure on consumption and investment, private and public. This is absorption: the economy absorbs goods and services for these various purposes. Absorption exceeds the national output or supply. Income is derived from output. Hence absorption exceeds income, and, because it does so, there is a current account deficit.

The argument then goes as follows. The current account deficit has to be reduced, and possibly has to be eliminated completely. Hence there is a problem. An obvious remedy would be to reduce absorption by some kind of tightening in monetary or fiscal policy. Domestic demand for importables will then fall, and this will reduce imports; in addition, domestic demand for exportables will fall, and this will make more goods available for exports and so, to some extent, may increase exports. Excess demand for tradables can therefore certainly be eliminated if the cut in absorption is sufficient. But a reduction in absorption will also reduce demand for non-tradables. This is an unfortunate but inevitable by-product of this policy.

At this point a crucial assumption is introduced: the prices of non-tradables are rigid downwards. I shall reconsider this assumption in the next chapter, but it is a reasonable first approximation. Reduced demand will lead then, not to price cuts, but to excess supply, inventory accumulation, and eventually to reduced supply and unemployment. It must be remembered that relative prices have not changed, so that there is no inducement for resources to move out of non-tradables into the tradable-goods industries. Increased unemployment is thus inevitable. External balance has been attained at the cost of losing internal balance.

The next step is to point out that, if it is desired to attain two targets—external balance and internal balance—it is necessary to have *two* instruments. The absorption instrument is not enough. On its own it could not maintain the level of employment. The second instrument required is a switching policy. This is a policy that raises the domestic price of tradables relative to the price of non-tradables and so causes patterns of production and of absorption to switch. On the production side, resources will be induced to move out of production of non-tradables into the production of exportables and importables. This will reduce the excess supply of non-tradables, and so help to restore internal balance, and at the same time it will increase the supply of tradables, hence reducing excess demand there, and helping to improve the current account. On the demand side, the rise in the relative price of tradables will shift the pattern of absorption away from tradables and towards non-tradables, hence also reducing excess demand for tradables and excess supply of non-tradables.

A switching policy can therefore offset the effects of the absorption-reduction policy in the market for non-tradables. The reduction in absorption created excess supply of non-tradables, while switching eliminated it. Both the reduction in absorption and the switching policy reduced excess demand for tradables, and thus both improved the current account. It follows that when the reduction in absorption is associated with the right switching policy, the cut in absorption need not be as great as when the whole current account improvement has to be brought about by an absorption reduction on its own. If the current account balance were brought to zero, demand for tradables would be equal to supply of them. At the same time, demand for non-tradables will be equal to their supply. Thus, for the economy as a whole, absorption (expenditure) would eventually be equal to output (and hence income). If some current account deficit remains, absorption will finally still be greater than output.

We have seen that an absorption policy on its own would not be satisfactory because it would initially create excess supply of non-tradables. The supply of non-tradables would then decline until it became equal to the reduced demand, and unemployment would result. Similarly, a switching policy on its own would be no good. It could not succeed in improving the current account. To show this, let us imagine the relative price of tradables to go up as a consequence of a pure switching policy. In the first instance we can suppose demand for tradables to be reduced and supply to be increased, so improving the current account. But this is not the end of the story.

The market for non-tradables will be adversely affected. At constant absolute prices of non-tradables there will be excess demand for non-tradables as demand is switched towards them, while at the same time resources have been induced to move out of non-tradable production. Thus the prices of non-tradables will rise until excess demand for them has been eliminated. The reasonable assumption here is that the prices of non-tradables are flexible upwards, even though they are inflexible downwards. This price rise simply negates the initial switching policy. Finally, relative prices will have returned to where they started, and the original current account improvement will have been reversed. If the prices of non-tradables were somewhat inflexible upwards—not a very realistic assumption—there might in the first instance be some involuntary savings to match the excess demand, but eventually the excess demand would spill over on to tradables so, again, reversing the original current account improvement.

II. ROLE OF DEVALUATION

An alteration in the exchange rate is seen in this model as the major switching device. I am assuming that the country concerned is small, so that it faces given world prices for its imports and exports. Let us think of Mexico here. We suppose that the prices of the many goods it buys and of the oil and manufactured goods that it sells are constant in dollar terms, quite unaffected by Mexican supply, demand, or pricing policy. When the peso is devalued, the peso prices—i.e. the domestic prices—of the tradable goods go up. There will be a uniform percentage rise in the prices of all exportables and importables, including prices of exportables sold at home and prices of import-competing goods. In this simple model, tradable prices rise by the full extent of the devaluation. If the rate of pesos to the dollar has risen from 10 to 12 pesos, all tradable prices rise 20 per cent.

If the prices of non-tradables stay constant, there will then be a rise in the relative price of tradables, this relative price change bringing about the desired switching. It was noted earlier that the prices of non-tradables are assumed to be rigid downwards. But they are not assumed to be rigid upwards, so a rise in their prices must be avoided if the switching effect of the devaluation is not to be negated. Hence, there must be an appropriate reduction in absorption associated with the devaluation if the latter is to be effective as a current account-improving device.

Devaluation is seen in this approach as an exogenous or parametric policy device. There is a market for foreign exchange, and the central bank pegs the price in this market by buying or selling foreign exchange. If there is excess demand for foreign exchange (which is excess supply of the home currency, the peso) the price does not rise because the central bank is selling some of its foreign-exchange reserves. The bank then makes a policy decision to raise the price of foreign exchange, and this requires it to sell less in a given time period. The peso is thus devalued, and we study the effects of this devaluation on domestic production and absorption. In the presence of international capital mobility this matter is actually a little more complicated: essentially, monetary policy will be the instrument that determines the exchange rate. I shall return to this below. For the moment, it is sufficient to assume that, one way or another, policy can bring about a desired change in the exchange rate.

In this and later chapters I shall always refer to dollar prices as being foreign prices and peso prices as being domestic prices. Given the small-country assumption, a devaluation leaves dollar prices unchanged but raises peso prices of tradables. The peso price of tradables relative to non-tradables can be described as the real exchange rate. This is a useful definition, though not the only interpretation of this term. There is a real depreciation when this relative price rises, and a real appreciation when it falls. If the price of non-tradables is constant, a nominal depreciation will thus lead to a real depreciation, which is the assumption I have been making so far.

Devaluation has not only a relative price or switching effect. It may also have an effect on absorption. It may itself bring about some of the necessary disabsorption in our example. It is even conceivable that it brings about, by chance, all the disabsorption that is needed. Indeed, it may even overshoot the mark and produce too much disabsorption. I shall take this matter up again in Chapters 4 and 5, so I only deal with it briefly at this stage.

The simple point can be made as follows. Suppose that fiscal and monetary policy kept the level of nominal expenditure constant. This is sometimes suggested as a monetary policy target. It would result, for example, from a constant nominal money supply combined with an unchanged velocity of circulation. The devaluation would then have reduced real expenditure because it will have raised the average domestic price level. (The prices of tradables have risen while the prices of non-tradables have remained unchanged.) Thus, absorption in real terms will have fallen. Just looking at the demand side, the rise in the price of tradables, with total nominal expenditure constant, will lead to a rise in demand for non-tradables on account of a switching (substitution) effect and a fall on account of a disabsorption (income) effect.

The main point to note is that the appropriate disabsorption policy—i.e. fiscal or monetary policy, or both—must take into account whatever automatic disabsorption has already been brought about by the devaluation. This is a consideration which has tended to be underplayed in this approach. We have supposed that the appropriate disabsorption policy will take place, and have stressed the problems that arise if there is a failure to disabsorb sufficiently—or if there is too much disabsorption—but we have not focused on the details of the disabsorption policy and how much is brought about automatically by devaluation.

III. THE USEFULNESS OF THE BASIC MODEL

This basic model is undoubtedly very useful, and focuses on important matters that are not always clearly understood. It brings out a particular role for the exchange rate. Without disabsorption the current account cannot improve, and—in the case considered—a devaluation cannot improve the balance of payments, except perhaps temporarily and except insofar as it is allowed to have a disabsorption effect. But a devaluation conceived of as a switching device is still necessary because it makes it possible to avoid reducing employment and aggregate output while the disabsorption policy improves the current account.

It is particularly important to emphasize that, when one starts in internal balance, some disabsorption is necessary if the current account is to improve. The disabsorption represents a cut in real spending and thus, in a sense, is a sacrifice. To the extent that the devaluation itself brings about some disabsorption, it produces some of the sacrifice. A relative price change on its own—pure switching—may seem like a soft option, a gimmick that improves the current account and yet avoids real expenditure cuts. But this is shown to be wrong. If there is no disabsorption, there will be no improvement.

In many countries it is often suggested that a balance-of-payments problem should be dealt with by the imposition or tightening of import restrictions. Somehow it is thought that this can be painless. But a system of import quotas, like a devaluation, is a switching device. Both disabsorption and switching are likely to be needed. Yet, it has not always been realized that without the appropriate disabsorption—a politically painful process—import restrictions are unlikely to have any beneficial effects on the balance of payments, other than, perhaps, in the very short run. This, of course, leaves aside the large issue of the choice between import restrictions, whether in the form of quotas or tariffs, and devaluation.

The model improves on earlier models by distinguishing between tradables and non-tradables. The important switching effect of a devaluation comes about because the price ratio between these two categories of goods—the real exchange rate—is being altered. The terms of trade—i.e. the price ratio between exportables and importables—do not need to alter. In earlier models a devaluation usually worsened the terms of trade. This is certainly a possibility, as we shall see below—and it is highly likely in the case of large economies—but it is not inevitable.

IV. SOME SIMPLE EXTENSIONS OF THE BASIC MODEL

The model obviously needs to be applicable to a world of floating exchange rates and high capital mobility if it is to be currently relevant. Indeed, as I have already noted in Chapter 1, increasing international capital mobility has been the principal development in the world economy affecting exchange rates and current account balances since 1973. I shall use models with capital mobility in later chapters, so that what follows is very simplified. At this point one can show that absorption and switching can still be manipulated by policy when exchange rates float and capital mobility is high. The famous Mundell-Fleming model is the relevant one here.

Absorption would be reduced by fiscal contraction. A monetary contraction would also reduce absorption insofar as it managed to raise interest rates and thus restrict credit to the private sector. But if the economy is small in the world capital market and capital mobility is very high, a monetary contraction would have little or no effect on domestic interest rates and hence absorption. Fiscal policy alone could fill the role of managing absorption.

The role of monetary policy would be to manage the exchange rate. A monetary expansion would tend to lower interest rates, thus lead to short-term funds flowing into foreign currencies, and so depreciate the domestic currency. In the extreme case (sometimes called perfect capital mobility), the domestic interest rate could fall below the world interest rate only if an appreciation were expected. With static expectations, the domestic interest rate would be equal to the world interest rate, apart from any risk factor. Essentially, monetary policy would simply determine the exchange rate. A monetary contraction would appreciate the exchange rate. Thus, to simplify a little, fiscal policy could be targeted on absorption, and monetary policy on the exchange rate. Absorption and the exchange rate would be targeted on so-called internal and external balance.

The present model tells us that—*if* internal balance, however defined, is to be maintained—a change in a current account must be associated with an appropriate change in the real exchange rate, the latter brought about (given certain assumptions) by an appropriate change in the nominal exchange rate. That is the essence. For example, if the US budget deficit is expected to be reduced, and this is likely to reduce the current account deficit, there will also have to be real depreciation, which may have to be brought about by nominal depreciation. The converse also follows. If a real depreciation is desired or predicted, there will have to be a decline in absorption which, when capital is internationally highly mobile, would have to be brought about by fiscal contraction. The whole approach could be applied to a country which wishes to reduce a current account surplus rather than a deficit. In that case maintenance of internal balance would call for an increase in absorption, since switching alone in the form of real appreciation would lead to unemployment.

In Chapter 4 I shall discuss in detail the case where a country has an investment boom financed by capital inflow. It will thus run a current account deficit and, for the time that capital inflow is available, such a deficit could be described as external balance. In this case the movement from slack investment into investment boom and capital inflow would be associated with real appreciation.

One might balk at the concept of an importable good used in this type of model. This implies that import-competing goods are perfect substitutes for imports, so that the domestic prices of import-competing goods are fully determined by the domestic prices of imports. Because of product differentiation there is rarely such close substitutability. While it is a matter of degree, in principle one could assume that there is no domestic production of importables at all—that all are actually imported—and then one could include all import-competing goods in the non-tradable sector. This would change nothing in the basic analysis.

One should allow for changes in the composition of absorption. I assume here that monetary policy can affect absorption, which means that capital mobility is not too high. A given reduction in absorption can be obtained with various combinations of fiscal and monetary policies—some increases in personal-income tax, some increases in corporate tax, some decreases in government spending, some credit contraction to the housing sector, and so on. But changing the mix of these policies may have a switching effect. For example, if the non-tradable content in housing expenditures is greater than in spending out of corporate profits, a shift in the pattern of an absorption reduction which involves higher corporate tax but makes relatively more finance available for housing will have a switching effect similar to a devaluation: it will switch expenditures away from tradables towards non-tradables.

Thus one really needs to know the composition of absorption policy in order to determine how much deliberate switching (exchange-rate) policy is needed. This parallels the earlier point that the absorption content in the switching policy of devaluation affects the extent to which further deliberate disabsorption is needed. The model is deprived of some of its simplicity when one realizes that very few policies do not have both an absorption and a switching content.

V. TERMS-OF-TRADE EFFECTS INTRODUCED

Any possible changes in the terms of trade have been ignored so far. The effects of absorption changes and of devaluation on the terms of trade clearly need to be taken into account. The simplicity of the basic model hinges on the assumption that the country concerned is genuinely small, so that it cannot affect its terms of trade. The terms of trade can certainly be allowed to alter for exogenous reasons, but the quantity of its imports the country buys must not affect its import prices, and the quantity of its exports that it unloads on world markets similarly must not affect their prices. With this assumption a devaluation has the same proportionate effect on the domestic (peso) prices of exports as of imports. Furthermore, it becomes justifiable to treat exportables and importables as if they were part of one composite commodity—the tradable—since there is no relative price change within the composite.

If one wants to allow for terms-of-trade effects, one should, at the minimum, have a three-good model—exportables, importables, and non-tradables—for the single country. The main ideas can be explained if one superimposes on the basic model a foreign-price effect on the export side.[2] We continue to assume that the country cannot affect its import prices in foreign-currency (dollar) terms. But now, the more it exports, the more the dollar prices of exports fall. There is a downward-sloping foreign demand curve for exports. Since the dollar prices of imports are constant, export prices can be measured in terms of imports.

Both the reduction in absorption and the switching policy (devaluation) will increase the quantity of exports for the reasons that follow from the basic model. This increased export quantity will then cause export prices in dollars to fall. In addition it will modify the original increase in exports because the fall in the dollar prices of exports will cause their domestic-currency (peso) prices to fall somewhat relative to the situation before this terms-of-trade effect. Since the increases in the domestic prices of exportables induced switching between exportables and non-tradables in the first place, the net result will be a lesser rise in the quantity of exports. But some rise in the export quantity will

---

[2] Appendix 2.2 represents geometrically the effect of a devaluation on exports, including the J-curve effect.

remain, at least provided production and demand patterns respond to relative price changes.

The crucial question remains whether the rise in the quantity of exports will lead to a rise in their foreign-currency (dollar) value. The quantity has gone up but the dollar price has gone down. If it leads to a fall in the dollar value—that is, if the foreign elasticity of demand for the country's exports is less than unity—then the analysis has to be modified in a significant way. On the other hand, if the elasticity is greater than unity, there is no problem at all. All the preceding discussion stands. It remains true that both a reduction in absorption and a devaluation will increase the quantity and dollar value of exports. Even when the dollar value of exports falls when the quantity rises, the main argument could still stand. A reduction in absorption might still improve the current account, because the improvement on the side of imports might outweigh the worsening on the side of exports; and similarly in the case of a devaluation. Of course, the terms-of-trade effect represents a real loss to the country; therefore, the reduction in real absorption that has to go with a given balance-of-payments improvement has to be larger than in the absence of such an adverse terms-of-trade effect, as also has to be the devaluation required.

VI. THE J-CURVE EFFECT

Here the J-curve effect should also be noted. The foreign-currency value of exports might fall in the short run as the result of a devaluation even before the quantity of exports increases. The peso price might be rigid in the short run, perhaps because of contracts or administered pricing, so that the dollar price must fall to the full extent of the devaluation. This leads to the so-called J-curve effect: at first the dollar value of exports falls, and then later, as peso prices rise and export supply responds, the dollar value of exports rises. The peso price could have been increased immediately after the devaluation without sales being lost as a result, but it was not. Alternatively, it might be increased somewhat, but not as much as is possible on a short-run market basis. The dollar price will then fall when the country devalues, and if the quantity does not increase much, the value of exports will fall, just as in the case where the foreign elasticity of demand was less than unity.

The moral of the J-curve is that one must not get impatient about the effects of a devaluation or an appreciation on the current account. The initial effects of a change in the exchange rate may be perverse, but in time prices and supply adjust to produce the expected results—at least provided absorption policy is appropriate at the same time. In 1985 the yen started appreciating steeply relative to the dollar (strictly, the dollar depreciated relative to the yen and other currencies). This was naturally expected to reduce the dollar value of Japanese exports to the United States, at least relative to trend. But at first it rose. It took time for the supply of Japanese exports to slacken off and for prices to adjust. This effect was even more noticeable with respect to US exports. It took time for supply to increase, and at first the adverse terms-of-trade effect dominated. Inevitably, economists and other observers became impatient, and even suggested that new theories of international trade—which would show that real exchange rates were somewhat ineffective—had to be developed. But, other than in asset markets, economic effects of price changes usually operate slowly.

The terms-of-trade effect just discussed can be important. But I shall ignore it in the next two chapters in order to focus on other matters. Thus I shall return to the so-called small-country assumption where the country concerned faces given import supply and export demand prices abroad. But this does not mean that the discussion to follow is not relevant for large countries; it means only that for such countries something should really be added about terms-of-trade effects—and this would have to be done even for those countries that are not really large but are nevertheless significant world suppliers of some of their exports.

Absorption and Switching for Internal and External Balance

In Fig. 2.1 tradables are shown on the vertical axis and non-tradables on the horizontal axis. TT' is the constant employment transformation curve, employment on this curve being at the internal balance level. Initially production is at the point B, determined by the slope of the line $G'G$, which indicates the initial price ratio or real exchange rate. Income measured in non-tradables is OG. Initial expenditure measured in terms of non-tradables is OH and the initial absorption point is D. Thus expenditure exceeds income by GH. The indifference curve tangential to $H'H$ at D represents a constant level of real absorption. Demand and supply for non-tradables are equal. But demand for tradables exceeds their supply by BD, this being the initial current account deficit.

If expenditure is reduced but the price ratio (real exchange rate) is kept unchanged, the absorption point will move down OZ towards O. The curve OZ traces out the pattern of demand between tradables and non-tradables as expenditure changes. If expenditure were reduced to OG, it would be equal to income at the internal balance employment level. Demand would be at C. But there would be a residual current account deficit and excess supply of non-tradables. If expenditure were reduced further, to OF, demand would move to E. There would be current account balance, but excess supply of non-tradables of EB. The latter would lead to reduced production of non-tradables, and hence unemployment, and finally the production point would be at E.

There is internal and current account balance at A, where an indifference curve is tangential to the transformation curve. JJ' is tangential to the transformation curve at A, and its slope indicates the real exchange rate appropriate to internal and external balance. (External balance is defined here as representing a zero current account balance.) A switching policy could establish this price ratio, bringing the absorption pattern to some point on the curve OZ', while the appropriate absorption policy could bring the absorption point to A.

A pure switching policy—one that kept real absorption constant but raised the domestic price of tradables—would bring the absorption point to K, which is on the same indifference curve as the initial point D. This

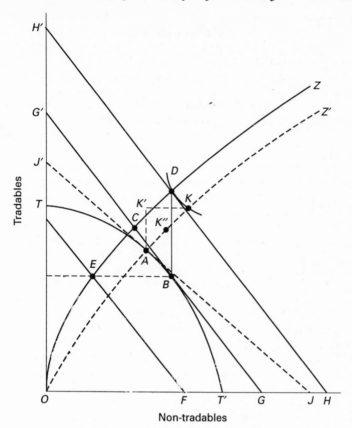

Fig. 2.1. Absorption and Switching

would yield excess demand for non-tradables of $K'K$, which would raise their price, and so negate the original switching, returning absorption to D.

One can imagine the restoration of external balance, while maintaining internal balance, to be reached in various ways. First, there might be a switching policy, possibly incorporating some disabsorption in real terms, bringing the economy to some point on OZ' below K, such as K''. This could be a devaluation. Then expenditure would be reduced by fiscal or monetary policy to OJ (measured in non-tradables), bringing the absorption point to A. Alternatively, first expenditure might be reduced to the level of internal balance income, bringing the absorption point to C, and then switching brings it to A. In this case switching will involve a fall in real absorption (since the indifference curve through *A* is below that through *C*) but it will also involve a rise in nominal expenditure (with a given price of non-tradables), the expenditure increase (again, in terms of non-tradables) being *GJ*.

Finally, a country may start in current account and internal balance (at point *A*), and need to go into current account deficit in order to absorb capital inflow. Absorption must then rise and the real exchange rate must appreciate, the movement being from *A* to *D*.

APPENDIX 2.2

Export Value, the Terms of Trade, and the J-curve

In Fig. 2.2 the vertical axis shows the price of exports in terms of foreign currency (dollars). The dollar price of imports is assumed to stay constant. The horizontal axis shows the quantity of exports. DD is the foreign demand for exports. S_0S_0 is the initial supply curve of exports. Initial equilibrium is at A.

Reduction in domestic absorption

This reduces domestic demand for exportables and thus shifts the export supply curve to the right, say to S_1S_1. If the terms of trade were given, the new equilibrium would be at B. With a terms-of-trade effect and prices flexible, equilibrium moves to C. The terms of trade have deteriorated. The quantity of exports has risen but by not as much as when the

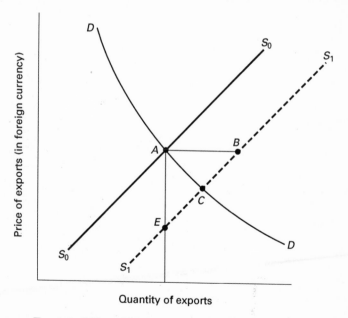

FIG. 2.2. Effect of Devaluation on Exports: J-Curve

dollar price was fixed. The dollar value of exports will rise if the elasticity of foreign demand is greater than unity.

Devaluation without a J-curve effect

A devaluation lowers the dollar price for a given peso (domestic currency) price, and thus shifts the supply curve to the right. More is supplied for a given dollar price. In the absence of a terms-of-trade effect, equilibrium moves to B, and with a terms-of-trade effect, it moves to C. The dollar value of exports will again rise if the demand elasticity is greater than unity.

The J-curve effect of a devaluation

We ignore the absorption effect. At first, the peso price stays constant and supply does not increase. The dollar price must thus fall to E, and the dollar value of exports falls to the same extent. Gradually the peso price rises and the dollar price recovers until C is reached.

REFERENCES

The "two-targets two-instruments" approach to balance-of-payments theory originated in Meade (1951). Also a landmark in this field, which introduced the concept of switching, is Johnson (1958a). The geometric small-country model with traded and non-traded goods, which forms the basis of the approach in this chapter, was first presented in Salter (1959), and is generally known as the "dependent economy model".

On the real exchange rate, including measurement issues and reasons why the equilibrium real exchange rate might change, see Edwards (1989a, 1989b) and Little et al. (1993).

3

Income Distribution, Wage Rigidity, and Balance-of-Payments Policy

THE present chapter deals with two related issues. First, how would a devaluation combined with fiscal contraction affect the distribution of income between various sectors or factors of production, and, in particular, how would it affect real wages? Second, what happens if the assumption of rigid prices of nontradables is reconsidered and if the possibility of real-wage rigidity is introduced?

Without taking distributional effects into account, it is difficult to explain varying attitudes to balance-of-payments policies in different countries and in different sectors of the community. The analysis of distributional effects provides the foundation for the political economy of devaluation. Hostility to devaluation can often be explained by its adverse effect on some sectors of the community. Similarly, one cannot understand why some policies have failed when they ought to have succeeded on the basis of our simple model. If there is some tendency to real-wage rigidity, the role of devaluation as a useful instrument of policy is in doubt. Real-wage rigidity (or real-wage resistance) will be introduced in Section VIII.

I. INCOME DISTRIBUTION: EFFECTS OF SWITCHING

A switching policy such as a real devaluation represents a relative price change. Prices of tradables rise relative to those of non-tradables. Clearly, there will be gainers and losers. One can put this in the most general terms. Consider a country with many industries, all with different factor intensities. In addition, there are many factors of production. Devaluation raises prices of exportables and of goods that are close substitutes for imports, and lowers relative prices of goods that are only distantly substitutable.

Factors specific to, or intensive in, the tradable industries will tend to have their real incomes raised; and the reverse for factors specific to, or intensive in, the non-tradable sectors.

Switching also has income distribution effects because of demand differences. When the prices of tradables rise relative to those of non-tradables, then those people who are heavy consumers of tradables are likely to lose relative to those who have preferences for non-tradables. For example, if foods are primarily non-tradables, and the share of expenditure on food is higher for wage-earners than for others, a rise in the relative price of tradables would shift income distribution towards wage-earners on this account.

Some distributional effects of real devaluation are rather obvious. Profits in industries producing tradables will tend to rise and in non-tradables will tend to fall. An example that applies to many developing countries can be given. Peasants who produce for export are likely to gain from devaluation while urban workers, producing manufactures for the local market that are effectively non-tradables because of import restrictions, are likely to lose. The urban workers will be buying food from the rural sector, as well as buying imported consumer goods, the prices of which have all been raised by devaluation. Profits in manufacturing industries will also fall because the cost of imported inputs will rise.

II. MUST DEVALUATION LOWER REAL WAGES?

It is often said that a devaluation must reduce real wages, at least if it is to be effective. Yet there seems to be no general, theoretical reason why wage-earners as a whole would lose from a relative price change. One could well imagine that wage-earners in exportable industries gain even though those in non-tradables activities lose. To get an overall adverse effect on real wages, more specific assumptions must be introduced.

The simplest model is one derived from standard trade theory. There are two sectors, tradables and non-tradables, and two factors, labor and capital, their returns being wages and profits, respectively. There is a uniform wage rate throughout the economy and also a single profit rate (rate of return on capital). One might then assume that non-tradables are labor-intensive relative to tradables. This seems a reasonable assumption, given the simplicity of the model, because non-tradables usually include a heavy component of services, which are indeed labor-intensive relative to production of commodities. In this model a rise in the relative price of tradables would indeed reduce real wages.

Another possibility is the cost-plus model. This is the model that people often have in mind. The nominal wage is given, and there is a constant percentage profit margin in the non-tradables sector. Hence, the price of non-tradables is given, which is the assumption maintained in the previous chapter. A devaluation raises the domestic currency prices of tradables and hence the profit margin in the tradables sector. With the prices of tradables higher, the average price level rises and so, with given nominal wages, the real wage must fall.

A decline in the real wage as a result of devaluation could also be caused by a combination of a given nominal wage and some downward rigidity in the price of non-tradables. Prices rise more readily than they fall. Hence, prices of tradables rise while prices of non-tradables do not fall, or do not fall much, even though absorption has decreased. In the very short run, prices of all domestically produced goods, whether tradables or non-tradables, may indeed be rigid, or somewhat sluggish, but the domestic currency prices of imports must still rise as a result of devaluation. Hence, again, real wages must fall.

On balance, it is very likely that a real devaluation would lower real wages, but one can think of contrary cases, and certainly of some sectors of the labor force that would gain. It is quite likely that an export boom generated by devaluation would raise nominal wages of some categories of workers in export industries by more than it has raised the cost of living facing them.

If we go beyond the small-country model, we must allow for the possibility that a devaluation worsens a country's terms of trade. This strengthens the likelihood that a devaluation lowers the overall real wage. In terms of pesos, the prices of imports rise more than the prices of exports. Wage-earners gain from higher export prices but lose from higher import prices, and are likely (though not certain) to lose.

Again, one can refer to a standard two-sector trade theory model, namely one where there are home-produced goods, some of which are exported, and foreign goods. In this model, no distinction is made between tradables and non-tradables. A real devaluation is thus the same as a decline in the terms of trade. The relative price of home-produced goods falls as a result of devaluation, and this brings about switching in the pattern of demand both at home and abroad. In simple models the peso price of home-produced goods and the dollar price of foreign goods is given, so that a devaluation lowers the dollar price of home-produced goods (and raises the peso prices of foreign goods) and thus worsens the terms of trade. Both the real wage and the rate of profit will fall. There is a general loss in real income and not necessarily any redistributive effect.

III. INCOME DISTRIBUTION; EFFECTS OF EXPENDITURE REDUCTION

Having looked at the effects of switching on income distribution, we must now look at the other aspect of current account improvement: the reduction of aggregate expenditure or absorption. I shall now assume that a fiscal contraction is brought about either by reducing government expenditure or by raising taxes.

In order to introduce the real income effects of these fiscal changes into our analysis, we must distinguish earned income, disposable income, social income, and total income, and similarly for the components of income—wages and profits. Earned income is the pre-tax income derived from production. Our analysis so far has only been concerned with earned income, and when I have referred to the real wage, it has been the earned real wage. I shall call this the product real wage—the earned wage related to the prices of domestically produced products. Disposable income is earned income plus transfers minus taxes. Social income is the value of the services provided by government non-transfer expenditure, and total income is the sum of disposable and social income. Changes in the pattern of domestic output induced by switching policies affect, as we have seen, the pattern of earned income. Now we introduce the effects of tax increases and government expenditure reductions in order to determine what happens to total real income and to its components, total real wages and total real profits. To isolate these effects for the moment, we hold earned income and its components constant.

If the public expenditures that are reduced gave no one any satisfaction—being neither transfers nor a form of social income—then there would be no effects on total real income. This is an extreme case. If services are cut, both the social wage and the disposable wage are likely to be reduced, so that the total wage falls on both counts. Some government revenue may have been used, as in some developing countries, to subsidize food and so keep down the cost of living to the wage-earner, in which case cutting this expenditure will reduce the total wage. Perhaps business loses out in government services, or through failure to maintain public infrastructure, so that the real value of total profits falls. If public investment has been cut, then the real total incomes of those members of the community that could expect to benefit from these in the future have fallen. On balance, it is certainly likely that expenditure reductions would lead to some cut in real total wages. When the fiscal deficit is reduced by an increase in taxation, a real total wage cut is even more likely. It is inevitable that some of the burden of higher tax rates or expansion of the tax base would fall upon wage-earners.

A fiscal deficit must have been financed in some way. Perhaps it was financed by foreign borrowing. Essentially the following argument also applies when the deficit is financed in various other ways discussed in the next chapter. Reducing borrowing will then reduce the obligation on future taxpayers to generate primary fiscal surpluses needed for payment of interest and amortization.

Given a tighter fiscal policy now, future tax rates can be lower, or non-interest expenditures greater, than if current policy had not been tightened. The expectation of these favorable consequences of tighter fiscal policy represents a rise in real income for taxpayers, who include wage-earners. This effect is often ignored, and could outweigh all the other effects, but is unlikely to do so if wage-earners heavily discount expected future incomes.

IV. INCOME DISTRIBUTION: SWITCHING AND EXPENDITURE REDUCTION COMBINED

To the income distribution effects of switching one must thus add the real income effects of the expenditure reduction. It is likely that the real total wage will fall on both counts: the earned real wage (or product real wage) will fall as a result of switching—at least if non-tradable industries are labor-intensive or other relevant and plausible conditions discussed earlier apply; and the disposable real wage will fall even more because of tax increases and reduced transfers, while the social wage will fall because of reduced expenditures. By contrast, the real income of capital before tax and before taking into account reduced benefits from governments' expenditures might rise as a result of switching—and must do so when non-tradables are labor-intensive—but it might nevertheless fall once the adverse tax and government expenditure effects are added in. In other words, earned profits may rise and yet total profits may fall.

It is interesting to calculate for various countries or episodes the distributional effects of a balance-of-payments adjustment program which includes both devaluation and fiscal contraction. For example, if one considers the rural sector of a primary product-exporting developing country, its members will gain from the direct effects of the devaluation but may well lose from reduced expenditures by government in the rural areas. Public employees providing non-tradable services are very likely to lose, while import-competing manufacturing industries may gain from higher prices for their final products (unless they are fully protected by quantitative import restrictions) but lose from the higher cost of imported inputs as well as from higher taxes.

When one takes these income distribution effects into account, it is not difficult to see why countries have often been reluctant to make significant discrete alterations in their exchange rates, whether to devalue or to revalue. The expenditure reduction that needs to go with the devaluation is likely to have adverse effects on various sections of the community, including wage-earners—at least if prospective benefits from reduced future public sector interest payments are ignored or not rated highly. In addition, there may be a redistribution against some sectors. In the case of devaluation a fall in real wages on this account seems likely.

V. EXCHANGE RATE PROTECTION

If a real devaluation is likely to reduce the general level of real wages but raise profits in export industries—and possibly also raise real wages of labor specific to export industries—then a real appreciation will have the opposite effect. Its effects on export and import-competing industries will be adverse. If absorption stayed constant, the switching effect of appreciation would reduce employment and output. One might then assume that appreciation would be associated with an increase in absorption, possibly brought about by fiscal expansion. Tax reductions or public expenditure increases might benefit the tradable industries so that, conceivably, the adverse effects on them of the appreciation could be offset. In any case, the whole of the preceding analysis clearly applies in reverse to an appreciation.

Leaving aside the favorable effects of fiscal expansion, it is in the interests of producers of tradables that a real appreciation be avoided. From their point of view, the more depreciation the better. A government may follow a set of policies that brings about real depreciation, or that modifies a real appreciation that might otherwise have taken place. If the motive is to favor export and import-competing industries—and no need is actually seen to reduce a fiscal or current account deficit—then the policy might be described as one of *exchange rate protection*. Producers of tradables are protected at the expense of producers of non-tradables.

There have been times when countries have developed large current account surpluses, the best examples being Germany, Japan, and Taiwan. This has not necessarily been undesirable, as I shall discuss in later chapters. But at certain times governments or monetary authorities have deliberately intervened in the foreign exchange market so as to prevent appreciations of their currencies, and they have avoided fiscal expansions that they might otherwise have undertaken, because of a concern that appreciation and reduced current account surpluses would have adverse effects on tradables producers. These have been policies of exchange rate protection. The motive of such a policy is distributional—to favor a particular sector implicitly at the expense of others. The rate of return on foreign exchange reserves that are accumulated as a result may well be less than the social returns that could be obtained by expanding private or public investment at home. Hence, some loss is incurred for the sake of achieving the protectionist objective.

I come back to this issue of the adverse effects of appreciation in the next chapter when discussing the effects of private capital inflow. Now I return to the case of a country which runs a current account deficit and requires a real devaluation.

VI. FACTOR PRICE FLEXIBILITY

A crucial assumption of the model expounded in the previous chapter has been that the prices of non-tradables are rigid downwards. Hence, reduced demand for non-tradables resulting from a reduction in total absorption would lead to excess supply and thus unemployment, rather than to a fall in their prices. A switching policy has thus been necessary to maintain the level of employment. Furthermore, we have supposed that the combination of absorption and switching policies has prevented the prices of non-tradables from rising. It follows that the absolute rise in the domestic prices of tradables resulting from a nominal devaluation has led to an equivalent rise in their prices relative to those of non-tradables. It is this relative-price effect—or real devaluation—that has led to switching of the production and demand patterns.

Now I shall look at three alternative assumptions. First, one might assume that commodity and factor prices are flexible downwards. This is the neo-classical assumption. Second, one might assume that nominal wages, but not the prices of non-tradable commodities, are rigid downwards, and in addition are prevented from rising by the combination of the two policies. And third, one might assume some real rather than nominal rigidity, and in particular, downward rigidity of real wages.

If commodity and factor prices were flexible downwards, there would be no need for a switching policy. Starting in current account deficit and full employment (or equilibrium employment), absorption would be reduced in order to eliminate the deficit. In the first instance this might yield excess supply of non-tradables. So their prices would fall. As demand for labor fell, wages would fall. The price fall would bring about the same rise in the prices of tradables relative to non-tradables as the nominal devaluation would have done. The only difference in the final outcome is that this time the average price level—of tradables and non-tradables combined—falls, instead of rising. In both cases a real devaluation has resulted.

The main point is that there is now automatic switching. The prices of non-tradables will fall until full (equilibrium) employment in the non-tradable sector has been restored; this is brought about by a movement of resources out of this sector into tradables, induced by the price fall, and by a shift of demand towards it, also induced by the price fall. There is thus no need for an instrument designed to maintain internal balance, since price flexibility automatically maintains internal balance. The instrument would only be needed if the maintenance of price stability—in the present case, prevention of price declines—were an objective of policy.

VII. DOWNWARD RIGIDITY OF NOMINAL WAGES

The second alternative assumption is to let nominal wages be rigid downwards, rather than the prices of non-tradables. This assumption would be more in conformity with the usual Keynesian models, and does seem more realistic. It does not actually make a great deal of difference to our story. I shall consider here two possible models.

One possibility is that there is a constant percentage profit margin in the non-tradable sector, this being the cost-plus model. In that case, with the nominal wage given, the price of non-tradables also stays constant. This is a plausible interpretation of the rigid commodity-price assumption of the basic model. A second possibility is that commodity prices are flexible and that there is specific capital in each sector. As labor is drawn out of non-tradables because of the greater profitability of tradables, and demand for non-tradables falls, the prices of non-tradables fall and, with given nominal wage rates, the profit margin falls there. The main point is that, with constant nominal wages, we end up with the relative prices of tradables having risen not only because their prices have risen owing to the devaluation but also because the prices of non-tradables have fallen. The switching effect of a given devaluation is therefore strengthened.

What is the best assumption to make—wage and price flexibility, nominal wage rigidity, or perhaps some kind of real wage rigidity? No one would suggest that prices and wages are instantaneously flexible downwards. Until the 1970s few people would have seriously considered a model where nominal wages were flexible downwards: the influence of Keynesian theories as well as common sense was too strong. But models have been developed—notably the monetary models of the balance of payments—which do seem to make that assumption. I have doubts about the assumption, but nevertheless, some argument for it can be made along the following lines.

It can be argued that all this analysis must be superimposed on a situation of general inflation. We imagine all prices to be rising continuously. Relative price changes are then brought about by some prices rising faster than others. The assumption that excess supply for labor will not cause nominal wages to fall—the assumption of nominal-wage rigidity downwards—must then be restated as the assumption that the continuous rise in the level of nominal wages will not be affected by excess supply of labor. An assumption of downward flexibility of nominal wages can then be reinterpreted as meaning that excess supply of labor will soon lead to a slackening of the rate of nominal-wage increase until the excess supply has been eliminated. It may never be necessary for nominal wages to fall absolutely.

This argument was more applicable in the 1970s and early 1980s, when inflation was high in many countries, than in the 1990s. A currently relevant variant of the argument is that, even with low price inflation, nominal wages would normally be rising steadily owing to productivity growth, so that excess supply of labor would lead to a slackening of the rate of increase of nominal wages rather than to absolute falls in nominal wages—just as in the case of general inflation.

Perhaps the right approach is to suppose that in the short run there is some, if not absolute, downward rigidity, even in the rate of increase in wages, but in time flexibility emerges. The basic model, with its fundamental Keynesian assumption, is a short-run model, and the issue then simply becomes how short the short run is, whether indeed it has been becoming shorter in recent years, and to what extent policy should be concerned with the short run.

VIII. REAL-WAGE RESISTANCE

It is often said that a devaluation will lead to a compensating rise in nominal wages designed to avoid a fall in real wages, and that this real-wage resistance will negate the effects of a devaluation, making it pointless. Switching as a result of policy is simply not possible. The only way to get an improvement in the current account is to reduce absorption appropriately, even at the cost of unemployment. The unemployment consequent on the cut in absorption is the true cost of downward inflexibility of real wages. Eventually unemployment will moderate real-wage resistance and thus induce real wages to fall, but devaluation alone will not bring it about. This is an extreme way of putting the real-wage resistance argument, but let us analyze its implications in more detail. I shall consider the case where fiscal contraction involves some fall in real total wages, and a switching policy, such as devaluation, leads to a further fall because non-tradables are labor-intensive relative to tradables.

Let us first suppose that nominal wages have stayed constant, and the appropriate disabsorption policy combined with devaluation has brought about the desired current account outcome while retaining internal balance. Real wages—interpreted in the broad sense of total real wages—have fallen both because of the devaluation and because of the fiscal contraction. After a while nominal wages rise to compensate for that part of the real-wage cut brought about by the devaluation itself. The switching effect will then be completely reversed, the prices of non-tradables rising to the same extent as the prices of tradables. Some unemployment and external imbalance will result. To achieve the desired current account improvement, absorption will have to be reduced further, and hence the departure from internal balance will be even greater.

But this is not all. Nominal wages may also rise to compensate for the effect of fiscal contraction. For example, suppose that tax rates on wage-earners were raised. The pre-tax (earned) nominal wage may then be pushed up to bring the post-tax real wage back to where it was originally. This extra rise in the pre-tax nominal wage would have an additional switching effect, actually raising the prices of non-tradables relative to tradables above where they were in the very first place. This is the same effect as if there had been an appreciation with constant nominal wages.

If there is indeed real-wage resistance, it may not be possible to attain both internal and external balance. Essentially the point is that the real wage that is apparently insisted on by wage-earners exceeds the marginal product of labor at the level of employment identified with internal balance. A devaluation is unable to reduce the pre-tax (earned) real wage, while tax and expenditure changes which affect wage-earners adversely actually lead to a compensating increase in the pre-tax wage.

This discussion gives an indication of tendencies in many countries, especially in Europe. But complete real-wage resistance is an extreme case. While there may be formal or informal indexation of wages to the cost of living, in practice it is usually incomplete. Nominal wages may not respond to changes in income tax rates, in transfers, or in public expenditures. The only fiscal changes that would affect the cost of living directly—and thus nominal wage rates—would be changes in indirect taxes and in prices of public utility services, the latter affected by the extent to which public enterprise losses were being subsidized out of the budget.

The adjustment of nominal wages to the cost of living is usually lagged, so that for some time devaluation and fiscal contraction can reduce the real wage. Nevertheless, if it is generally expected that full adjustment of nominal wages to the cost of living will eventually take place, appropriate switching of resources and demand patterns will not take place. Firms will see little point in expanding output of tradables if the increase in profitability is soon expected to disappear as wage costs catch up with the higher sales prices (in domestic currency) made possible by the devaluation.

Given that there is real-wage rigidity, how can two kinds of real-wage rates be reconciled? There is the real wage that the trade unions insist that their members receive—the real total wage, which might be called the income real wage and takes into account taxes paid and subsidies and transfers received by workers. Then there is the pre-tax (earned) real wage facing employers, which is defined in terms of the sales price of domestic products. It is the product real wage and determines employment. The higher the product real wage, the lower employment. A particular product real wage paid by employers will yield the socially desired level (or internal balance level) of employment. The problem is that the union-determined income real wage may be too high, given the desired fiscal deficit and the product real wage required by internal balance. How can they be reconciled?

First, a government can borrow abroad and use the resources

obtained to subsidize wages directly or indirectly, perhaps by reducing taxes that impinge on wage-earners, by subsidizing public services, or by increasing transfers of various kinds. Hence, the product real wage can be sufficiently low to yield internal balance while labor gets the higher income real wage it wants. The obvious objection is that an external deficit involves debt service payments and, in any case, may not be able to go on forever. The country cannot indefinitely live beyond its means. If borrowing is domestic and crowds out domestic investment, a cost is still incurred by future taxpayers and reflects to some extent the value of potential investment forgone.

Second, the gap can be eliminated by raising the product real wage towards the rigid income real wage. But this will reduce employment below the internal balance level. The hope may be that eventually the desired income real wage will be reduced by the high level of unemployment that may result. Experience has shown that wage demands do certainly respond to levels of unemployment, sometimes quite quickly, and that income real wages are only rigid in the short run. The obvious objection here is that unemployment imposes costs through losses of output and additional social costs, and that the short run is often long enough to be painful.

Third, there might be a domestic redistribution of income towards wages. For example, profits might be taxed in order to subsidize wages. This assumes that real profits, unlike real wages, are not resistant to a reduction. Here there are various objections. Taxing profits directly or indirectly involves various distortions and disincentives, as well as reducing funds for investment. If capital is highly mobile internationally, taxing profits above international levels will, after some lag, lead to an outflow of capital. In any case, it may, of course, not be feasible to subsidize wages to the extent necessary. The revenue yielded by a profits tax at the maximum revenue level may simply be insufficient. Furthermore, the desired or target income real wage may not be a constant: it may continuously run ahead of the willingness of society to make the transfer. It is not a policy that I am advocating, but it is a possibility for dealing with a short-term problem.

There are also indirect ways of taxing profits or other non-wage incomes in favor of wages so as to sustain a desired income real wage. Protection might be provided for labor-intensive products.

Instead of devaluing when a current account has to be improved, tariffs or import restrictions on labor-intensive products might be imposed instead. Resources will be switched from non-tradables to import-competing industries, so that switching will take place. But the export industries, and those import-competing industries that are not protected, will lose relative to the devaluation alternative, because resources will not be switched from non-tradables into these industries. Factors intensive in these tradable industries that are not protected will lose relative to what would have happened if switching had been induced by a devaluation and thus there had not been discrimination in favor of certain industries.

An example comes from developing countries. In the past—when protection was fashionable in developing countries—many developing countries implicitly taxed their rural export sectors in favor of the urban sectors producing import-competing products. In this way they maintained high urban real wage levels and also imposed costs on themselves through forgoing some of the gains from international trade.

IX. THE ROLE OF DEVALUATION, IF ANY

Finally, I come to a simple but extremely important proposition about the efficacy of devaluation. It follows from the main themes of this chapter. Consider two characteristics of our basic (essentially Keynesian) model. First, the prices of non-tradables are rigid downwards or, alternatively, the nominal wage is. Second, devaluation can reduce real wages. Here I shall focus on nominal wage rather than price rigidity since there is much evidence that the former is generally much greater than the latter. I am also assuming, realistically, that, with a given nominal wage, a devaluation does reduce real wages, at least in crucial sectors. If the nominal wage were not rigid downwards, there would be no need for a deliberate switching policy, since switching would be automatic in response to unemployment in the labor-market. Wages and non-tradable prices would fall, as required. Devaluation substitutes for a fall in nominal wages, and if nominal wages would fall in any case, there is no need for a devaluation. These are both ways of attaining the fall in real wages that is normally necessary. On the other hand, if the real wage were inflexible downwards, a devaluation would be ineffective. *To make devaluation necessary, nominal wages have to be inflexible, and to make it effective, real wages have to be flexible.*

In practice, nominal wages are not utterly inflexible downwards, allowing time for adjustment, while real wages are rarely utterly rigid. Devaluation may not be absolutely necessary since in time wage and price flexibility could do its job, but it may fulfil a useful short-run role. Similarly, real wages may not be absolutely rigid, but in time the efficacy of devaluation may disappear as nominal wages catch up with the rise in the cost of living caused by devaluation. Thus, some judgment is required in deciding whether a devaluation is indeed necessary and effective in an appropriate time period. But this simple proposition focuses on central issues which I shall take up again in Chapter 8 when discussing the costs of forgoing the exchange rate as an instrument of policy.

REFERENCES

The analysis of devaluation with nominal wage rigidity is presented more rigorously in Jones and Corden (1976). See also Dornbusch (1975). The concept of exchange rate protection—originally applied to the policy response to a natural resource (oil) discovery that would otherwise appreciate the real exchange rate—comes from Corden (1981).

4

Fiscal Policy, Monetary Policy, and Capital Mobility

This chapter introduces capital mobility, and pursues some details of monetary and fiscal policy. One cannot talk about balance-of-payments theory without introducing money explicitly. Does it make any difference whether a budget deficit is financed by the sale of bonds or by borrowing from the central bank? What are the mechanisms by which a budget deficit creates a current account deficit and a real appreciation? It turns out that various, apparently very different mechanisms, may yield very similar real outcomes. I shall also discuss the monetary approach to the balance of payments which was at one time very fashionable and which is still of interest. Another topic is the real appreciation problem: can a real appreciation, with its adverse effects on export industries, be avoided when capital flows into a country and there is a private investment boom? In general, this chapter assumes high, and sometimes perfect, international capital mobility, and makes the small-country assumption, though the analysis is also relevant for large countries.

I. THE SAVINGS AND INVESTMENT APPROACH

The most useful framework for analysis of the current account is the savings and investment approach. The current account deficit is equal to the excess of national investment, government and private, over national savings, both government and private. Alternatively, it is equal to the government's budget deficit plus the private financial deficit, the latter being the excess of private investment over private savings. This approach follows from the even simpler proposition that the current account deficit is equal to the excess of absorption over income. These, of course, are no more than identities, but they are identities that must be satisfied, and are helpful for analysis. If a particular policy—for example, an increase in protection—would not change the fiscal position, nor increase private savings or reduce private investment, then, also, it would not improve the current account. The same applies to the effects of a devaluation. One approach to studying the effects on the current account of any policy change is, then, to study separately how it might affect these various components.

Let us use this approach to analyze, first, the effect of a devaluation on the current account and, then, the effect of a fiscal expansion.

A devaluation switches expenditure towards non-tradables and at the same time switches labor and capital in the opposite direction, that is, it reduces output of non-tradables. Assuming initial internal balance, it would then bring about excess demand for non-tradables. To maintain internal balance, absorption must be reduced at the same time. That was the story of Chapter 2. The decline in absorption might be brought about by fiscal or by monetary contraction. Reducing absorption implies greater savings, public or private, or lower investment, public or private. The devaluation on its own does not necessarily improve the current account; the improvement is brought about by the associated disabsorption policies, which reduce investment or increase savings.

But there are many other channels through which a devaluation can increase savings or reduce investment, some of which I shall discuss later. The most important one is the Keynesian channel. If there is initially a Keynesian situation of excess capacity and unemployment, disabsorption policies may not be needed to improve the current account. The switching of domestic expenditures towards non-tradables will raise real incomes, and if the marginal propensity to save is positive, this will lead to higher savings and thus a current account improvement. It will also lead to higher tax revenue and, with given government expenditures, an improved fiscal balance and hence further current account improvement. Frequent arguments that a devaluation on its own can improve the current account imply a Keynesian story of this kind—a story where there is some scope for real incomes and output to rise as a result of devaluation because output is initially below the internal balance level. It is important to remember that this assumption is often valid only in the short run.

Consider now the effects on the current account of a change in the budget deficit. Must budget and current account deficits move together or be related in some way? This is the twin deficit issue much discussed in the United States. If private savings and investment stayed constant, an increase in a budget deficit caused, say, by an increase in government expenditure, must indeed be matched by a similar increase in a current account deficit. The interesting question is to what extent private savings and investment would be affected by changes in fiscal policy. If a change in the budget deficit leads to a lesser or a greater change in the current account deficit, then the private sector financial balance—the excess of private investment over private savings—must have altered. There are many possible channels through which this could happen.

The most obvious channels are two that come out of the simple Keynesian model. A fiscal expansion is likely to raise real incomes, at least in the short run, and given a positive marginal propensity to save, total private savings will then rise and thus modify the deterioration in the current account deficit resulting from the fiscal expansion. The current account deficit will rise by less than the increase in the budget deficit. Increased domestic private savings will have financed at least part of the higher budget deficit. Such a Keynesian effect is surely important, even though it may be temporary. Some of the rise in absorption resulting from higher government spending is satisfied in this case out of higher domestic output. In addition, financing of the fiscal expansion may cause the interest rate to rise, thus crowding out some domestic private investment, and possibly raising savings.

There are two other possible effects of a fiscal expansion on private savings and investment. These are concerned with expectations. Citizens may foresee that the budget deficit implies the need for increased taxes later. Hence they may increase their savings now so as to avoid a sharp decline in consumption later. In other words, they seek to smooth consumption over time. This is the Ricardian equivalence effect which I discuss further in Chapter 11. In that case, it is at least possible that a fiscal expansion does *not* lead to an increased current account deficit, or, at least, that the effect on the current account is modified. Second, expectations of future tax increases, or of inflation brought about by the budget deficit, might reduce private investment, and thus also modify the effect on the current account.

II. THE TWO DEFICITS

An increase in a budget deficit brought about by a rise in government spending or tax cuts is likely to worsen the current account deficit or reduce a surplus. But it follows from these examples that changes in the two deficits need not be the same, nor, indeed, must a country that has a current account deficit have a budget deficit, or vice versa. It is obvious that there is also scope for variations in private savings and investment. Furthermore, there can be a reverse effect: a change in private spending may affect the budget deficit. For example, a private investment boom may raise real incomes and output in the country, hence raise the tax base and increase government revenue even with given tax rates, and so improve the fiscal position. Nevertheless, the current account will deteriorate, because the increase in private investment will be greater than the decline in the budget deficit.

In 1985 the general government balance of the United States was almost equal to the current account balance, at 3 per cent of GDP. The Federal government deficit was actually over 6.6 per cent but it was substantially offset by the surpluses of the states. (The general government fiscal balance combines the net balances of all levels of government.) In 1989, again, the two deficits were quite close, with a general government deficit of 1.7 per cent of GDP and a current account deficit of 2 per cent. Furthermore, allowing for some lag, the shift in the United States into large current account deficit in the early 1980s more or less coincided with the increase in the Federal deficit.

These rather similar changes and magnitudes of the two deficits in the United States led to the twin deficit concept. Sometimes it was said that there were two distinct problems, the fiscal problem and the current account problem. This was clearly wrong. The correct interpretation was that the US current account deterioration around that time was caused principally by the sharp shift in the fiscal policy of the Federal government—the Reagan effect. Yet at various times there have also been other factors at work.

The US recession of 1990–1 both worsened the fiscal balance

and improved the current account. The improvement resulted, essentially, from a rise in the private savings propensity and a fall in private investment. At the same time, the tax base fell and unemployment benefit payments increased, so that the budget deficit increased. The current account improvement since 1988 has also been attributed to the dollar depreciation that began in 1985, and that brought about the necessary switching. This explanation might imply a Keynesian story: depreciation raised real incomes and hence savings. More plausibly, after a lag, depreciation made possible some fiscal contraction (reduction of the budget deficit relative to GDP) without the United States having to depart from internal balance, at least until 1990.

In 1988 and 1989 Britain had a private spending boom, which led both to a current account deficit and a budget surplus. This was a fairly unusual combination, essentially because budget surpluses have been unusual in the 1980s. The opposite combination—budget deficit and yet current account surplus—has been more common. In the 1980s this was the normal situation of Germany, and, until 1988, of Japan. In 1988 and 1989 Japan's general government was in surplus (though the central government was in deficit) while current account surpluses continued. Thus, one can find examples of all combinations of fiscal and current account imbalances. In particular, it is not inevitable that a country which has a budget deficit also has a current account deficit, even though an increase in the former is quite likely to lead to an increase in the latter, or to a reduction in a current account surplus.

III. EFFECTS OF A BUDGET DEFICIT: FLOATING EXCHANGE RATE REGIME

If private savings and investment do not change, an increased budget deficit must lead to an increased current account deficit. That follows from the savings-and-investment approach. But where do monetary policy and the exchange rate regime fit into this story? In particular, does it matter how the deficit is financed? We must distinguish three forms of financing of the budget deficit: the government could directly sell bonds abroad, possibly denominating the bonds in foreign currency; it could sell bonds on the capital market at home; and it could borrow from the central bank. These three methods can be described as foreign borrowing, bond-financing (meaning bond-financing in the domestic market, thought of as distinct from the foreign capital market), and monetization. I shall now assume a floating exchange rate regime.

The simplest case is the one where the deficit is financed by the sale of bonds at home. This case is represented diagrammatically in Appendix 4.1. It is the classic Mundell–Fleming story applicable to the United States and many other countries. In its simplest version it assumes perfect capital mobility. Absorption rises and (for the moment, with constant private savings and investment) the current account worsens to the extent of the increased fiscal deficit. The interest rate rises, capital is thus drawn into the country, and capital inflow appreciates the domestic currency until the domestic interest rate is again equal to the world rate (apart from the influence of exchange rate expectations). In the case of a large country, notably the United States, the world interest rate would, of course, rise, and this may reduce private investment somewhat. If capital mobility is imperfect (the more realistic case), the domestic interest rate will stay somewhat above the world rate.

Extra spending resulting from the fiscal expansion will tend to raise demand for the country's own goods, while the appreciation will have the opposite effect. There is no general presumption as to what the net effect will be—expansionary or contractionary. But if the country concerned were small in the world capital market, and capital mobility were perfect (as in the simplest version of the Mundell–Fleming model), the interest rate would return to the initial world level; in that case, if the real money supply stayed constant, the net expansionary effect would be zero. But that is only a special case. The net result may well be an expansion of demand for home-produced goods.

In this bond-financing case just described, the government borrows domestically from the private sector, diverting some of the private sector's savings away from other borrowers, and foreign capital then flows in to replace the diverted funds. Thus the government borrows from the private sector and the private sector borrows abroad. Of course, in addition, foreigners may be buying the government's bonds directly on the domestic market. The domestic capital market is an intermediary between the government and foreign savers. People are often misled by this mechanism. If the nation is getting into debt owing to its current account deficit, is that caused by private or by public borrowing? In this case, foreign borrowing is undertaken by the private sector, but essentially public borrowing is the cause of the deficit.

The budget deficit may be monetized, rather than financed, by a sale of bonds on the open market. In that case, the government sells its bonds to the central bank, and the central bank creates money as a result. But continuous money creation would be inflationary, and I shall examine that case in the next chapter. Here I shall assume that the central bank is committed to avoiding inflation, and hence must prevent a continuous rise in the money supply. Inflation will be introduced in the next chapter. The central bank must thus engage in offsetting open market operations in the form of a continuous sale of bonds. With one act the central bank increases the money supply, and with another it reduces it. Thus it has passed on to the capital market the bonds it initially purchased from the government. The increased supply of bonds on the market raises the interest rate, draws capital in from abroad, and appreciates the exchange rate. The government has sold its bonds to the central bank, the central bank has sold them to the public on the domestic market, and private agents on the domestic market have sold bonds abroad or borrowed in other forms. The story is finally the same as when the government sold the bonds directly in the market, except that the central bank has been one more intermediary in the chain.

Of course, if the government had sold its bonds directly abroad (the foreign borrowing case), there would have been no intermediary. The extra foreign exchange acquired by the government as a result of its borrowing, less the foreign exchange content of the initial increase in absorption resulting from the budget deficit, would have appreciated the exchange rate and brought about the necessary switching.

The conclusion is that in all three cases the increased budget deficit leads to an increased current account deficit, and thus to new borrowing abroad. Also, in all cases it leads to nominal and real appreciation. But in two cases extra borrowing abroad is done by the private sector, and in the third, by the government itself. And in the monetization case the central bank is an intermediary. The accumulation of foreign debt may lead to long-term debt-servicing problems, which might be resolved by inflation. But here I am only concerned with short-term mechanics.

I shall not trouble to spell out in detail what happens when the exchange rate is fixed by sterilized intervention. The fundamental outcome of the budget deficit—increased net indebtedness to foreigners and real appreciation—will be much the same. Real appreciation will be brought about by domestic prices rising, rather than nominal appreciation. Unless the government borrows abroad directly, the deficit will be financed out of the central bank's foreign exchange reserves rather than by private capital inflow.

IV. THE MONETARY APPROACH AND THE RESERVES

In the 1970s the monetary approach to the balance of payments was fashionable, and it was sometimes argued that it provided the best framework for balance-of-payments analysis. This has turned out to be quite wrong; nevertheless the approach sheds useful light on some matters and is worth discussing briefly. It can be used for analyzing exchange rate behavior in a floating rate system, but here I deal with the fixed exchange rate case.

A current account deficit can be financed by foreign borrowing by the government, by private capital inflow, and, finally, by drawing down the central bank's foreign exchange reserves (R). The monetary approach focuses just on the determination of R. Its main point is that changes in R reflect changes in the demand for money and in the supply of domestic credit. The interesting question is why changes in the reserves should be the focus of concern, and that will be discussed below.

The basic idea of the monetary approach is the following. The money base, M, consists of the central bank's foreign assets, R, and of its domestic assets, D. An open market purchase of bonds, or a purchase of bonds to finance a government deficit, will raise D. The supply of the money base, M, has to be equal to demand, at least in equilibrium. The monetary approach shows how, given a fixed exchange rate and capital mobility, various policies or exogenous shocks bring about monetary equilibrium through variations in R. To put it simply, $M = R + D$. If M has to rise because the demand for money has risen, and D is constant, R

must rise. If M has to stay constant because the demand for money is unchanged, while D rises, R has to fall.

Let us spell this out. Suppose that the demand for money rises because the price level has risen. How is equilibrium brought about? One way would be for D to be increased by open market operations. But let us assume now that D is held constant. In the absence of international capital mobility, equilibrium would be restored by a rise in the interest rate, which would reduce the demand for money again. In that case, the supply of the money base, M, would not need to change. Now we allow for international capital mobility. A rise in the interest rate will then lead to capital inflow and, given intervention to keep the exchange rate fixed, this will raise R. It will thus raise M and so bring about the required increase in the supply of M in response to the increased demand for M. If the interest rate cannot finally rise above the world rate, the whole adjustment must take place through the rise in R.

To sum up, the change in R is part of the adjustment mechanism to an imbalance between demand and supply of money. If capital mobility is imperfect, adjustment takes place both through the interest rate—which changes the demand for money—and through R—which changes the supply.

Next, consider the situation where there is an expansion of domestic credit, D. This time the demand for money does not change initially. But the central bank creates credit (increases D) either because it hopes to raise M in this way, or because it has been unable to resist requests for extra credit either from the private sector or from the government. Most likely, credit creation finances a budget deficit, a case of monetization of the deficit. The tendency for the interest rate to fall will lead to an outflow of capital, hence a fall in R, and thus, finally, to no rise in M, or a lesser rise than otherwise. The rise in D has been offset, or partially offset, by the fall in R. This is the offset factor.

In the extreme case of perfect and instantaneous capital mobility, the offset is complete; in that case, the central bank cannot change the money base other than by changing the demand for money in some way, for example by bringing about price rises through a devaluation, which would increase the demand for money. With a given demand for money, every increase in domestic credit by the central bank will be fully offset by a reduction in its foreign exchange reserves: an increase in domestic credit will fail to increase the money supply, but will reduce the reserves to an equal extent.

This approach is directly applicable to the analysis of a balance-of-payments crisis in a fixed exchange rate regime. Suppose there is a potential balance-of-payments crisis because R is steadily falling. If the demand for money is constant, the fall in R means that D must be rising. The flow of new domestic credit must be equal to the decline in reserves in each time period. Of course, the demand for money may also be rising over time, as a result of growth or of increased monetization of a relatively underdeveloped economy. It may also be falling because of financial innovation. Thus the fall in R does not have to be exactly equal to the rise in D. But the implication is that, if the decline in R is to be arrested, there has to be a decline in D, that is, a reduction in domestic credit. If R is the policy target, D must be the policy instrument.

Finally, let us go back to the case where the demand for money has risen because the price level has risen. This rise in the price level might have been caused by an increase in nominal wages, for whatever reason, or perhaps by a devaluation. Our story so far has been the following. An increase in the demand for money leads to an increase in the supply of money through international capital mobility. The actual or incipient rise in the interest rate resulting from higher money demand leads to capital inflow, which then raises R, and hence M. In this story a change in savings and investment, and hence the current account, plays no role. But there is in fact an additional mechanism by which an increased demand for money leads to a rise in R, though it is surely less important. It does not depend on international capital mobility. Rather, it works through a temporary rise in savings and thus through the current account. The monetary theory of devaluation is built on the reasoning that, through this mechanism, a devaluation temporarily improves the current account and brings about a once-for-all rise in reserves.

Suppose that the demand for money has risen because prices or real income have risen, while D is kept constant. Not only will the public seek to move out of bonds into money (which leads to a rise in the interest rate and capital inflow) but it will also move out of goods into money—i.e. increase savings—to restore or raise the real value of money balances. A given rise in prices, caused, for example, by a devaluation, will lead to a temporary rise in savings. The rise is only temporary, because it will come to an end once the real value of money balances has reached the desired level. A once-for-all stock adjustment leads to a temporary change in flows. Higher savings, of course, improve the current account and thus (for given capital inflows) raise R and thus M.

To summarize, an increase in the demand for money increases R, and thus M, through two mechanisms: through higher capital inflow and through a current account improvement. Both the increased capital inflow and the current account improvement will be temporary, unless the rise in prices is continuous and is not equalled by a continuous rise in D.

V. THE MONETARY APPROACH: SOME QUESTIONS

One should ask some basic questions about the monetary approach to the balance of payments. I noted above a simple formulation of a balance-of-payments problem in terms of this approach. If R is the policy target—and it is implicit that it is—then D must be the policy instrument.

This is a neat conclusion, which was at the core of the International Monetary Fund (or Polak) model of the 1950s and 1960s that the enthusiastic advocates of the monetary theory of the balance of payments gave much prominence to later. Yet the conclusion has only limited significance. It does not go to the heart of the matter. Suppose there is a budget deficit and it is being monetized, so that D is rising, and hence R is falling. The decline in R can indeed be stopped by ceasing to monetize the deficit. But this may lead the government to borrow abroad instead, or to sell bonds in the domestic market. Unless something can be done about the budget deficit itself, the change in the government's financing policy that stops the decline in R will leave the current account—and hence the net foreign asset position of the country as a whole—unchanged. Surely, the focus has to be on the budget deficit itself, or on the current account, rather than on domestic credit creation.

It is true that, in the absence of an ability of the government or its residents to borrow abroad, a current account deficit could only be financed out of reserves, so that the monetary approach and a concern with the current account would come to the same thing. But that is not the way the world is now—or was in the 1970s for all developed and most developing countries. Control of domestic credit is not sufficient to ensure that the country does not borrow abroad excessively. Even a focus on the current account may be questioned, and I come back to that issue in Chapter 6.

Yet, having noted this doubt, a limited justification for the monetary approach can be given. This approach is useful as a supplement to approaches outlined earlier that focus on the real economy: on absorption, savings, investment, and the real exchange rate. It comes into play when the concern is with the ability of the central bank to defend a fixed nominal exchange rate. This ability depends on its reserves and also on its own foreign borrowing capacity. Since the latter is never assured, the reserves become a target of policy, and the policy instrument is then D.

The underlying idea is that the fixed exchange rate commitment is the method of inflation control. The fixed exchange rate determines the inflation rate, making it equal (more or less) to the weighted average inflation rate of trading partners, apart from temporary inflation required to bring about any required real appreciation. And the maintenance of a minimum level of foreign exchange reserves affects the ability to maintain the exchange rate. Hence, from this point of view, domestic credit policy must be directed to the maintenance of R. By contrast, in a floating rate regime, D affects the exchange rate directly: an increase in D increases the money supply, which leads to capital outflow and so depreciates the exchange rate.

The government of a country with a history of high inflation may wish to make a credible fixed exchange rate commitment. For example, the Argentine government had this objective in 1991. It can do so by committing itself not to increase D. Hence the Argentines introduced a "convertibility law" which embodied this commitment. Of course, R could still fall if the demand for money fell. But once the commitment is made, the demand for money is more likely to rise. On the other hand, such a commitment does not rule out bond-financed budget deficits or direct foreign borrowing by the government.

VI. CAPITAL INFLOW AND THE REAL APPRECIATION
PROBLEM

Many countries have gone through the following—somewhat confusing—experience. The country has a private investment boom financed to a great extent by foreign capital inflow. The capital inflow may take the form of direct investment, of portfolio investment, or of short-term capital inflow that responds to higher domestic interest rates resulting from the boom. Perhaps the capital inflow represents the reversal of earlier capital flight. If the exchange rate floats, or at least is fairly flexible, it will appreciate. If, at the same time, a fairly stable domestic price level is maintained by a tight monetary policy, there will be a real appreciation. The increased spending resulting from the investment boom combined with the switching effect of the real appreciation will together generate a current account deficit equal to the capital inflow. Basically the story is the same as when the addition to spending came from the government, rather than the private sector. It is the reverse of the story of Chapter 2, where absorption and the current account deficit had to decrease, and a real depreciation was required.

The familiar problem is that the loss of competitiveness of export and import-competing industries brought about by real appreciation is very unwelcome. This is the real appreciation problem. Many governments, at many times, have been preoccupied with this problem. Exporters will be adversely affected and will surely complain. The flexible exchange rate system will be blamed.

The irony is that the investment boom and capital inflow will have resulted from a restoration of confidence in the country's economic management, which itself was caused by an earlier reduction or elimination of a budget deficit combined with real depreciation. Because of the earlier depreciation and reduction in domestic demand for factors of production, export industries had become more competitive and, after a lag, an export boom developed. Now, capital streams in because of this success, possibly even aiming for investment specifically in export industries. This experience represents the fruits of success, and yet carries problems with it. A good example was the experience of Mexico in 1991 and 1992. The by-product of capital inflow was a real appreciation which threatened to damage the very industries whose success had stimulated the inflow.

A further problem is that the capital inflow and investment boom may well be temporary, and hence in due course a real depreciation is likely. Of course, firms making the investments should be aware that the real appreciation may be partially or wholly reversed. This expectation should affect their investment decisions. But investors are not always adequately far-sighted. Furthermore, it may not be possible to reverse the rise in real wages that real appreciation will have brought about.

It is usually suggested that the obvious solution is to intervene in the foreign exchange market so as to prevent appreciation. This would be an attempt at exchange rate protection, a concept introduced in Chapter 3. The nominal exchange rate would be manipulated to protect the tradables goods industries. What happens in that case? I shall now assume that the exchange rate is kept completely fixed, any nominal appreciation being prevented.

The initial increase in demand for domestic goods resulting from the investment boom is likely to raise prices and so still produce a real appreciation. It is true that if there is initial unemployment and excess capacity (a Keynesian situation), some, or possibly even all, of the extra demand would lead to higher output rather than prices. But this may be only a short-term effect. Eventually prices are likely to rise, in which case there will still be a real appreciation even though the nominal exchange rate is fixed. While nominal appreciation has been avoided, real appreciation—and hence loss of competitiveness—has not. Indeed, the fixed exchange rate outcome may be worse than the flexible rate one, because the price rise may set off inflationary expectations, unjustified though this would be if the reason for the price rise were understood.

Could the problem be solved by sterilizing the monetary effects of capital inflow?[1] This is an important question since it is often thought that this is the solution. In fact, it is not a solution, but in some circumstances sterilization may moderate the real appreciation effect. With a fixed exchange rate, capital inflow increases the money supply. But the central bank could, at least for a time, offset this effect with an open market sale of bonds or other

[1] See Appendix 4.1 for an exposition with the help of diagrams of the rather complex argument of this and the next two paragraphs.

monetary action having the same effect. Hence, it may be possible to avoid an increase in the nominal money supply (or an increase greater than normal). This means that the investment boom would lead to a rise in the domestic interest rate. Assume for the moment that it is possible for the domestic interest rate to rise above the world rate. The higher interest rate will crowd out some domestic investment and consumer durables spending, so that the net expansion of demand resulting from the investment boom will be reduced. But there will still be some expansion of demand (since that is why the interest rate has risen with a constant money supply), so there will still be some tendency to real appreciation and some current account deficit. Because of foreign financing of the investment boom, the reserves will continually accumulate, and hence the central bank would have to sell bonds continuously.

This story assumes imperfect capital mobility since the domestic interest rate rises above the foreign interest rate and apparently stays that way. With perfect capital mobility the domestic interest rate could only exceed the foreign interest rate if depreciation were expected, but no such expectation has been introduced here. In fact, it would not make sense to expect depreciation. It is more likely that appreciation would be expected, in which case more capital would flow in. In any case, the higher is capital mobility, the more difficult it will be to prevent an increase in the money supply, since the higher interest rate would induce more capital inflow.

The important point to remember is that the domestic investment boom was not initially caused by an increase in the money supply. Even if a rise in the money supply were completely prevented by sterilization, there would still be a boom, though the rise in the interest rate would indeed moderate it. If the money supply increases—as is inevitable if there is high international capital mobility—this moderating effect will not operate.

One might ask whether there is any way of avoiding real appreciation completely. Leaving aside fiscal policy, one approach might be to stop the whole process: stop the capital inflow and stop the investment boom. Exchange controls might seek to prevent or moderate capital inflows. It is difficult to enforce exchange controls after a regime of high capital mobility has come to be established, but let us consider the possibility anyway.

The domestic interest rate could then rise above, and stay above, the world rate. The high investment demand of the boom industries would crowd out other domestic investment, and, indeed, the boom itself might be choked off completely with sufficient monetary contraction. There would be no increase in the current account deficit. But the objection to this policy is powerful: if the perception of profitable investment opportunities is soundly based, it will not be desirable to choke off an investment boom and forgo the opportunity of financing it from foreign savings.

At this point another possibility should be noted. There may be capital inflow even though there is no domestic investment boom to start with. This has been a common situation. For example, capital may flow in because the exchange rate is expected to appreciate. Given maintenance of the fixed exchange rate, the reserves will rise and the money supply will increase. The domestic interest rate will fall and credit will become more readily available as the money supply expands. A spending boom, leading to temporary inflation, will be induced. This spending boom will lead to domestic prices rising (given the fixed exchange rate) and thus, again, a real appreciation. A new equilibrium with a lower interest rate will be established, when the increase in the money supply will cease.

This is a case where the monetary expansion brought about by capital inflow in a fixed rate regime is actually the cause of real appreciation. It is to be distinguished from the earlier case, where there was a domestic boom and hence there was some real appreciation even before there was any monetary expansion. The diagram in Appendix 4.1 brings out the contrast.

In this case, sterilization of the monetary effects through open market operations or increases in reserve requirements of commercial banks could avoid the real appreciation problem only if capital mobility were sufficiently imperfect. Otherwise, there would be massive capital inflows as long as the exchange rate was expected to appreciate and the domestic interest rate had not fallen sufficiently. In practice it has become more and more difficult for countries to deal with this problem as capital mobility has increased.

VII. FISCAL STABILIZATION AND THE REAL APPRECIATION
PROBLEM

There is a way of moderating the real exchange rate effects of a
private investment boom. Fiscal policy might act as a stabilizer.
Fiscal contraction could offset the effects of an investment boom.
This idea needs to be explained in detail, since it is the main or
only way of avoiding the real appreciation problem. If a fiscal
contraction in the form of a budget surplus, or reduced deficit,
were combined with the private investment boom, real appreciation could indeed be avoided. This would be true both in a floating and in a fixed rate regime.

Let us consider the fixed rate regime. The investment boom
would increase demand for domestic goods and the fiscal contraction would reduce it. Thus, if the extent of the fiscal contraction were just right, temporary domestic inflation could be
avoided completely—i.e. internal balance could be maintained,
with no tendency for prices to rise. Hence there would not be any
real appreciation. If the marginal propensities to import out of
private investment and out of government spending and transfers
(assumed to have been reduced) were the same, the net effects of
investment boom and of fiscal contraction that maintained internal balance would be for the current account balance to remain
unchanged. On the other hand, if the import content of the
investment boom were greater, some net rise in the current
account deficit would result.

The political difficulties of cutting government spending or
raising taxes, and doing so quickly, are considerable. Hence, such
fiscal stabilization in response to a private investment boom may
not be a practical policy. Furthermore, a shift from public to private spending, possibly large and temporary, would create redistributive effects, and hence problems that are similar to a real
appreciation. There would be losers from higher taxes and
reduced government spending. For example, if the government
reduces its construction program, workers and firms in the construction industry will lose. This, of course, would present no
problems if they had also been the beneficiaries of the private
investment boom. On the other hand, if there is a particular concern with the prospects of recently revived export industries, such
a fiscal stabilization policy may still be the right approach, or at

least a desirable element in a policy package, in spite of its adverse redistributive effects.

An orthodox Keynesian stabilization policy has usually been understood as a policy that smooths out fluctuations in demand for domestic goods. In a floating rate regime, it can be achieved by monetary policy (allowing for the usual lags and problems of short-term management). For example, an increase in demand for domestic goods resulting from an investment boom could be offset by sufficient real appreciation. Such a policy could keep the demand for home-produced goods constant even though there has been an investment boom. Some appreciation will, in any case, result from the rise in the interest rate brought about by the investment boom, but monetary policy can ensure that real appreciation is sufficient. Yet, even if successful, such a policy would not stabilize the real exchange rate. For that purpose fiscal policy is needed irrespective of the exchange rate regime. If stabilization through fiscal policy is not possible, a country must learn to live with temporary relative price changes, including real appreciations. They are the inevitable by-products of fluctuations in private and public spending, whether on investment or consumption.

VIII. INTEREST PAYMENTS AND DEVALUATION

It remains to introduce an important qualification to the analysis of Chapter 2. A distinction must be made between the current account and the primary balance of payments on current account. The primary balance excludes interest and dividend payments. Here we will only be concerned with interest, and disregard dividends, so that the primary balance can be defined as the non-interest current account. If C is the current account deficit, H is the primary deficit, $r^{\star}$ is the world (dollar) interest rate, and F is the country's foreign debt denominated in dollars, while dF represents the increase in debt, we have

$$dF = C = H + r^{\star}F$$

$r^{\star}F$ represents interest payments on initial debt.

The whole of the analysis of Chapter 2 and subsequently applies to the primary balance, H, only. This balance is determined by absorption and switching policies. If a country wishes to eliminate a current account deficit completely (make C zero) and is a net debtor—i.e. has a commitment of interest payments abroad, so that r^*F is positive—its policies must produce a primary surplus. (If r^*F is positive, and C is to be zero, H must be negative, a negative H being a surplus.) If a current account deficit continues, the foreign debt, F, will grow; hence, the interest bill will grow, unless the interest rate falls. To repeat, the simple statement in Chapter 2 that the objective is to improve the current account must be restated in terms of the primary balance only. It is this balance that is directly affected by the policy instruments that determine absorption and switching.

All this is simple arithmetic. Of course, there are longer-run implications of the growth of external debt, especially if it grows faster than GDP. These fall beyond the scope of this chapter. Here I shall discuss interesting issues concerning the effects of a devaluation on interest payments, and, indirectly, on absorption. These effects of devaluation have been important for developing countries. Here there have been some misunderstandings. The central issue is whether a devaluation must have an adverse effect on the fiscal balance and the current account through raising interest payments.

Consider the situation of all the indebted developing countries in the 1980s. In the 1970s their governments had been borrowing abroad, acquiring dollar-denominated debt. A large part of the governments' interest and amortization obligations were fixed in terms of dollars. In the 1980s, many of them devalued. The purpose of the devaluation was to increase exports. Such a devaluation raised the peso (domestic currency) cost of debt service. Did this mean that the countries incurred losses from devaluation through this channel? Does a devaluation increase the interest burden?

Let us make the small-country assumption of given terms of trade and an exogenously given interest rate. In that case, a devaluation changes neither the dollar returns on the initial quantity of exports, nor the dollar cost of imports, nor the dollar cost of debt service. Thus a country should be no worse off as a result of devaluation. In peso terms the interest bill will be higher, but peso returns on exports will have risen to the same extent. The simple view that the devaluation imposes a loss on the indebted country because of the higher peso cost of interest payments is thus wrong. Yet there is more to be said.

The government has to make interest payments in dollars, while dollar export income is received by the private sector. Of course, export income may also be received by the government, but let us assume, for the moment, that it goes mainly to the private sector. Hence, the devaluation creates a potential fiscal problem. The peso cost of the government's interest bill goes up, even though its peso revenue does not rise directly. Conceivably, the problem could be resolved—and sometimes is resolved— through taxing the peso gains of the exporters to finance the government's higher peso interest bill. But this would defeat the purpose of devaluation, which is to improve the incentives to producers of tradables.

A fiscal problem is thus created by the devaluation through its impact on the peso cost of the government's interest bill. It will make the reduction of absorption that is required to improve the primary balance more difficult. The extra taxes required may create distortion and collection costs. Perhaps more important, higher taxes are very likely to encounter political resistance. The same applies, of course, to attempts to reduce government non-interest expenditures. This is an adverse side-effect of devaluation that has to be taken into account. Through raising the peso cost of interest payments on dollar loans, devaluation intensifies the fiscal problem.

Yet the effect of devaluation on interest payments is not the whole story. To see the fiscal effects of a devaluation in full perspective, we must go back to some ideas from Chapter 3. It was shown in that chapter that devaluation has important redistributive effects. A devaluation creates gainers and losers through differential effects on various sectors of the community as consumers and producers. For example, consumers of imports lose and producers of exports gain, most people, of course, being affected both as consumers and producers. This analysis also applies to the fiscal situation of the government.

As just shown, the government will lose through higher debt service. (Interest payments represent payments for an invisible import, so the government is a consumer of imports here.) As a consumer it will also lose because the peso costs of its direct imports (for example, military equipment) will rise. On the other hand, it will gain in peso revenue from taxes on trade, which for many developing countries are significant. Most important in some countries, notably the oil exporters, the government might actually own or be a major shareholder in one or more export industries, and it would then receive higher peso profits as a result of devaluation. Hence, the net budgetary effect of a devaluation could go either way. In the 1980s many of the heavily indebted developing countries certainly found that the debt overhang intensified their fiscal problems.

APPENDIX 4.1

A Bond-financed Budget Deficit and Capital Inflow

Fig. 4.1 is the familiar *IS–LM* diagram. It is used here to represent the standard Mundell–Fleming approach expounded in the text of the effects of a bond-financed fiscal deficit. The starting point is at A, the given world interest rate is r_0, the initial level of real income is Y_0, and the *LM* curve is drawn for a given real money supply, M/P. With perfect capital mobility and assuming no expected exchange rate changes, in equilibrium (allowing for lags), the domestic interest rate must be equal to r_0.

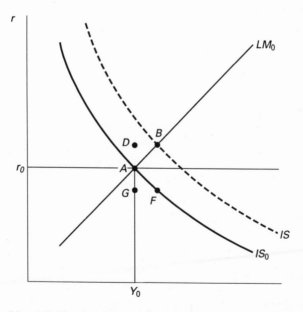

FIG. 4.1. Mundell–Fleming Model: Effect of Bond-financed Deficit and of Investment Boom

Bond-financed deficit and floating exchange rate

The extra demand for home-produced goods generated by the fiscal deficit shifts the *IS* curve from IS_0 to IS_1. If capital were not internationally mobile and the prices of domestic goods, P_h, were constant, equilibrium would move to *B*. Depreciation of the exchange rate to restore current account balance would move the *IS* curve further to the right (not shown).

Given capital mobility, the higher interest rate would lead to capital inflow and appreciation of the exchange rate, the switching effect of which shifts the *IS* curve down again (i.e. reduces the demand for home-produced goods). With perfect capital mobility and a given world interest rate, this must go on until the domestic interest rate is back at r_0. If the *LM* curve stayed constant, the final equilibrium would thus be at *A*, where the demand for home-produced goods, and hence *Y*, is back at its initial level. In this case, the real appreciation exactly offsets the effect of the extra government spending on demand for home-produced goods.

A slight modification is that the *LM* curve will move to the right (the real money supply will increase) because the average price level (*P*) will fall. This is because an appreciation will lower *P* and thus raise M/P for given *M*. The net effect is then expansionary.

Private investment boom with fixed exchange rate

Fig. 4.1 can also be used to represent the case where there is a private investment boom rather than increased government spending. It is represented by a shift of the *IS* curve to the right. If the price level did not rise and there were no capital mobility (other than the inflow which finances the investment boom), equilibrium would move to *B*. We now introduce capital mobility, and also assume that P_h rises whenever *Y* is above Y_0.

In the absence of sterilization, final equilibrium would again be at *A*, the *IS* curve having moved down because of the price rise and hence real appreciation, and the nominal money supply (*M*) having increased so that the real money supply, and hence the *LM* curve, stays constant. This ensures that equilibrium gets back to r_0, where capital inflow (other than that generated by the investment boom) ceases, and the reserves do not change. The capital inflow that remains is just sufficient to finance the current account deficit.

Now assume complete sterilization. This means that the nominal money supply is held constant, the increase in reserves being offset by a sale of bonds. The real money supply must then fall as *P* rises. Equilibrium (if one can call it that) will be at *D*, with the domestic interest rate greater than r_0. This is the case of imperfect capital mobility described in the text. There will be a continual accumulation of reserves, the monetary effects of which are offset by a continuous sale of bonds by the central bank. This is not a sustainable equilibrium.

Expected appreciation and capital inflow

Finally, consider the case discussed in the text where there is no investment boom initially (the *IS* curve does not shift) but capital flows in because the exchange rate is expected to appreciate. Given perfect capital mobility, the money supply will increase until the domestic interest rate is reduced sufficiently, leading to an equilibrium such as *F*, if P_h is constant. If P_h rises to bring *Y* back to its initial level, there will have been a real appreciation. Such a real appreciation shifts the *IS* curve to the left and would bring equilibrium to *G*.

REFERENCES

The classic Mundell–Fleming model is expounded in every textbook of international economics. The original articles are Fleming (1962) and Mundell (1963). See also Bruce and Purvis (1985) and Marston (1985) for more elaborate discussions.

Numerous articles have presented the monetary approach to the balance of payments. It originated with David Hume and had its modern revival in the writings of Robert Mundell. Many of the relevant papers have been collected in Frenkel and Johnson (1976). A survey which includes a review of the empirical literature up to the late 1970s is Kreinin and Officer (1978). See also Frenkel and Mussa (1985). A pioneer of the monetary approach was Jacques Polak, who was for many years the Director of the Research Department of the International Monetary Fund. He developed in Polak (1957) a simple fixed exchange rate monetary model which has been much used in the Fund's work on developing countries.

On capital inflows and real appreciation in several Latin American countries in the early 1990s, see Calvo et al. (1993). This episode, partly caused by the reduced demand for funds in developed countries owing to the recession and partly by the economic reforms in the countries themselves, provides an example of the real appreciation problem.

5

Inflation and Exchange Rate Policy

In this chapter I introduce inflation. Is a devaluation inflationary? Should an exchange rate commitment be used as a *nominal anchor* to keep the inflation rate down in inflation-prone countries, acting as a discipline on credit creation and reducing inflationary expectations? This nominal anchor approach can be contrasted with the *real targets* approach to exchange rate policy. Finally, what is the relationship between inflation, current account deficits, and the exchange rate?

I. IS A DEVALUATION INFLATIONARY?

One might think it obvious that a devaluation is inflationary. Devaluation raises the prices of imports in terms of domestic currency, and some might regard that as inflationary. Furthermore, it switches demand towards non-tradables, while reducing their supply and—in the absence of a reduction in absorption—that will create excess demand for non-tradables and so raise their prices. Finally, devaluation may cause nominal wages to rise and generate a devaluation–wage–price spiral. Yet it has also been argued by some that a devaluation can be contractionary. Clearly, some sorting-out of the various possible effects and processes is called for.

I shall begin with the assumptions of Chapter 2: the country's terms of trade are given (the small-country assumption), and the starting situation is one of internal balance. A current account deficit needs to be reduced.

The devaluation raises the peso (domestic currency) prices of tradables. Here it is worth stressing that the peso costs of imported inputs will rise, so that non-tradables that use such inputs are also likely to go up in price. At this first stage we assume that nominal wages are constant. The initial rise in prices of tradables and non-tradables can be called the primary cost-inflation and is a once-and-for-all price adjustment. It might also be called *adjustment inflation*. If one thinks of inflation as being a process of a continuous rise in prices, then inflation is really a misnomer in this case, even though the adjustment will certainly look like inflation in the year or so when it works its way through the economy. If that were the only effect on prices of a devaluation, then it would have brought about a bubble in the inflation rate, something that can be observed in the inflation histories of many countries.

Next comes the secondary cost-inflation. Nominal wages are likely to rise because prices have risen. Wages may not rise sufficiently to restore real wages, but there is bound to be some increase in wages. In other words, there is formal or informal wage indexation, at least to a partial extent. Higher nominal wages mean higher costs for producers, and thus higher prices of non-tradables, and also of tradables insofar as the latter are not perfect substitutes for imports or exports (the prices of which are given by world markets and the new, devalued, exchange rate). And as domestic prices rise, nominal wages will rise further, prices will rise further, wages will rise further, and so on. Hence, a price–wage spiral is started. This process is *spiral inflation*. If nominal demand does not expand at the same time, the continuous increase in prices will cause real demand (real absorption) to decline, and hence unemployment will result, so that the wage increases may be slowed up. Thus, unless the price rises are accommodated by appropriate monetary expansion, the spiral will eventually cease. But that leads us to consider the demand side. What happens to absorption?

If real absorption stayed constant, and there was initial internal balance, the switching effect of devaluation would certainly be demand-inflationary by creating excess demand for non-tradables, and so leading to a continuous rise in their prices until the real effects of the devaluation disappeared. In other words, finally the nominal devaluation would not have led to a real devaluation. The devaluation will have raised the peso prices of tradables (p_t), and the subsequent inflation will have raised the prices of non-tradables (p_n), so that finally the p_t/p_n ratio would not change. This inflationary process may take some time, but would also be temporary. Of course, if absorption were appropriately reduced by fiscal or monetary contraction, as indicated by the analysis of Chapter 2, this effect would not operate.

I have already noted in Chapter 2 that various policy instruments affect absorption and switching at the same time. One thinks of devaluation as essentially a way of switching expenditure away from tradables and output towards tradables. But it may also affect absorption. The interesting question to be considered here is whether the devaluation itself would reduce or raise real absorption and thus have an expansionary or contractionary effect before any changes in fiscal or monetary policies take place. Is it possible that the devaluation brings about directly the reduction in real absorption that is needed to avoid excess demand for non-tradables? The answer is that it certainly is possible, though by no means inevitable. It is also possible that it has the opposite effect, namely, that it leads to an increase in real absorption.

Essentially, there are three channels through which a devaluation could affect real absorption—through changing the real money supply with a given nominal money supply, through changing the fiscal situation, and through altering the distribution of income in the private sector.

If the nominal money supply stayed constant, then cost inflation, both primary and secondary, would reduce the real money supply, raise interest rates, and so bring about demand deflation: real absorption would fall. But with high international capital mobility and a fixed-but-devalued exchange rate, the nominal money supply would not actually stay constant even if domestic credit were fixed in nominal terms. The initial reduction in the real money supply resulting from devaluation would attract capital inflow, raise the reserves, and so increase the nominal money supply.

A more important effect is on the budget. We have already noted in the previous chapter that a devaluation is likely to change the fiscal situation: for example, it may worsen it because of the higher peso costs of interest payments on foreign debt denominated in dollars. If the private sector's extra peso income resulting from devaluation were wholly spent, while the government did not reduce its own non-interest expenditures—hence going into deficit or increasing a previous deficit—real absorption would rise. The initial impact of the devaluation would be expansionary, quite apart from the switching effect; hence, the policy-induced decline in absorption required to maintain internal balance would have to be even greater. On the other hand, increased revenue from export and import taxes, or from export industries the profits of which go to the government, would improve the budget, and so have a contractionary effect.

There are, in fact, many channels through which a devaluation could affect real absorption. Just one other way may be mentioned because it played a big role in a literature that was concerned with the possible contractionary effects of devaluation.

The devaluation has redistributive effects, and the marginal propensities to save of gainers may differ from those of losers. For example, a devaluation that reduces real wages (as can usually be expected) will shift incomes from wages to profits. It is likely that the short-term marginal propensity to save of wage-earners is generally less than that of those who benefit from higher profits. In that case consumption spending out of a given aggregate income of wages and profits combined will fall, and so real absorption will fall. The reduction of spending by wage-earners will be greater than the extra spending that resulted from higher profits. Of course, higher profits may stimulate investment, and that can be an offsetting effect on absorption.

It has always seemed to me that the concern about contractionary devaluation has been misplaced. Such a contractionary effect through a reduction of absorption should hardly be a matter of concern provided it can be foreseen when fiscal (or monetary) policy is made. After all, when the devaluation reduces absorption, the extent of fiscal contraction that is required to maintain internal balance after a devaluation is less than otherwise. Hence, the political problem involved in cutting government expenditures or raising taxes is less. The possibility that a devaluation might be contractionary certainly does not yield an argument against devaluation.

II. THE EXCHANGE RATE AS NOMINAL ANCHOR

The exchange rate policy of a country that is inflation-prone might be dedicated to the single target of maintaining a low inflation rate. In other words, the exchange rate might be its nominal anchor. The exchange rate would provide an anchor that limits its rate of inflation. This has been a popular idea—and has been much debated—though, as we shall see, it can create big problems and, indeed, crises.

In a nominal anchor regime, a country prone to high inflation fixes the exchange rate of its currency to the currency of another country that has a tradition of low inflation. Perhaps the other country—the anchor country—has an independent central bank that is likely to ensure low inflation. In 1990 Argentina fixed its exchange rate to the US dollar for this reason, and at times the dollar has also been the anchor for various central American countries, including Mexico. When Britain joined the Exchange Rate Mechanism of the European Monetary System in 1990, the objective was similar: sterling was to be tied to the Deutschmark (DM) and this would ensure a rate of inflation for Britain eventually about the same rate as that of Germany. I shall return to discussing the British experience in Chapter 7. The nominal anchor objective has also been a motive for other countries, notably France and Italy. If the anchor country's low-inflation policy is firmly established, and the fixed exchange rate commitment is perceived also as firm, possibly being embedded in some law (as in the case of Argentina recently) or in an international agreement, the nominal anchor policy may achieve its two purposes. These concern discipline and credibility.

First, the exchange rate commitment should act as a discipline on the country's own central bank not to create more domestic credit than the growth in the country's demand for real money balances and the foreign exchange reserves can support. Excessive credit creation would lead to a decline in reserves and a foreign exchange crisis, eventually forcing an abandonment of the fixed-rate regime. It is at this point that the monetary theory of the balance of payments becomes very relevant.

The common experience in many countries, especially developing countries, has been that fiscal deficits are monetized: credit is provided directly to governments to finance a budget deficit, the central bank buying the government's bonds. Monetary discipline, then, implies fiscal discipline. The same conclusion follows if the government finances its deficit by selling its bonds in the market, and the central bank then feels obliged to engage in open market operations (buying bonds) to prevent interest rates from rising. Again, credit expansion results from an expansionary fiscal policy.

Second, the exchange rate commitment should be credible, so that it is really believed in the goods, labor, and foreign exchange markets that a rate of inflation equal roughly to that of the anchor country (allowing for differences in relative productivity growth) will be maintained. This expectation concerns especially the prices of traded goods. Credibility in the labor market is particularly important. Nominal wages in the tradable goods sector should—on average, allowing for minor fluctuations—not rise faster than the rate of price inflation of tradables in the anchor country, combined with expected productivity improvements. This will then affect also the wages and prices of non-tradables.

If the inflation rate of nominal wages in general is greater—leading also to a similar rate of inflation in non-tradables—there will be a continuous real appreciation, making tradables less and less competitive. Such loss of competitiveness will lead either to a growing current account deficit or to growing unemployment, or both. It is the outcome that can be expected when a previously high-inflation country pegs its exchange rate to the dollar or the DM but the exchange rate commitment is not credible in either the labor or the goods market.

In assessing the nominal anchor approach to exchange rate policy, one needs to ask a number of questions.

The first question is whether it is really desirable to tie down a country's monetary policy so as to achieve a low inflation rate. Perhaps high inflation, whether temporary or permanent, serves some good purpose. Why try to discipline the government or central bank of an inflation-prone country? The implication of the anti-inflation view is that inflation is undesirable because of the various distortions and redistributive effects it brings about. Yet governments may find inflation useful. The implication of the nominal anchor approach, with its aim of imposing discipline on governments, is that the short-run interests of politicians do not in this case (if ever!) coincide with the longer-run national interest.

Inflation is a form of tax—the inflation tax—which may be the easiest tax to impose to finance government expenditures. When a central bank gives the government credit to finance its expenditures and this leads to a continuous increase in the money supply and hence causes inflation, a tax is, in effect, being imposed on the public's holdings of money, the real value of money balances being continuously devalued. With regard to the money base, the benefit goes to the government. In addition, if there is an element of surprise inflation, as there usually is—so that expectations of the rate of inflation are less than actual inflation—a tax is also imposed on holders of government debt. In that case, nominal interest rates will not compensate for the decline in the real value of the government's debt when the latter is denominated in domestic currency.

If the government is deprived of revenue from the inflation tax, it will either have to reduce expenditures or raise other forms of taxes. The latter will also have distortion and collection costs, and this must certainly be taken into account. The implication of the nominal anchor approach is that, even allowing for the costs of alternative taxes, the inflation tax is a very inefficient one.

Another reason for inflation is very familiar. Governments often find it in their short-term interest to boost the economy, and hence employment and output, with demand expansion. In the short term they may well be successful. But at the same time such a policy will increase inflationary expectations: next time a given increase in output will be associated with a higher inflation rate.

A body of macroeconomic theory develops this argument rigorously, and it cannot be expounded in detail here. The main point is that expectations are likely to adjust to the frequent pursuit of such an expansionary policy, and finally the country will end up with no more employment and output than if it had avoided such short-term Keynesian policies. The country will just be saddled with a higher rate of inflation. The argument is that governments should be prevented or disciplined from following such short-term policies. If the discipline is perceived to be credible, inflationary expectations will decline appropriately.

The second question about the nominal anchor approach is whether the attainment of low inflation should be the only target of exchange rate policy. The alternative to the nominal anchor approach to exchange rate policy is the real targets approach. The real targets approach—as presented in Chapter 2—hinges on some flexibility of real wages combined with downward rigidity or sluggishness of nominal wages. The nominal exchange rate is used not as an instrument to keep the real exchange rate constant, nor as a nominal anchor against inflation, but to bring about necessary real adjustments. It has a role in achieving real targets, such as its switching role when the current account has to be improved. Suppose a country has a need to improve its current account and starts in internal balance. There is need for a real devaluation. Could this be brought about without nominal devaluation? If the nominal exchange rate stayed fixed but aggregate demand were contracted so as to improve the current account, eventually nominal wages and prices of non-tradables would fall. Eventually the market would therefore produce the necessary real devaluation. But use of the nominal exchange rate instrument speeds up the process of bringing about real devaluation and thus reduces or even avoids completely an increase in unemployment and loss in overall output. The downward rigidity or sluggishness of nominal wages often makes nominal devaluation desirable.

The crucial assumption is that a nominal devaluation can bring about a real devaluation. This means that the exchange rate acts in a *pro-equilibrium* direction. It helps the system to move to a new equilibrium real wage—or structure of real wages—that is acceptable in the labor market. An alternative possibility is that nominal wages would rise to compensate for the effects of nominal devaluation, so that finally the desired real devaluation would not be achieved. This is the case of real wage rigidity discussed in Chapter 3. If exchange rate policy sought to bring about a real devaluation that was not an equilibrium one—i.e. one that was not sustainable because of reactions in the labor market—we could say that it was an *anti-equilibrium* policy. This is the case described above where the government tried to pump up the economy in the short run, but the benefit soon disappeared as inflationary expectations adjusted. Eventually, such a policy only achieves more inflation. It would then be better to keep the nominal exchange rate fixed. The distinction between a pro-equilibrium monetary and exchange rate policy (the two going together) and an anti-equilibrium one is very important, and I shall return to it in Chapter 8 and Appendix 8.1.

Countries encounter various shocks, originating externally or internally, and the exchange rate usually does at various times have a pro-equilibrium role along the lines outlined in Chapter 2. From this point of view, forgoing the use of the exchange rate instrument for the sake of the anti-inflation target is thus a cost. It is the cost of not being able to use the exchange rate to achieve a real target—in this case, the required real devaluation. One can argue that, for an inflation-prone country, the central issue of exchange rate policy is the choice between the nominal anchor and the real targets approach.

The third question posed about the nominal anchor approach to exchange rate policy is whether there are not other ways of achieving the objectives of discipline and credibility. Because of the possible switching role of exchange rate policy, might not alternatives be preferable? Clearly, a government could simply set out to pursue a non-inflationary monetary policy while allowing the exchange rate to float or to alter it frequently. If the government pursues this policy long enough—as Germany has—it will acquire credibility, and hence inflationary expectations will be appropriately reduced. Thus there certainly is an alternative. It seems a sensible alternative, and normally is preferable to a nominal anchor policy. Furthermore, it is obvious that not all countries can follow the nominal anchor approach. There has to be at least one anchor country. Various countries, notably Britain, the United States, and Germany, have filled this role. Low inflation in the anchor country depends on the direct maintenance of fiscal and monetary discipline there, and an historic commitment to discipline will ensure the necessary credibility.

For a previously inflation-prone country—a country with a long history of inflation—the establishment of credibility may take a long time, so that wages and prices will continue to rise at excessive levels, and a policy of monetary restraint alone would lead to high and perhaps increasing unemployment. The attraction of the exchange rate commitment is that it is well defined. From this point of view it is preferable to a general commitment to low inflation. A commitment to intervene in the foreign exchange market so as to maintain a particular exchange rate is a clear rule and signal, even though, for reasons discussed, it also requires domestic credit restraint.

In the 1970s the fashionable operating rule designed to yield discipline and low-inflation credibility was the monetarist one: maintaining a defined rate of money supply growth, while combining this with a floating or flexible exchange rate regime. This was Milton Friedman's recommendation. The money growth target was meant to provide the necessary discipline. But this version of applied monetarism went out of fashion in the 1980s because of the difficulty of defining money and the instability of the velocity of circulation, the latter resulting, among other causes, from the liberalization of financial markets.

It should also be borne in mind that if the pursuit of a constant money supply target fails to achieve credibility—so that wages and prices continue rising at an excessive rate—the problem is the same as when the exchange rate target fails to achieve credibility, a possibility to be explored below. In both cases unemployment will result. Since a tight money policy in a floating rate regime would lead to higher interest rates and nominal appreciation, there would also be real appreciation. This was the experience after the Thatcher government took over in 1979 and pursued a tight monetary policy with the aim of attaining a monetary target.

III. WHAT HAPPENS IF THE NOMINAL ANCHOR FAILS?

The nominal anchor may fail either because discipline is not achieved in spite of the fixed exchange rate commitment, or because credibility is not achieved.

Consider first the discipline problem. The government may be unable or unwilling to reduce its fiscal deficit sufficiently and may not be able to borrow in domestic or foreign markets to finance it. So the central bank creates credit to finance the fiscal deficit, and, given the fixed exchange rate commitment, this leads to a continuous decline in foreign exchange reserves. Hence, at some stage the central bank will have to cease intervening on the foreign exchange market to maintain the exchange rate, since it will run out of reserves.

The central point is that the objective of tying the government's hands with respect to one instrument of policy—the exchange rate—is meant to constrain it also with respect to another instrument—domestic credit creation (meaning, usually, fiscal policy)—and if the second constraint is not achieved, a crisis will result. Some net domestic credit creation can of course be justified by growth in the demand for real balances. In addition, the money supply can increase when the foreign exchange reserves increase owing, for example, to a terms-of-trade improvement. Furthermore, credit creation may finance not a central government deficit but rather the private sector or—as has been very common—semi-independent state-owned enterprises.

But the main point remains: domestic credit creation must be controlled to fit in with the commitment to maintain the fixed exchange rate.

The nominal anchor may also fail because credibility in the labor market has not been achieved. Wages may continue to rise at excessive rates, even though there may, in due course, be some decline in the rate of wage inflation. Employers and trade unions may not believe that the exchange rate commitment will be sustained. Their expectations may thus be adaptive, influenced by past inflation or past failures, rather than by the new commitment. Such expectations could be entirely rational, the past being a better guide to the future than the promises of the government.

The two requirements of discipline and credibility are distinct, though connected. Discipline may actually be maintained, but nevertheless credibility may not be achieved. In that case, continuous real appreciation will lead to growing unemployment and excess capacity. On the other hand, discipline may fail to be attained while, for a time, credibility is achieved. In that case there will not be any real appreciation, but the foreign exchange reserves will decline. In both cases the system will be in danger of breaking down. There is also a connection between the two requirements. Credibility clearly depends on the perception as to whether discipline will be achieved. The more it has been achieved in the past, or, in the case of a high-inflation country, the clearer is the evidence of a shift to a disciplined fiscal policy, the more likely is the achievement also of credibility.

One must distinguish the implications of failure of credibility in the labor and goods markets—which will bring about continuous real appreciation—from failure of credibility in the foreign exchange market. Attempts at fixing nominal exchange rates have frequently broken down in crises because of runs on the currency. The foreign exchange market does not wait for a failure of discipline to reduce the foreign reserves to zero. Nor does it wait until a government chooses to devalue in order to stop or even reverse the real appreciation, and hence loss of competitiveness, that has resulted from a failure of credibility in goods and labor markets. The market anticipates one or both of the two failures just discussed. Hence, it expects a devaluation or an end to the fixed exchange rate regime, and brings about quickly by *force majeure* what it anticipates. There have been many such episodes—for example, the crises of sterling and of the lira in September 1992.

Failure of credibility in the foreign exchange market is thus crucial and precipitates the crisis. But, if there is some rationality in the foreign exchange market, it will be influenced by expectations about discipline and about labor-market responses.

If a country seeks to use the exchange rate as a nominal anchor, but fails—and possibly tries many times, and fails many times—the result will be a jerky real exchange rate path. While the nominal exchange rate is kept fixed, the real exchange rate will appreciate, with all the familiar adverse effects on export and import-competing industries, and with excessive consumption of imports and excessive use of imported inputs by tradable and non-tradable industries alike. Then a crisis will bring about a big real devaluation. If the nominal exchange rate is again fixed after that, there will again be real appreciation, followed eventually by another crisis, another devaluation, and so on.

It is also relevant that foreign exchange crises have sharp political costs; they discredit whichever government is in power at the time, and especially the finance minister. They are likely to reduce confidence in the political system. Before the crisis a finance minister feels obliged to proclaim his or her commitment to the exchange rate parity, that being part of the attempt to achieve credibility. Hence, the minister is discredited when the crisis actually forces an abandonment of the commitment. The nominal anchor policy cannot be recommended to a finance minister who is risk-averse.

I shall take up all these issues again in Chapter 7, when dealing with the European Monetary System, and also in Chapter 16. At this point, having in mind developing countries, one can conclude as follows: there is some argument in favor of using a fixed exchange rate commitment as a nominal anchor for an inflation-prone country where the establishment of discipline and of credibility is a serious problem. But it is not a strong case, essentially for two reasons. First, the exchange rate still has a pro-equilibrium role in pursuing real targets, notably in response to adverse exogenous shocks that require a real depreciation which would not be brought about quickly enough by downward flexibility of domestic prices and wages. Second, the costs of failure, in the form of foreign exchange crises, are severe.

IV. THE BUDGET DEFICIT, INFLATION, AND THE CURRENT
ACCOUNT

I turn now to a situation where a nominal anchor, if there is one,
fails. The need to reduce or eliminate a current account deficit
has led to an increase in inflation. The country moves from a
low-inflation equilibrium to a high-inflation one. Perhaps the
terms of trade have suddenly deteriorated, this has reduced government revenue from exports and hence increased the budget
deficit, and the extra deficit is financed by monetization—i.e. by
borrowing from the central bank. Hence, the rate of growth of
the money supply rapidly accelerates. This discussion is very relevant for studying the experiences of Latin American countries in
the 1980s.

If it is attempted to maintain a fixed exchange rate, the foreign-
exchange reserves will certainly decline, and, in the absence of
foreign borrowing, will rapidly evaporate. Assuming that capital
mobility is imperfect, domestic expansion to finance the budget
deficit will lead not just to a decline in reserves but also to a continuous expansion of the money supply and of domestic demand,
and hence to inflation of non-tradable prices and of wages; thus
there will be real appreciation, with its adverse effects on the tradable sectors. The current account will deteriorate, the deficit
being financed out of the reserves. Very soon the exchange rate
will have to be floated or frequently depreciated. Hence, the rate
of inflation will rise. If foreign borrowing is not possible, the current account will have to get back to equilibrium.

One can imagine a new steady state where the rate of nominal
depreciation is equal to the excess of the domestic over the foreign rate of inflation, so that the real exchange rate stays constant. In this new steady state, increased private savings will
finance the increased budget deficit. The higher private savings
will have been generated by inflation. Inflation reduces the real
value of nominal balances held by the private sector (this being
the inflation tax), and the savings are designed to restore their
real value. In this way the extra base money that was created to
finance the budget deficit is absorbed by the private sector.

In this story a current account deficit has been reduced or
eliminated by a process that increased inflation. Increased inflation has generated the inflation tax, which has reduced absorption

through raising private savings, and so has improved the current account. This is exactly what happened in the crisis of the early 1980s that various Latin American countries, notably Mexico, faced. Yet this relationship between the current account and inflation seems to be a paradox. If the exchange rate were fixed, increased inflation would lead to real appreciation and a deterioration of the current account. But with a floating or flexible rate, real appreciation can be avoided, while absorption is reduced by inflation as well as by other policies. Hence, an increase in the rate of inflation is actually associated with an improvement in the current account.

Given a flexible exchange rate regime, there is a trade-off between the rate of inflation and the current account. Suppose a government has to cease borrowing abroad or drawing on its reserves, and yet is unable for political reasons to reduce the real value of ordinary government expenditures or raise the real value of (non-inflation) taxes. Hence, its primary deficit in real terms stays constant. Aside from borrowing domestically—for which there may be little scope left—the only avenue left is the inflation tax—the last-resort tax which, at the cost of possibly an ever higher rate of inflation, will finance the budget deficit. This is not a policy which I recommend, but because it has often been pursued, it is certainly worth noting. The government has to switch financing from borrowing abroad—which made possible a current account deficit—to borrowing from the central bank and so leading to a continuous increase in the money supply. This shift from current account deficit to inflation will require a once-for-all real depreciation (as does any improvement in the current account) and a continuous nominal depreciation. For a limited period the nominal exchange rate must thus depreciate by more than is required just to keep the real exchange rate constant.

REFERENCES

On contractionary devaluation, see Krugman and Taylor (1978), Lizondo and Montiel (1989), and Corden (1993).

The nominal anchor approach is discussed in Bruno (1991) with special reference to Israel, and in Aghevli *et al.* (1991). The contrast between the real targets and the nominal anchor approach is developed in Corden (1991*a*). There is a large literature describing the role of exchange rate policy in the inflation stabilization policies of various Latin American countries, including Argentina, Chile, and Mexico. All are described in Little *et al.* (1993). On Argentina, see Dornbusch and de Pablo (1990), and on Chile, Edwards and Edwards (1991).

This chapter refers to a body of macroeconomic theory that shows how a policy regime which allows a government discretion for short-term demand management is likely to lead to more inflation—and eventually to no more output—than a regime which ties a government to a credible low-inflation rule or some kind of commitment. The basic articles are Barro and Gordon (1983*a*, 1983*b*), and the argument is particularly well expounded in de Grauwe (1992).

6

Does the Current Account Matter?

THE previous chapters have emphasized the current account. In particular, external balance was defined in Chapter 2 in terms of the current account. This emphasis must now be reconsidered. I shall begin by making a rather stark contrast between two views of the current account, namely, the Old View and the New View. For all developed and many developing countries the New View is fundamentally the correct one, but it must be heavily qualified, which will be done later in this chapter.

I. THE OLD VIEW

Consider the following simple case to illustrate the Old View. A country is committed to a fixed exchange rate regime, though the possibility of devaluation is not ruled out. For whatever reason, there is little or no private international capital mobility. If such mobility does exist potentially, the private sector has little or no borrowing capacity abroad. Finally, the government or central bank cannot borrow abroad, other than short term for emergency purposes. Apart from such short-term emergency borrowing, notably from the International Monetary Fund, a current account deficit must thus be financed by use of the country's own foreign exchange reserves. This broadly describes the situation that did exist for all countries other than the United States in the early years of the Bretton Woods system.

In this situation, a country can run a current account deficit for a limited period. But no positive deficit is sustainable indefinitely. It must come to an end. If it keeps going, well before the foreign exchange reserves run out, there is likely to be a foreign exchange crisis generated by expectations of devaluation. Perhaps there is a steady and predictable inflow of direct investment, as there was into Western Europe in the 1960s. This makes a prolonged current account deficit possible, but no greater than the capital inflow. Hence, the sustainable deficit may not actually be zero. Some countries, such as Canada, have run current account deficits over very long periods because of a steady inflow of direct investment. In these cases external balance could be defined as a positive current account deficit limited by such capital inflow.

The practical conclusion is that the current account must be carefully watched so as to avoid a sudden crisis owing to a shortage of reserves. An increase in a current account deficit, or a shift from surplus or balance into deficit, is a matter of concern, even when the deficit is seen to be temporary and hence self-correcting. On the other hand, its causes—for example, whether an increase in it is caused by a rise in private investment, a fall in private savings, or an increase in the budget deficit—are irrelevant. Any current account deficit that is expected to last for a longer period in the absence of a policy change, and that exceeds predictable direct investment inflows, is "a matter for concern", to use a phrase that used to be popular in official circles. That is the Old View of the current account, which has certainly been commonly held.

It is obvious that a current account figure is a flow figure and what matters is the movement to a stock situation—i.e. the running down of foreign exchange reserves in the example I have given to a level that would lead to crisis. The only target can be a stock, such as a target foreign exchange reserves level, combined with a view about the optimal time profile of current account flows to attain the stock. Thus I do not distinguish the Old View from the new on this ground. Believers in the Old View know the difference between stocks and flows. When they show concern about a current account situation or about the prospective path of the current account deficit, they are concerned that it is not falling fast enough to attain the desired stock level (or ratio of the stock to, say, imports or GNP). At any point in time, external balance is that current account balance which is appropriate from the point of view of approaching the desired level of reserves, taking into account the possibilities of short-term borrowing and effects on speculative capital movements, possibly through leads and lags in payments for imports and exports.

The trouble is that times have changed. Most countries are no longer dependent on their foreign exchange reserves to finance a current account deficit. There *is* private capital mobility, and in addition a government that wishes to maintain its exchange rate can and does borrow directly on the international capital market to finance deficits. For all developed countries, as well as some developing ones, that is surely a correct description of their situation since the early 1970s and, to some extent, even earlier. Yet the old view has survived, at least until very recently. While it may still be justifiably applied to some developing countries with limited borrowing capacity, it is clearly not applicable—or must be heavily qualified—for all developed countries.

II. THE NEW VIEW

Hence, I now come to the New View. In its most general form, it can be put as follows. The current account is the net result of savings and investment, private and public. This follows from the savings-and-investment approach expounded in Chapter 4. An increase in a current account deficit can be caused by an increase in investment or a fall in savings, or any combination of these, again distinguishing private and public investment and savings. Indeed, there are many kinds of investment, and many different agents who may save, so it is not just a matter of four variables. If, just for exposition, we simplify by aggregation and suppose that there are just two agents, the private sector and the public sector, and just two decisions for each, the investment decision and the savings decision, one can conceive of an optimal outcome when all four decisions are optimal.

There are some problems about this approach because the four decisions are not necessarily independent. But, to proceed, the optimal outcome will carry with it a particular current account level at any point in time. Yet this cannot really be described as the optimal current account at which policy should aim, because it could result from various combinations of savings and investment, public and private, and not just from the optimal combination. The current account that would result from the optimal levels of saving and investment could also be a by-product, for example of a situation where the budget deficit was too high and private investment too low. Looking at the current account figure on its own tells us nothing. One must look at the separate decisions.

An increase in a current account deficit might have been caused primarily by an increase in public sector borrowing, as in the case of the United States since 1982 or many developing countries that borrowed heavily on the world capital market from 1976 to 1982 and stumbled into a debt crisis as a result. Alternatively, it might have been caused by an increase in private investment combined with a decrease in private savings, as in the case of Australia, Britain, and Spain in the late 1980s. These are very different situations and require very different policy changes, if indeed they require policy changes at all. For example, if investment increased because the perceived productivity of investment had increased, and there is reason to believe that its marginal productivity was equal to or greater than the rate of interest on borrowed funds abroad, no policy change at all would be required. There are numerous factors determining optimal savings and investment, and also divergences between the actual and the optimal savings and investment levels, and it is these factors that are relevant for policy consideration.

A simple parallel from trade theory can be drawn here. I shall abstract from terms-of-trade effects for the moment, and assume that we are concerned with a small country facing given terms of trade and a given world interest rate. The trade volumes and trade patterns resulting from free trade are then optimal for a country if there are no domestic distortions, that is, if underlying production and consumption decisions are not distorted by taxes, subsidies or controls, lack of information, and so on. If there are distortions, the first-best policy is to remove them. Looking at what happens to the volume of trade tells us nothing about the distortions, and it is impossible to determine what the optimal trade volumes and trade patterns are, other than by seeing what happens, or speculating what might happen, if the distortions were removed.

In a decentralized system, it is necessary to get the traffic signs and signals right—which includes providing appropriate taxes and subsidies or other incentives to deal with externalities—and then the optimal traffic flow will result. The same applies to savings and investment decisions. Decentralized optimal decisions will lead to a net balance—the current account balance—which then will also be optimal. Looking at the net quantitative outcome on the current account balance will not tell us whether the outcome is close to or far away from the optimal one.

I put the New View in its strongest form in Corden (1977). Let me repeat it here, even though it will be qualified later. The argument was that one should assume that normally private savings and investment decisions are optimal unless there are particular, and strong, reasons to believe to the contrary. There is no reason to presume that governments or outside observers know better how much private agents should invest and save than these agents themselves. These private decisions should not be a matter for public policy concern, other than to ensure that there are no government-imposed distortions. Various divergences between social and private costs and benefits should be corrected, so that private decisions are made on the basis of price signals that indicate social and not just private costs and returns. But there is no need for concern with particular quantitative outcomes, and certainly not for any public policy quantitative targets. On the other hand, public sector behavior—i.e. the budget balance—is a matter for public policy concern and the focus should be on this. This does not mean that budget balances should be zero (however calculated), but only that a public policy issue of the appropriate fiscal policy does arise.

It follows that an increase in a current account deficit that results from a shift in private sector behavior—a rise in investment or a fall in savings—should not be a matter of concern at all. In the United States in the 1980s there was widespread confusion as to whether the problem (if any) was the budget deficit or the current account deficit, since they tended to move together from 1982. Sometimes it hardly seemed necessary to make the distinction. By contrast, developments in other countries, for example Chile in the late 1970s, Britain and Australia in the late 1980s, and Mexico in the early 1990s, highlighted the issue raised in this chapter. The central budgets moved into rough balance or even surplus, while current account deficits increased owing to private consumption and investment booms. Thus these countries did not have twin deficits, and one could clearly distinguish the current account issue from the fiscal policy issue which is, in principle, quite distinct.

III. IMPLICATIONS OF THE NEW VIEW: WHAT IT MEANS FOR
THE TARGETS-INSTRUMENTS APPROACH

In distinguishing the source of a current account deficit or of an increase in a deficit, it is important to keep in mind a conclusion from Chapter 4. The party that borrows abroad to finance a deficit is not necessarily the same party that is the initial source of the deficit. An increase in a budget deficit may be financed either by public borrowing or by private borrowing abroad. In the latter case the government sells bonds at home, but the higher interest rates lead to greater private capital inflow. When a current account deficit increases and this is financed by private capital inflow, the change may still be attributable to a shift in fiscal policy. Conversely, it is also possible that a current account deficit is financed by a decline in the central bank's foreign exchange reserves or by public borrowing abroad, even though the change is attributable to an increase in credit to the private sector, whether for private consumption or investment. For the purpose of analyzing the significance of a change in the current account, one should go back to the source—the change in savings and investment, private or public.

Suppose one accepts the New View of the current account in its extreme form. The budget deficit matters, but not the current account. Even here one must introduce a caution: the budget deficit, in its turn, depends on a series of separate decisions about government expenditure and taxation, and it could be argued that a fiscal deficit should no more be a target than a current account deficit should be. The objective must be the achievement separately of optimal public investment and consumption decisions. But let me stay with the simple proposition. A more important issue is whether the targets-instruments analysis of Chapter 2 must then be recast. The general answer is that it must indeed be recast, though the fundamental analysis is still relevant.

We would have two targets, namely the optimal budget deficit (or surplus) and internal balance. Fiscal policy instruments would be directed to achieving the optimal fiscal outcome. Absorption would be influenced by fiscal policy as well as by private savings and investment behavior, which can be regarded as exogenous for this discussion. It follows from Chapter 2 that, for any given level of absorption, a particular real exchange rate is required for internal balance. Assuming that the nominal exchange rate influences or determines the real exchange rate, exchange rate policy would then be targeted on internal balance. With high capital mobility, monetary policy would determine the exchange rate.

Finally, with high capital mobility, we have thus two instruments, namely monetary policy and fiscal policy; and two targets, namely the optimal fiscal outcome and internal balance. Absorption and the current account are by-products. The analysis of Chapter 2 is still relevant. It highlights the relationships between absorption, the real exchange rate, and internal balance, relationships that remain crucial ingredients in a revised targets-and-instruments approach. Yet it has to be added that upon closer examination every target, whether the current account, internal balance, or the budget balance, turns out to be questionable, being no more than an approximation to a more complex examination of the underlying factors. The simple targets-instruments approach is no more than a first step to deeper analysis.

The next step is to consider qualifications to the New View. Given capital mobility, would policy-makers really be justified in ignoring changes in the current account when these are attributable to changes in private saving or investment behavior rather than to the budget balance?

IV. THE REAL EXCHANGE RATE AND EXCHANGE RATE PROTECTION

Let us now assume that a country's current account deteriorates, perhaps quite suddenly and sharply, owing to a private spending boom, that is, a rise in private investment or a fall in savings. The interest rate will tend to rise, which draws in capital from abroad, and the real exchange will appreciate as a result of some combination of rise in domestic prices and nominal appreciation. If the authorities wish to avoid temporary inflation—leading possibly to the generation of inflationary expectations and hence longer-term problems—these developments will be associated with some monetary contraction, which may avoid the rise in domestic prices and which will appreciate the nominal exchange rate further. In any case, there will be a real appreciation, with familiar redistributive effects affecting producers of tradable goods adversely, and probably raising real wages, at least in the nontradable sectors. This is a version of the real appreciation episode analyzed in Chapter 4. I assume here that there is no change in fiscal policy, though the budget balance could, of course, be affected by these developments. Naturally, foreign debt will build up as a result.

The question now is whether the current account deficit and build-up of foreign debt are matters for public policy concern. One can think of several channels through which, conceivably, they might be. The first follows from the real exchange rate implications of an increase in a current account deficit, however caused.

A movement into current account deficit, or a greater deficit than before, is (other things being equal) associated with real appreciation. Much of the concern with current account deficits and their sustainability is often connected with what I called in Chapter 4 the real appreciation problem. The concern is with the adverse distributional effects of changes in current accounts. If a current account goes into deficit in the way described, the problem can be of two kinds. First, the actual distributional effects of the change may be thought undesirable, and will certainly be perceived as such by losers, namely producers of tradables. Second, the current account deficit may be predicted to be temporary, being based perhaps on an inevitably temporary investment boom, or it may be unsustainable because of a growing debt–GDP ratio or a growing ratio of the country's debt instruments in international portfolios, leading to an increasing risk factor and an inevitable adjustment to a lower deficit. The temporary nature of the deficit, and hence of the real appreciation and national output patterns that go with it, are often thought to be undesirable because they are sources of instability. Hence, there is a natural pressure for exchange rate protection—i.e. measures that will avoid or moderate the real appreciation for the benefit of the tradable industries.

These two concerns—the immediate distributional effect and the dislike of a temporary shock—are somewhat contradictory. If distributional effects are temporary, they are, presumably, less sectorally damaging than if they were permanent. And if they are known to be temporary, they should not lead to costly reallocations of resources which will later be regretted as the real exchange rate depreciates again when the boom and the capital inflow come to an end.

It has to be borne in mind that an unsustainable deficit is not necessarily undesirable. An investment boom may be perfectly sound—the expected marginal productivity of capital exceeding the foreign rate of interest—yet it will inevitably be temporary. It can be interpreted as a sound stock adjustment—a switch in the nation's asset portfolio out of financial assets into real assets because the expected profitability of real assets has improved. Similarly, an apparent consumption boom is often really a boom in the acquisition by households of consumer durables and here, again, it can be regarded as an adjustment of asset portfolios.

It can certainly be conceded that stability of the real exchange rate, and hence of the size and profitability of the tradable relative to the non-tradable sectors, could be desirable, other things being equal; it could be one of a number of arguments in a plausible social welfare function. This suggests that some public policy action designed to modify or offset, at least in part, the current account and real exchange rate effects of a private sector boom could be justified. This, as I have noted, is the motive of exchange rate protection, and would be brought about by some fiscal contraction combined with monetary expansion or with direct intervention in the foreign exchange market designed to moderate the appreciation of the currency. If the exchange rate floated, fiscal contraction alone would do the job. But such a fiscal stabilization policy is likely to make the budget balance non-optimal from other points of view—government spending becoming too low or taxes too high—an adverse effect which would have to be traded off against the objective of real exchange rate stability. Furthermore, a fiscal stabilization policy aimed at the real exchange rate is subject to all the modern critiques of short-term demand management and stabilization policies.

Before leaving the real exchange rate issue, I should note that there could be a real-wage ratchet effect which may sometimes provide an additional argument in favor of some real exchange rate stability.

Real appreciation is likely to raise real wages, at least in the non-tradable sectors. It may be difficult to reduce real wages later when the real exchange rate needs to depreciate because the investment boom has come to an end and so the incentive for capital inflow has declined. If the nominal exchange rate is fixed, nominal wages will not fall, as they should, and if the nominal exchange rate is flexible, nominal depreciation may fail to bring about real depreciation because of real-wage rigidity. In other words, while the real wage is flexible upwards, it may well be inflexible, or sluggish, downwards—surely a common situation.

In this case, with real depreciation—and hence switching—not possible when the private spending boom has ended, unemployment will result. The implication of this argument is that fluctuations in capital inflow and hence the current account can have a ratchet effect on real wages. An increase in capital inflow and thus the current account deficit raises real wages, while a decline in inflow and the current account does not reduce them.

V. UNSOUND PRIVATE BORROWING AND THE SIGNALLING ROLE OF THE CURRENT ACCOUNT

I come now to another qualification of the New View, one that is undoubtedly important. Perhaps the private spending boom that gave rise to the current account deficit is unsoundly based. This could be because the government or central bank was understood to have provided implicit or explicit guarantees for domestic borrowers (a moral hazard problem) or because, for whatever reason, the country is just experiencing the usual unsound private sector boom destined to end in a bust. Even without guarantees involving the possibility of rescue operations, private losses are bound to be spread to the public sector, if only through reduced tax collections.

Basically I am assuming now either that there is a divergence between private and social interest (a domestic distortion) or that myopic private agents subject to a boom mentality do not really know what is best for themselves, and, in doing themselves and their shareholders and creditors harm, are also harming society as a whole. In Chile in the 1970s the government ended up taking over the foreign debts of private borrowers, and during the brief borrowing boom there appeared to have been a perception of implicit guarantees for private borrowers. In the Australian boom-and-bust of the 1980s there was a wide perception that leading Australian entrepreneurs who went heavily into debt did not really know what they were doing or, to put it mildly, showed poor judgment.

If there is no moral hazard problem, the suggestion that an unsound boom may justify public policy action to restrain it implies a belief that the official authorities may have more knowledge or judgment than the private agents creating the boom. But why should governments know better, when would we know that they know better, and can they be relied upon to act appropriately even when they do know better? These are questions which need to be asked, though universally valid answers can hardly be given. In my view there is some presumption that private agents would act at least as wisely in their own interest as government officials or politicians, but sometimes officials may indeed be more sensible or better informed. In any case, the moral hazard case may well predominate.

There may, then, be a case for policies that either moderate the boom through monetary contraction (in the absence of high capital mobility), or offset its effects through fiscal contraction. The move into sharp current account deficit can then be regarded as a warning signal of a problem. The deficit matters in the sense that it needs to be watched. It has a signaling role. This argument does not mean that a current account deficit must always be moderated or avoided, but only that a spending boom which caused it possibly should be. It is still necessary to look in detail at the sources of the deficit, as taught by the New View. Not all booms are unsound, or even partially so, so that second-guessing by the authorities is not necessarily justified. On the other hand, sudden movements into current account deficit owing to private spending booms suggest some risks for the public sector—risks of tax revenue losses and the need for bail-outs—so that a risk-averse government may well be wise to engage in some stabilizing fiscal measures or (in the absence of high capital mobility) on credit restrictions for private borrowers.

One might ask whether the availability of the international capital market is the source of the problem, since the current account deficit is only possible because foreign borrowing is possible. Suppose there were tight exchange controls which prevented foreign borrowing, or that foreigners were simply not prepared to lend to the booming country, possibly because of foreign restrictions on capital outflow. In that case, extra spending by some domestic sectors would be financed by crowding out domestic spending elsewhere. A current account problem would certainly be avoided. But would the country be better off?

On first thought one might conclude that there would surely also be a problem if an unsound private spending boom manifested itself not in a current account deficit, but in higher interest rates, leading to crowding out sound domestic investment. Surely the source of the problem is the unsound boom and not the fact that it is financed abroad. In fact, the matter is more complicated. The unsoundness of the boom is indeed a distortion, leading to a departure from optimality, but it is possible that an additional distortion, such as exchange controls, could, on balance, lead to an improvement.

There are two opposing factors at work. On the one hand, a higher domestic interest rate would probably discourage some of the unsound investment, this being a beneficial effect of not being able to borrow abroad. Unsound investment is reduced. On the other hand, the higher domestic interest rate would bring about a reduction of some sound investment which yielded an expected rate of return higher than the potential cost of foreign funds. The excess of the risk-adjusted domestic interest rate over the foreign interest rate brought about by exchange controls would be a measure of this distortion at the margin. Failure to take the opportunity to finance sound investment through foreign borrowing would be the cost of imposing exchange controls.

VI. CONTAMINATION EFFECT AND COUNTRY RISK

The more private agents or governments borrow, the larger the share of their equities or the debt instruments they issue in international portfolios. The larger this share, the greater the risk factor will be, and thus the interest rates that borrowers have to pay, or the lower the prices of their equities. This is obviously not an argument for keeping current account deficits to zero, since there cannot be any presumption that the existing stock of the nation's financial assets held abroad happens to be optimal to start with. Furthermore, the risk factor surely depends also on the state and prospects of the economy, which depend, among other things, on the way in which the borrowed funds have been used. The expected time paths of the debt-GDP and debt-export ratios may shed some light on the risk factor.

But all this is not really relevant for the central issue of whether the current account—as distinct from the build-up of *public* debt held at home or abroad—should be a matter of public policy concern. The real issue is whether changes in the risk factor resulting from increased borrowing are wholly internalized for the various agents, private and public, or whether there is some externality or contamination effect. If changes in the risk factor were wholly internalized—so that increased borrowing by one agent would not raise the risk factor facing another agent—there would be no public policy issue on this account resulting from current account deficits.

This is the key point. There has to be an externality. In the absence of an externality, individual agents will incorporate expected adverse effects of their own increased borrowing wholly in their own borrowing—and hence savings and investment—decisions. Other borrowers in the country will not be affected. In the absence of externalities, the New View does not have to be modified because of the risk factor.

Yet there is surely a possibility that borrowers do contaminate each other, so that there is an externality. Markets are concerned with country risk and do look at a country's total debt ratios. It is not unreasonable to presume that the more some private agents of a country borrow, the higher have to be the interest rates that are paid both by the government of the country and by other private agents. Perhaps this is not always so and, if markets are sensible, they will also look at the details—how much went into consumption, how much into investment, and so on. Yet such a concern of markets with country risk is not wholly irrational and can be explained by considerations already discussed.

Governments may have to rescue private agents in trouble, and so may encounter more financial difficulties themselves as a result of excessive private borrowing (hence increasing the need for rescheduling their own debts, for example). Conversely, private agents may have to rescue governments in trouble through paying higher taxes to finance mounting sovereign debt service obligations. In that case increased government borrowing may lead to higher interest rates facing private borrowers. Furthermore, if some private agents get into trouble, governments may have to raise taxes or reduce government services to finance their rescue, and this would then create financial problems for other private agents.

We have thus an important qualification to the New View resulting from the existence of country risk: from this aspect, at least, the current account as a whole, and not just the sources of its changes, is relevant. Decentralized decision-making could lead to excessive borrowing from a national point of view. But this qualification will only become relevant once debt ratios and current account deficits exceed certain levels, and particularly when increased borrowing is for consumption rather than for investment.

VII. CONCLUSION

Where does all this leave us? It is clear that in making a normative judgment about a current account balance, and especially about any big changes in it, it is necessary to go behind the scenes and see what has happened to the elements that gave rise to changes in private and public savings and investment. In special cases where there are no possibilities of foreign borrowing, this may not be necessary. Any prolonged current account deficit, and sometimes even a brief one, is a problem, unless financed by foreign aid or limited foreign exchange reserves. But, generally, more depth of analysis is required. There can be no general presumption that a current account deficit is undesirable.

The real exchange rate implications of current account deterioration are clearly important, and sometimes may justify some policy response in the form of stabilizing or moderating fiscal policy. Furthermore, the possibility that private spending decisions are non-optimal or unsound cannot be ruled out, especially if there are moral hazard possibilities. The contamination or country risk considerations I have discussed can be important. It follows that the current account cannot be ignored, especially for its signaling role, but the determinant of it which should be watched most closely is the budget deficit, for that is where the primary policy problem is likely to lie. Sometimes it may really be sufficient for public policy to ensure an optimal fiscal policy combined with optimal taxation or subsidization (if any) of private savings and investment, and then to allow the current account to take care of itself. The latter was the view I espoused as a general principle in Corden (1977).

REFERENCES

This chapter is closely based on Corden (1991*b*) which expounds the contrast between the Old View and the New View, and develops more fully the qualifications to the latter. Earlier doubts about the significance of the current account appeared in Corden (1977) and in Salop and Spittaller (1980). A number of theoretical articles imply or state the New View and provide intertemporal analyses of external balance. They usually assume that national savings and investment are determined independently and optimally, so that a time path for the optimal current account emerges. See Bruce and Purvis (1985), Frenkel and Razin (1987), Stockman (1988), and Pitchford (1989).

The current account issue has been hotly debated in Australia. From 1986 to 1990 the Australian current account deficit averaged 4.8 per cent of GDP, while there was an average budget surplus of 1 per cent of GDP. The decline of the fiscal deficit from 3 per cent of GDP to a small surplus in 1986 was associated with an increase in the current account deficit from 3.7 per cent of GDP to 5.5 per cent. Both private investment and consumption rose, and one explanation for the latter was undoubtedly financial liberalization. Many Australians have written on this issue. The initiator of the debate and principal proponent of what is here called the New View was John Pitchford. See especially Pitchford (1990).

EMS and Monetary Integration

7

The European Monetary System

THE European Monetary System (EMS) has been the most significant and effective international exchange rate arrangement operating since the breakdown of Bretton Woods. It was instituted in 1979 amidst much skepticism, but lasted, though with limited participation, until August 1993, and formally was still operating at the beginning of 1994. Its effective revival is not inconceivable. It is worth studying not only as a major episode in recent international monetary history but also as an example of an (almost) fixed-but-adjustable exchange rate system. It has provided the inspiration for various proposals for international monetary reform that I shall discuss later. Its history raises several interesting issues, including the use of an exchange rate commitment as a nominal anchor.

I. OVERVIEW: A TALE IN THREE ACTS

The EMS should be clearly distinguished from the European Monetary Union (EMU) proposal, dealt with in the next chapter. I shall now summarize the four main features of the EMS. Formally these still exist, so that one cannot really talk about the EMS in the past tense. Thus I follow with a present tense account. But it may well be that one is really describing a historical episode that came to an end in August 1993, because the effectiveness of the system had certainly ended, possibly temporarily, at that date.

The first and main feature is the Exchange Rate Mechanism or ERM. This is a bilateral exchange rate grid—that is, a set of central, bilateral rates which those members that have committed themselves to the ERM maintain. Until August 1993, the permissible margin of fluctuations on either side of a central rate was 2.25 per cent for most countries, except for some countries, notably Italy (and also Britain and Spain while they were within the ERM), where it had been 6 per cent. In August 1993, as the result of a crisis, the margin was increased to 15 per cent. For each bilateral rate the relevant two central banks have to intervene to an unlimited extent to keep the rate within the margins, buying and selling each other's currency. Thus the aim is (or was) to maintain short-term bilateral exchange rate stability. All the exchange rates together do, of course, fluctuate relative to outside currencies such as the dollar and the yen.

Second, there are credit facilities, both short term and medium term. Short-term credits are unconditional, while policy conditions are attached to medium-term credits. Since the Basle-Nyborg Agreement of September 1987, short-term credits can also be used for intervention when an exchange rate is within its margin.

Third—and this is a very important feature—there has never been an irrevocable commitment to the central rates. They can be changed or realigned after appropriate discussions. In practice they were often realigned even when the actual rates were within the margins. Thus the ERM is not formally a system of firmly fixed rates.

Finally, there is the ECU—a basket of currencies which is supposed to be used as a unit of account and to determine when intervention takes place. In practice, the ECU has turned out to be of no significance. The system has evolved not as an ECU-based but as a DM-based system. I shall discuss the role of the DM below, but the ECU can be ignored.

It is participation in the ERM, not the EMS, that matters. Britain has always been a member of the EMS. It could participate in certain meetings, and the pound sterling has always been included in the ECU basket. But Britain was a participant in the ERM for only two years.

The original participants in the ERM were Germany, France, Italy, Belgium, Denmark, Ireland, and the Netherlands. Spain joined in 1989, Britain in 1990, and Portugal in 1992. (In addition, in 1991 Sweden, Norway, and Finland linked their currencies unilaterally to the ERM, as had Austria earlier.) From 1979 to 1987 there were eleven realignments, the important ones having been of the lira and the French franc relative to the DM. Then there was a long period—from 13 January 1987 to September 1992—when there were none at all. The central rates were firmly fixed. Until late August 1992 many people believed that the ERM had been transformed into a fixed exchange rate system. On 17 September 1992 Italy and Britain left the system, possibly temporarily, while there was the first of a number of devaluations of the Spanish peseta within the system.

The story of the EMS or ERM is thus a tale in three acts. In Act I, which lasted until January 1987, there were many realignments, so that the ERM was in no sense a fixed rate system. But it did give some short-run exchange rate stability. In Act II, which lasted until September 1992, there were no realignments. The ERM seemed to have become a fixed rate system, though always with some possibility of realignment or departure from the system. Act III was inaugurated by the crisis of 16 September 1992—known in Britain as Black Wednesday. There was a further crisis at the end of July 1993 that led to the drastic widening of the margins, and this act is still playing.

The motive for the system changed significantly from the first to the second act. In the first act the motive was to produce some short-term exchange rate stability, and, where possible, even longer-term stability. In the second act, it was to provide a nominal anchor for anti-inflationary policy—to discipline domestic monetary policy and influence expectations. This was a classic nominal anchor episode of the type discussed in Chapter 5. In the third act, this objective broke down.

Finally, an important date should be noted here. In July 1990 France and Italy completely removed all capital controls. This was part of the Single Market Program agreed upon in 1988. Germany, Britain, and the Benelux countries had removed controls much earlier. I shall return to the significance of this event shortly.

II. MINI-BRETTON WOODS BUT BETTER

During Act I, lasting from 1979 to January 1987, the system could be described as follows. It was a mini-Bretton Woods system embodied in the world-wide floating rate system. The Deutschmark (DM) floated relative to the dollar, the yen, sterling, and various other currencies, while the franc, the lira, and the other currencies in the ERM were (almost) fixed in the short-term relative to the DM. Of course, they were not completely fixed because of the margins of fluctuation around the central rates. The central rates were frequently adjusted, so that the ERM was, like the Bretton Woods system, a "fixed-but-adjustable system". It differed from the Bretton Woods system because the adjustments were much more frequent and thus individually smaller and because the short-term credits provided were more generous. Hence, crises were averted.

At this stage the system did not bring about complete convergence of inflation rates, since Italian and French inflation rates—especially the former—were far above those of Germany. I shall return to the issue of inflation convergence below. But the ERM did bring about some degree of intra-European nominal exchange rate stability, avoiding the sort of gyrations to which the dollar was subject at the time. Inevitably, real exchange rates did not stay constant. Whenever the Italian inflation rate was higher than the German rate and the lira was not realigned, Italy would suffer real appreciation, which would be wholly or partially reversed once a realignment in the form of devaluation of the lira took place.

One can only understand the EMS if one understands the special role of the DM in relation to the dollar. When there are capital movements out of the United States, they tend to go into the DM rather than into the other EMS currencies, so that—in the absence of the ERM—the DM would appreciate not only relative to the dollar but also relative to the other European currencies. This tendency put great strains on the system since, because of the inflation differentials, the natural tendency is for the DM to appreciate in any case, a tendency that in the Act I period regularly forced realignments. On the other hand, appreciation of the dollar helps the system by keeping the DM relatively low. In the early years of the EMS, from 1981 to 1985, the dollar was appreciating, and this helped the system greatly, reducing the pressure for realignments. But there have been various episodes of strain, for example in 1992, when monetary expansion in the United States depreciated the dollar.

This dollar effect also helps to explain the German interest in the establishment of the EMS. From 1976 to 1978 the dollar depreciated owing to monetary expansion in the United States under the Carter administration. This was reversed by the Volcker deflation that began at the end of 1979. The DM appreciated not only relative to the dollar but also relative to other European currencies. German industry thus lost competitiveness. German trade with the United States, and competition with the United States in third markets, is less important than trade and competition with other European countries, notably France. Germany was thus eager for the effects of disturbances to the dollar to be shared with her Community partners, and thus wanted intra-European exchange rate stability. In an EMS system with stable exchange rates, all the participating currencies together would appreciate together relative to the dollar. After its huge appreciation from 1981 the dollar started depreciating again from February 1985, and there is no doubt that from then on German real appreciation was much less than it would have been in the absence of the EMS.

Originally the EMS was meant to be a symmetrical system, based on the ECU. One might ask how it came to be a DM-based system in the same way that the supposedly symmetrical Bretton Woods system came to be a dollar-based system. There were many realignments that involved depreciations, especially of the lira and the franc, and in each case these were depreciations relative to all the other currencies, including the DM (though sometimes several currencies were realigned at the same time). But the DM itself was never deliberately appreciated relative to all the others.

If Italy was losing competitiveness relative to Germany owing to Italy's inflation being higher, it was Italy that felt the need to take action, not Germany. Intervention at the margin would require a German contribution, but usually intervention was intra-marginal. Hence intervention was principally by Italy, with the help of the credits provided in the system. Insofar as Germany did intervene, it always ensured that the effects were sterilized. Italy had to adjust its monetary policies to the needs of the system, that is, to maintain its chosen parity, while German monetary policy was determined by domestic considerations and, above all, by the desire to keep inflation low. When realignments came to be expected, the interest rates of France or Italy, or whichever country's parity was involved, would rise, but there would be no change in the German interest rate. In general, this asymmetry met with the approval of the governments of the non-German members because they could see that the DM provided a non-inflationary anchor for the system. But I shall come back to the anchor role below.

As I have noted, the motive for constructing the system was to bring about some degree of exchange rate stability. Europeans (not including the British) were heavily committed to this objective. Giavazzi and Giovannini (1989) have stressed that this was the motive initially, not the aim which later became important, namely making the DM the nominal anchor for the monetary policies and the expectations of other countries. There were a number of reasons for the European aversion to exchange rate instability.

First, continental Europeans had bad memories of competitive devaluations in the 1930s, and the French looked back with no pleasure to their floating rate experience of the 1920s. Second, the economies trade heavily with each other, much more than with the world outside Europe. They are very open economies, an openness that was of course boosted by the establishment of the Common Market. Hence, they have had much more to gain from exchange rate stability than the United States or Japan, or even Britain. Third, it was difficult to run the Common Agricultural Policy (CAP)—with its centrally determined fixed internal prices—when exchange rates were changing. This is a complicated subject (like everything to do with the CAP), and here it is sufficient to note that special subsidies had to be introduced to compensate farmers who lost from their country's appreciation. Floating rates would be particularly inconvenient. These complications threatened the survival of the CAP, so that inevitably the French had a strong motive to favor exchange rate stability.

During Act I the system was a success. Indeed, many economists were surprised that it survived, bearing in mind that considerable divergences in inflation rates remained. After all, the Bretton Woods system had crashed, a fixed-but-adjustable system having been shown to be incompatible with high capital mobility.

What were the reasons for survival and success? First, Italy and France, the two relatively high inflation countries, maintained exchange controls that were at least partially effective—as evidenced by careful studies of interest rate differentials and their movements. Hence, capital mobility was imperfect. This was the most important single reason for the survival of the system.

Second, realignments were frequent and could thus be relatively small. Unlike in the Bretton Woods era, they were not reluctant. Realignments took place before crises built up. Third, the realignments were always mutually agreed upon. Hence, the new rates were more likely to be maintained since financial resources from Germany would be potentially available to sustain them. It was a system built upon co-operation rather than conflict and certainly not just upon unilateral decision-taking. The Bretton Woods system was also meant to be such a co-operative system, but in practice it did not operate in this way. Fourth, short-term credits were more ample. Finally, the margins around the central rates allowed for some flexibility, especially for Italy.

III. THE ERM AS NOMINAL ANCHOR

Between 1983 and 1985 there were no realignments, and a shift to the nominal anchor approach could already be perceived, especially in the case of France. After the eleventh realignment in the ERM in January 1987, Act II was inaugurated, though not formally, of course. There were no further realignments until 1992. In 1988 Spain joined the ERM, and in 1990 Italy's band around its central rate was narrowed to 2.25 per cent, the same as that of the other members. In October 1990 Britain joined. Also in 1990 the French government explicitly committed itself to a franc that would never be devalued within the ERM. This was a confirmation of the strong franc or *franc fort* policy that had actually been practiced since 1987, and arguably since the substantial devaluations that had taken place in 1982 and 1983. Later Norway, Sweden, and Finland unilaterally linked their currencies to the ERM.

The logic of the system was now clear. The German central bank—the Bundesbank—had low-inflation credibility. This was based not only on its independence from government and its own anti-inflationary tradition but also on the fact that it had support for conservative monetary policies from the German public. Because of its success in achieving its widely approved aims, the Bundesbank had high prestige. Other countries tried to import the Bundesbank's credibility by tying their currencies to the DM. This was a classic nominal anchor policy. But, since monetary policies were still independent and hence realignments or even complete departures from the ERM were not ruled out, credibility of the exchange rate commitments could not be complete.

How did the system affect inflation rates? To analyze the effects of the EMS on inflation, one must focus primarily on what happened to the inflation rates of France and Italy. One would not expect the German inflation rate to be affected significantly, since German monetary policy stayed, as I have noted, quite independent.

Both French and Italian inflation rates started falling in 1983—i.e. after the realignments of that year. By 1992 it was clear that there had been a great deal of convergence towards the German inflation rate. The French inflation rate was 13 per cent in 1980 and 1981, and was down to 6 per cent in 1985. It dropped drastically from 1986, and by 1992 was 3 per cent, actually lower than that of Germany. One must attribute this outcome to French tight monetary policies. But can one really say that French monetary policies were determined by the exchange rate commitment? The commitment might not have been made, or might have been broken in the form of a realignment, had the French authorities wished. Rather, tight monetary policies were made politically acceptable and generally credible by being tied to an exchange rate commitment which could be presented as being necessary for the survival of the European Community, and especially the common market. But interest rate differentials and also wages behavior showed that credibility of the *franc fort* was never complete.

The Italian inflation rate fell from 20 per cent in 1980 and 1981 to 11 per cent in 1984, and by 1992 was 6 per cent. This was certainly a remarkable achievement and, as in the case of France, connected with the EMS. But for the whole Act II fixed exchange rate period, the Italian inflation rate was 5–6 per cent, well above that of Germany and France, so that there was continued real appreciation of the lira (about 18 per cent from 1987 to 1992)—and hence the prospect of trouble. Inevitably the fixed exchange rate commitment was not fully credible, as indicated by interest rate differentials and wages behavior.

It is worth remembering that from 1983 inflation rates of all major OECD countries declined, notably those of the United States and Britain. Membership of the ERM was not needed to bring this about. On the other hand, it is true that the extent of the French and Italian declines, especially from 1986, was exceptional. The survival for nearly six years (1987–92) of an effectively fixed rate system (or narrow-margins system) was remarkable. It was particularly surprising because France and Italy had completely removed capital controls in July 1990. There was a widespread belief that this would create problems for the system—since speculation against exchange rates would become much easier. Hence, by early 1992 many observers were surprised that the fixed exchange rates had lasted. As I have noted, inflation rates had certainly converged, but the Italian inflation rate was still relatively high and considerable real appreciation of the lira had taken place.

In retrospect, it is clear that one reason why the system survived without realignments by 1992 was that the ERM began to be seen as a stage in the progress towards monetary union (EMU) to which the Maastricht Treaty appeared to have committed the members, including Britain. Here it is relevant that if countries wanted to follow the agreed Maastricht process, they would try to avoid realignments. As long as this was believed, high credibility attached to the existing exchange rate grid.

IV. THE BREAKDOWN AND AFTER

Now we come to Act III, with its two crises, one in 1992 and one in 1993. In August and September 1992, there was heavy foreign exchange speculation against many ERM and ERM-linked currencies, other than the DM, but including the French franc, the lira, and sterling. Various countries raised their interest rates, but speculation continued. The crisis came on 16 September—Black Wednesday. On 17 September the lira and sterling left the ERM, and the Spanish peseta was devalued. Pressure against various currencies, including the franc, continued later, and the peseta was subsequently devalued several times more. But the French franc, as well as the Dutch, Belgian, and Danish currencies, stayed in the system.

It is easy to say that this partial breakdown of the near-fixed exchange rate system was inevitable. The inevitable actually took a long time to happen. There were some fundamentals that made it inevitable, and some cyclical and political factors that caused it to happen when it did.

First, German unification led to a combination of fiscal expansion and monetary contraction—and hence to higher interest rates—in Germany. Fiscal expansion resulted from the need to subsidize East Germany, and monetary contraction was designed to avoid higher inflation. Actually German inflation did increase, reaching 5 per cent in 1991 and 1992, but no doubt it would have increased more in the absence of tight money policies. Higher interest rates meant that capital was inevitably drawn into Germany.

Second, the coincidence of this German expansion with recession elsewhere intensified the problem. Other countries—some of which, like Britain, were in recession or, like France, had a major unemployment problem—were reluctant to raise interest rates to the same extent.

Third, the recession in the United States led to monetary expansion there, and hence depreciation of the dollar and DM appreciation. This DM appreciation relative to the dollar then caused the other currencies that were in the ERM also to appreciate against the dollar. I have already mentioned this effect: dollar depreciation tends to increase tensions in the ERM.

Fourth, there was the most fundamental factor: Italian, Spanish, and British inflation rates had failed to converge earlier to German inflation rates, so that there was accumulated real appreciation. In Britain it was widely argued that sterling entered the ERM in 1990 at too appreciated a rate.

Finally—and this was the main political factor—doubts about the commitment of countries to the EMU process as charted by the Maastricht Treaty developed. The exchange rate breakdown came shortly after the Danish referendum when a majority of the people voted "No" and shortly before the French referendum about the outcome of which there were doubts. (There turned out to be a small "Yes" majority.)

It is interesting that in 1992 it was possible to maintain the *franc fort*. The superficial explanation is that the franc had become credible. But why had it? In 1992 it was often said that the French franc at its existing parity had become credible because the French fundamentals were right. The French inflation rate was actually below the German one, and the current account deficit was small. There was no reason for devaluation. But this ignored the fact that French unemployment was high and some French politicians and opinion-makers advocated Keynesian remedies—lower interest rates and thus inevitably devaluation. The basic assessment that the market had to make was whether a French government would engage in monetary expansion policies to reduce unemployment. The market looks not only at current fundamentals—which include the level of unemployment—but also at likely policy responses to these fundamentals.

The socialist government's commitment to the *franc fort* policy was rooted both in the French dislike of devaluations and in the 1982 experience when a newly elected socialist government was forced into devaluation as a result of engaging in monetary expansion when other countries, notably Germany, were following tight money policies. Furthermore, expectations about the policies that might be followed by an alternative government formed by opposition parties are always important. It seemed unlikely that a right-wing government would follow more expansionary policies than the surprisingly orthodox socialist government had.

In any case, this confidence in the *franc fort* policy did not last. When the Bundesbank decided not to lower its discount rate at the end of July 1993, there was strong pressure on the French franc and also the Belgian and Danish currencies, leading to heavy intervention to keep the currencies within the narrow margin. But the markets were more powerful, and on 1 August it was decided that the margin should be widened to 15 per cent. The central rates were not changed, and a narrow margin remained for the Dutch guilder. Tight monetary policies continued to be maintained by France, so that the franc actually depreciated very little, but one can no longer say that the ERM provides a nominal anchor or, indeed, any significant constraint, given such a wide margin.

In Chapter 4 I discussed the real exchange rate implications of capital inflow. It follows from the basic theory that, if a country swings from current account surplus into deficit, then—other things being equal—a real appreciation will be required. These ideas can be directly applied to the implications of German reunification. From having been a large net lender on the world capital market, Germany became a net borrower. The German current account surplus in 1990 was $47 billion, which was actually the largest in the world in that year, higher than Japan's. One year later Germany had a current account deficit of $20 billion.

Naturally one would expect the DM to appreciate in real terms not only relative to the dollar and the yen but also relative to its EMS partners. This might have been brought about by devaluations within the ERM of the other currencies, a policy that was favored by the Bundesbank. In the absence of these devaluations, real appreciation of the DM could only be brought about either by inflation in Germany or deflation elsewhere. Germany was rightly reluctant to inflate—though in fact the inflation rate did rise—and the others, notably Britain, were reluctant to deflate. It followed that tight monetary policies in Germany ensured that there would either be deflation in other countries—more than they wanted—or exchange rate adjustment, in this case forced by the market. If countries wanted to import anti-inflation credibility from the Bundesbank, they should have welcomed the latter's commitment to a low-inflation monetary policy. Given the nominal anchor approach, the unusual situation created by German unification called for a once-for-all (and clearly once-for-all) appreciation of the DM relative to all other currencies.

That is the end of the story of the EMS and the ERM—at least for the time being. I shall come back to options for the future in Chapters 9 and 16. But, before leaving this subject, I shall discuss in more detail the arguments for and against joining the ERM as it appeared in Britain in the 1980s. This debate highlighted the basic issue of whether it is desirable to accept a fixed-but-adjustable exchange rate regime for the sake of exchange rate stability and anchoring inflation. I also expound the issues in Appendices 7.1 and 7.2.

V. IN AND OUT BY BRITAIN: THE ARGUMENTS FOR AND AGAINST JOINING

Britain entered the ERM only in October 1990, but for at least five years before that its policy-makers agonized whether to join. Britain left again—with no immediate intention of rejoining—in September 1992. Since then sterling has floated, though there is certainly intervention, and interest rate policy does not completely ignore effects on the exchange rate.

British attitudes to exchange rate stability and the possibilities of making an exchange rate commitment were different from those in the rest of the Community. There was certainly no concern over the preservation of the Common Agricultural Policy. Historical memories included recollection both of the benefits of devaluation in 1931 and of the political cost of attempts to maintain a fixed exchange rate in face of sterling crises during the Bretton Woods period. There was also a widespread, deeply ingrained belief in the virtues of short-term fine-tuning through variations in the interest rate. Most important, Britain had removed exchange controls in 1979 and there was a huge market in highly mobile sterling. In the absence of complete credibility, it would be difficult to maintain a chosen exchange rate in the face of market forces.

In spite of all this, as early as 1985 the idea of joining the ERM had a strong appeal in Britain. The then Chancellor of the Exchequer, Nigel Lawson, became a believer and there was wide support for ERM membership. But Prime Minister Margaret Thatcher was adamantly opposed—until she reluctantly gave way in 1990, by which time Lawson had resigned, essentially over differences on this issue. Nigel Lawson in his memoirs (1992) lays out the arguments put by him and by Margaret Thatcher in 1985. These highlight the central issue of whether to adopt a fixed-but-adjustable exchange rate regime for the sake of maintaining economic stability, and especially low inflation.

Mrs Thatcher was not concerned about exchange rate instability. In her view there was no alternative to leaving exchange rate determination to market forces. She was certainly committed to fighting inflation. But, as she saw it, the anchor was either a tight money policy or—and this was probably her deepest belief—the strong commitment of Margaret Thatcher and her government to low inflation by following tight monetary policies. Particular measures of the money supply may not send out very accurate signals, but policy adjustments could be made to reverse short-term mistakes, and inflationary expectations would be kept down by public understanding of her strong anti-inflation commitment.

Nigel Lawson was motivated both by the need for exchange rate stability and by the need for a nominal anchor to keep inflation and inflationary expectations low—which were the two motives of the system that I have already discussed. He was influenced by the huge appreciation of the dollar from 1981 to 1985, which culminated in a remarkable speculative bubble that ended in February 1985 and was followed by depreciation which completely reversed the earlier appreciation within two years. The movements of the dollar had affected sterling in seemingly irrational ways—sterling having depreciated sharply in 1984—and this concerned him. In his view (and that of others) some degree of exchange rate commitment by the monetary authorities could moderate or even avoid speculative capital movements that compelled either exchange rates or interest rates, or both, to move so drastically. In addition he did not want a repetition of the sharp and unexpected appreciation of sterling in 1980 and 1981 that had resulted from the Thatcher government's policy of monetary contraction.

Mr Lawson believed strongly in the need for a nominal anchor and preferred rules over discretion. The Thatcher government—influenced by Milton Friedman—began with an almost religious belief in monetary targeting as the appropriate anti-inflation technique. A fixed, predictable rate of growth of the money supply was meant to be the nominal anchor. But the chosen measure of money—namely M3, known as "broad money"—had sent out very misleading signals. In 1980 and 1981 it was growing very fast, and yet the exchange rate was appreciating and Britain moved into a severe recession—all signs of tight, not loose, money. The reason was that financial liberalization had led to a move out of various assets into interest-bearing deposits that were included in the M3 measure. By 1985 various measures of money had been tried and all were found wanting. Insofar as it was attempted to manage the economy and attain low and steady inflation by looking at the state of overall demand, statistics indicating the state of demand came out with a lag, and early figures often turned out to be inaccurate. Thus Nigel Lawson and others came to be disillusioned with money supply and other measures as possible nominal anchors. The Europeans, notably France, seemed to do much better by, in effect, fixing to the DM.

One can summarize the contrasting views as follows. Mrs Thatcher believed that freedom to vary interest rates to achieve domestic objectives—including, above all, low inflation—should be the paramount objective. The interest rate should not be destabilized to maintain an exchange rate objective, as was inevitable when a fixed exchange rate is maintained while the regime is not fully credible, so that there are speculative capital movements. By contrast, Mr Lawson believed that a credible exchange rate commitment would provide an anchor for expectations and so moderate speculative capital movements. The need for undesirable interest rate variations would then be reduced. I compare these two positions in a diagram in Appendix 7.1.

The weakness of the Thatcher position was that it ignored the disadvantages of exchange rate instability for trade and rational long-term investment, as well as the difficulty of finding a suitable anchor for monetary policy and for inflationary expectations, other than the exchange rate. The primary weakness of the Lawson position was that it ignored the possibility that, for one reason or another, the nominal anchor might fail, above all because credibility in the foreign exchange market was not attained. It thus ignored the possibility of something like a Black Wednesday event. In effect, such a crisis can only be averted by a willingness to vary short-term domestic interest rates severely, ignoring all domestic considerations.

APPENDIX 7.1

A Fixed-but-Adjustable Regime: the Paradox of Expectations

In Fig. 7.1 the spot exchange rate e is shown on the vertical axis and the domestic interest rate r on the horizontal. An increase in e represents a depreciation. The given world interest rate is $r^\star$ and the risk premium is S. The curve E_0 is drawn for a given expected exchange rate, and also given $r^\star$ and S. It shows the return on foreign-currency deposits in terms of domestic currency: as e falls (appreciates), the return increases, since expected depreciation will increase. It follows from the interest parity formula (see Appendix 12.1) that, with capital mobility, $e = E_0$ when $r = r^\star + S$. Hence, we obtain the starting-point A. If the expected exchange rate depreciates, the curve will shift to a position such as E_1. Given such a change in expectations, if the spot exchange rate were to stay constant, r would have to rise as indicated by the move from A to W.

The line M_0 shows short-run money market equilibrium for a given initial money supply (M). (An increase in e raises the demand for M because it raises the domestic price level, and an increase in r lowers it). Say M is expected to increase to M_1. The expected exchange rate will then move to E_1. (This is the exchange rate compatible with the increase in M and a constant $r = r^\star + S$.) If the spot rate is to stay constant, M will have to fall to M_2, so that equilibrium W is attained.

The paradox—very evident in the September 1992 and July 1993 EMS crises—is that an *expected* increase in M (to M_1) which—if it had eventuated—would have increased the demand for domestic goods through its exchange rate effect, will bring forth an *actual* decrease (to M_2) if monetary policy aims to keep the exchange rate fixed. (A minor complication is that an increase in M might have led to overshooting, hence causing r actually to fall, so that a point such as D, instead of C, would initially have been attained if the exchange rate had not been kept fixed. In addition, r would have fallen because of imperfect substitutability of foreign for domestic assets. Thus—when it is attempted to keep the exchange rate fixed—an *expected* fall in r leads to an *actual* rise in r.)

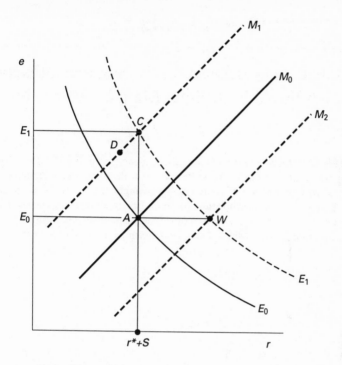

FIG. 7.1. Fixed Rate: Expectation of Devaluation leads to Decline in Money Supply

APPENDIX 7.2

The Choice between a Floating and a Fixed-but-Adjustable Regime: Margaret versus Nigel

In Fig. 7.2 the E curves have the same meaning as in Fig. 7.1. In a floating rate regime, with no commitment to a fixed rate, expectations will move around without any anchor. They might thus move to a position such as E_1. But the authorities would be free to allow some depreciation or rise in the interest rate, or both. They would choose some optimal combination (as perceived from their point of view) as represented by

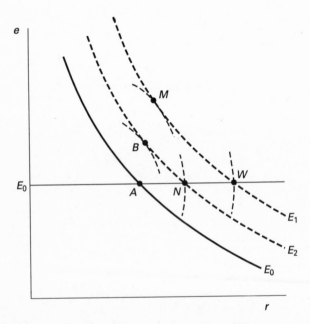

FIG. 7.2. Choice between Floating (Point M) and Fixed-but-Adjustable (Point N) Regime

point M, interest rate policy bringing this about. This is the Margaret Thatcher equilibrium. If there were a very strong aversion to any interest rate increase at all, M would be vertically above A. The attraction of this policy is that the government is "free to choose".

If a fixed exchange rate commitment were made, and this were utterly credible, the E curve would not shift at all from E_0 and equilibrium could stay at A. If, as is likely, the commitment is only somewhat credible, the curve will shift, say, to E_2, expected depreciation being less than if there had been no commitment. To maintain a fixed exchange rate, some rise in r will still be required, but less than in a floating rate regime. Assuming the exchange rate commitment is kept, the new equilibrium will be at N, the Nigel Lawson equilibrium. The attraction of this policy is that some stability of expectations has been obtained, and this has modified the extent of the required rise in r.

Two "surprise" equilibria

If a clear signal that a fixed exchange rate policy is being followed is not sent out—so that expectations move to E_1—while a fixed exchange rate policy is actually followed, equilibrium W will result, this being the Worst Equilibrium. It would result from a very foolish "surprise" policy. Alternatively, a fairly credible fixed exchange rate commitment may indeed be made—so that expectations move only to E_2—but it is reneged upon, so that the optimal point given the new expectations is chosen. Equilibrium B will then result, and this is the Best Equilibrium, but strictly only in the short run, since the surprise will affect the credibility of future fixed rate commitments.

In the diagram a set of indifference curves is drawn, indicating levels of short-run utility of the policy-makers. Ideally they want stability in both e and r, so that A is the maximum welfare point. M and B represent maxima given the relevant exchange rate expectations. Clearly B is the best (in the short run) and W the worst. But whether M (Margaret) or N (Nigel) is superior is not clear. Each has an advantage; Margaret allows policy freedom with any given expectations, and Nigel favorably affects expectations.

More can be done with this diagram. If the world interest rate rises, E_0 will shift to the right and so will the other curves for given expectations. Maintaining a fixed exchange rate will require a greater increase in r, and so M is more likely to be superior to N. If Nigel had known that German interest rates would rise as much as they did because of German unification, he might not have favored effectively fixing the pound to the DM.

REFERENCES

Giavazzi and Giovannini (1989) give a thorough account of the EMS until 1988. See also Giavazzi (1990) and Gros and Thygesen (1992). In Giavazzi and Giovannini (1990) the authors conclude that the EMS could not be copied outside Europe.

A detailed analysis of the EMS crisis of 1992 is in Goldstein *et al.* (1993) and a comprehensive account of both the 1992 and 1993 crises and their implications in International Monetary Fund (1993). Developments in the EMS are always reported in detail in the *Annual Reports* of the Bank for International Settlements.

Figs. 7.1 and 7.2 are based on diagrams used in Krugman and Obstfeld (1991, ch. 13).

8

Monetary Integration

In this chapter I look at the benefits and costs resulting from the establishment of a monetary union, and at various related issues—such as whether independent fiscal policies can continue in a union. The comparison will be with a flexible exchange rate regime where the rates float or are fixed but adjustable.

I. THE MEANING OF MONETARY UNION

A monetary union is an area with a single currency controlled by a single central bank. Different countries or provinces within the union cannot have their own moneys and thus exchange rates. Hence, the establishment of a monetary union by a group of countries deprives them of the individual freedom to manage their monetary policies. Of course, the value of the common currency of the monetary union (say, the ECU) can still float, or be adjusted at intervals, relative to outside currencies, such as the dollar and the yen.

The immediate relevance of this topic comes from the proclaimed intention embodied in the Maastricht Treaty of 1991 to establish a European Monetary Union. But the issue is more general. The most recent formation of a monetary union out of two previously independent countries was that of the new reunited Germany. Monetary unions could possibly be formed by other groups of independent countries, and existing countries—which are always monetary unions—could theoretically be broken up into smaller currency areas. The issue certainly arises in the former Soviet Union.

There are complex transition problems in a move from separate flexible exchange rate regimes to a monetary union. This raises some of the most hotly discussed issues for Europe which I shall discuss in the next chapter. Here I shall simply assume that the monetary union exists and compare it with its alternatives.

I shall refer interchangeably to an independent monetary policy and an independent exchange rate policy. Both of these are given up when a country joins a monetary union. In the short run there is some distinction between the two, provided capital mobility is imperfect, so that sterilized intervention in the foreign exchange market (which does not affect the money supply) has some effect on the exchange rate. The greater is capital mobility, the less significant is the distinction between the two. With high capital mobility—as there is in Europe—a policy change in the exchange rate cannot be sustained without a change in monetary policy. A decision to devalue, for example, implies a decision to expand the money supply appropriately to bring this result about. I shall discuss the effectiveness of sterilized intervention further in Chapter 12.

The normal definition of a monetary union includes not only the condition that there is a single currency and a single exchange rate relative to any given outside currency, but also that there is complete freedom of capital movements within the union. In the case of Europe this has been (more or less) achieved by the Single Market Program, and, indeed, international capital mobility is now so high that this aspect of the establishment of a European Monetary Union is no longer relevant. High capital mobility also exists between other countries, such as the United States, Japan, and Britain, where the question of the establishment of a monetary union among them does not arise.

Finally, a distinction must be made between a *pseudo-exchange rate union* and a *complete exchange rate union*. They are distinguished by the credibility of the commitment involved. In the former case (which was proposed at various times in Europe), there may be a commitment by the member states to establish irrevocably fixed exchange rates. But separate currencies controlled by separate central banks would still remain. The possibility of realignment of bilateral exchange rates would thus still exist. This is (to use terms I expound later) a "loose" and not a "solid" arrangement. The exchange rates would be fixed-but-adjustable, even though the proclaimed intention is not to adjust. The commitment is only credible once the major institutional change—the creation of a single currency controlled by a single central bank—

is made. That is a complete exchange rate union, an essential component of monetary union.

An ambiguous intermediate transitional arrangement is one where separate currencies are maintained but they are controlled by the single central bank of the union, and the central bank commits itself to maintaining irrevocably fixed exchange rates. Even then the commitment is probably not wholly credible, so that such an arrangement is not a complete exchange rate union. In any case, here I shall assume that the monetary union has a single currency.

II. THE PRINCIPAL BENEFIT AND THE PRINCIPAL COST OF MONETARY UNION

The principal benefit of a common currency is rather obvious. There are economies of scale in the use of money, and it is clearly convenient for a single money to cover as wide an area as possible. I have already noted that Europeans, other than the British, dislike floating exchange rates. Movements in the foreign exchange market do not always make sense. Floating rates are thought to have adverse effects on trade (though there is little empirical support for this view) and to be generally inconvenient. A related suggestion is that floating rates stimulate pressures for increased protection, presumably only in countries where the exchange rate appreciates. I come back to this idea in Chapter 14.

Possibly the transaction costs for trade and capital movements that are created by fluctuating exchange rates are small in proportion to total costs, at least for large transactions. But the uncertainties created for investment decisions are surely significant. When over a short period exchange rates can change by 10 per cent or more, they can quickly cancel out the effects of tariff reductions or labor-cost savings. New financial instruments make it more and more possible to hedge against these risks, so that the costs of unexpected exchange rate variations, both short and long term, are likely to decline in time. Hence, the advantage that a common currency has over a floating rate regime from this point of view will also decline, though it is unlikely to disappear. In the absence of monetary union the alternative to a floating rate regime is a fixed-but-adjustable exchange rate system. This avoids some of the problems of freely floating rates but invites exchange rate crises and losses by central banks.

It is important to bear in mind that changes in exchange rates can affect the whole price structure of a country and not just prices involved directly in international trade or capital movements. Thus a depreciation will raise the domestic prices of all exportables, including those sold at home. Undue fluctuations in such prices will have unnecessary and unpopular domestic redistributive effects.

The principal cost of a monetary union relative to the flexible exchange rate alternative is the cost incurred by a member country when its government loses the management of the domestic money supply as an instrument of policy. The union central bank will still have this instrument, but only for the union as a whole. When the world demand for French goods falls, the French government can no longer bring about a devaluation of the franc either relative to the DM or relative to the dollar. The central issue is whether an independent exchange rate (monetary policy) instrument for a potential member country of the union is likely to be effective and needed. There are three distinct considerations to be taken into account, namely, (1) the nature of wages behavior, (2) the likelihood of asymmetric shocks, and (3) the extent of different policy preferences. I have already discussed the first of these in Chapter 3, but I return to it here.

III. REAL AND NOMINAL WAGE RIGIDITY

If the real wage were rigid, possibly because of formal indexation of wages with very short lags, a nominal devaluation would not lead to real devaluation. There would then be no point in devaluing in response to an adverse shock. The exchange rate instrument would be useless, and hence there could be no cost of giving it up.

Alternatively, suppose that the nominal wage were completely flexible in response to labor-market conditions, this being the neo-classical case. A reduction of demand for labor would very quickly lead to a decline in nominal wages, and then prices of non-tradables, and, with a fixed nominal exchange rate, a real devaluation would result. The labor market would automatically equilibrate. The exchange rate would not be needed as an instrument of policy, and there would also be no cost incurred by giving up this instrument.

This then leaves the third—or Keynesian—case where the real wage is flexible but the nominal wage is rigid or sluggish. This was the case expounded in Chapter 2. A reduction of demand would not lead to a decline in nominal wages—or at least not a speedy decline—so that a real devaluation would not come about automatically when the demand for labor fell. Furthermore, a rise in prices would not lead to an increase in nominal wages sufficient to prevent a fall in real wages. Hence, a nominal devaluation (or a rise in domestic prices brought about in other ways) can reduce the real wage, at least for a significant period of time. Nominal devaluation leads to real devaluation. It is in this Keynesian case that the exchange rate is an effective and necessary instrument of policy. Hence, a cost is incurred in giving up this instrument. If the Keynesian case applies, we have an argument *against* monetary union, to be set against the argument in favor given earlier.

A central theme of the theory of optimum currency areas, owed to Mundell (1961) and McKinnon (1963), is that the smaller the size of an economy, the less successful nominal exchange rate adjustment would be in bringing about a change in the real exchange rate. It is less likely that nominal wages would be fixed in domestic currency terms when increases in the prices of tradable goods would have large effects on the domestic price level. The larger the share of tradables in the consumption basket, the more likely is it that nominal wages would rise after a devaluation. To some extent, rigidity of nominal wages may reflect money illusion, but the smaller the economy, and hence the larger the share of traded goods in consumption and production, the less this illusion is likely to be. Hence, small, high trading economies are unlikely to gain from being able to use the exchange rate as a policy instrument to affect real targets: they are not optimum currency areas. The Keynesian case does not apply to them.

That, at least, is the argument. But one can think of plenty of modest-sized economies, especially in the developing world, where nominal devaluations have led to real devaluations that have lasted for some time, so this argument against the prevalence of the Keynesian case must be treated with caution.

Nevertheless, it is obvious that, both for this reason and because of the loss of the utility of money when it covers a small area, very small economies are not optimum currency areas. Surely Monaco should not have its own flexible exchange rate.

It is notorious that there is considerable real wage rigidity in the potential member countries of a European Monetary Union, this being a major cause of the high level of structural unemployment. While wage increases do not instantaneously follow price increases, they do follow very quickly. Hence, after a little time, a devaluation turns out just to have raised prices without bringing about the desired real devaluation and switching effect. A great deal of empirical research has been done on this subject. For this reason it has been frequently argued—especially by the advocates of monetary integration—that the exchange rate is not a useful instrument of policy in Europe.

In my judgment the evidence supports the view that—while there is indeed some tendency for nominal wages to follow prices with a lag—nominal devaluations have had real competitiveness effects in Europe provided they were associated with the appropriate disabsorption policies. Several examples can be given from the period around 1982, and again from 1992–3. For example, de Grauwe (1989) cites the case of the Belgian devaluation of 1982. This is not to underplay the adverse effects on employment of some tendency to real wage rigidity, especially in Germany.

One conclusion clearly emerges. If there is some tendency for the Keynesian assumptions to apply, so that real wages in the tradable sectors can be reduced by devaluation, a cost is incurred by giving up the exchange rate instrument. The Keynesian effect is only likely to be short run, but it may be sufficiently long lasting to be significant for employment. If a monetary union were established, an alternative way of bringing about necessary changes in real wages—or in their rates of increase—would have to be found. The obvious answer is that nominal wages will have to be more flexible downwards. If monetary integration is indeed achieved by the Community, the neo-classical mechanism will have to replace the Keynesian mechanism. The vital importance for the success of EMU of strengthening downward wage flexibility is often neglected.

Actually, EMU could have the opposite effect. It might lead to trade union integration, leading to uniformity of wage rates throughout the area of the union. It is well known that within individual countries there is some tendency for wages in areas of relatively lower productivity to approximate, or even equal, those in high productivity areas, causing unemployment in the former. When a single money rules in both regions, differences in real-wage levels become more transparent. Furthermore, the general tendency to integration inevitably brings with it trade union integration. This adverse effect could be seen most dramatically as a result of German unification. The increases in nominal and real wages in Eastern Germany after unification were not caused solely by the establishment of a monetary union. Perhaps there was some need to raise East German wages so as to discourage emigration. But monetary union clearly made wage comparisons between East and West Germany much easier, and thus created a tendency for equalization.

IV. ASYMMETRIC SHOCKS

A shock may affect all the countries of the monetary union equally. There may be a general decline in demand or the terms of trade, and the effects may be much the same throughout the union. Particular industries may be affected relatively more adversely, but these industries may be operating in many member countries. Possibly the union as a whole needs to devalue in real terms relative to the outside world. In this kind of case, a single monetary policy may be appropriate and nothing may be lost when the individual member countries give up their exchange rate instrument. This is the case of a symmetric shock.

But shocks are highly likely to be asymmetric, some countries being affected differently from others. Some shocks may be quite specific to particular countries. A rise in the oil price affects countries differently. A decline in a particular large industry could have a major effect on one country and very little effect on another. A recession has differential effects on industries, and therefore countries. Political developments in one country (say, the election of a populist government) could lead to expectations of reduced profits and hence reduced capital inflow or greater capital outflow, thus requiring real depreciation. Alternatively, a new government could engage in fiscal expansion, increasing its borrowing on the capital market, and this would require real appreciation.

The most dramatic asymmetric shock in Europe in recent years was German reunification. Given the reluctance to raise taxes, the costs incurred by the government of the Federal Republic, in order to assist and subsidize its new citizens and their industries, led to substantial fiscal expansion. Hence, the interest rate rose and the current account swung from surplus to deficit. Interest rates rose even further because of a tight monetary policy designed to prevent (or tone down) an uncharacteristic rise in inflation in Germany. The shift in fiscal policy required a real appreciation which—in the absence of exchange rate adjustment—could be brought about either by temporary inflation in Germany or by declines in prices in Germany's principal trading partners. As I noted in the previous chapter, this development was one cause of the 1992 crisis of the European Monetary System. German reluctance to allow some temporary inflation compelled other countries to choose between deflation and devaluation. In the absence of the exchange rate instrument, and given downward wage rigidity (the Keynesian case) in the trading partners, the appropriate policy response was for Germany to accept some inflation. Yet this breach with sound German anti-inflation habits would probably have raised inflationary expectations, with long-term adverse effects.

Can anything in general be said about the likelihood of asymmetric shocks? Kenen (1969) has pointed out that large economies are likely to be more diversified than small economies, so that shifts in the fortunes of particular industries would not be so likely to affect the economy as a whole and thus require real depreciation or appreciation. Asymmetric shocks between two large economies, like France and Germany, are less likely. Hence they could form a monetary union without incurring a serious cost through losing their individual exchange rate instruments. On the other hand, when a relatively small, and hence more specialized, economy joins a monetary union either with another small economy or with a large economy, it is more likely to incur a cost. It is more likely to suffer asymmetric shocks.

It is interesting that this Kenen argument leads to the opposite result from the McKinnon (1963) argument given earlier. Kenen suggests that large economies do not need the exchange rate instrument, being less likely to suffer asymmetric shocks. McKinnon suggests that small economies cannot use the exchange rate instrument since they will not have a sufficient degree of nominal wage rigidity or sluggishness. In the Kenen case, real exchange adjustment is not necessary, or is less necessary, for large economies, while, in the McKinnon case, for small economies real exchange rate adjustment cannot be brought about (for a reasonable length of time) by nominal exchange rate changes. One can summarize this apparent conflict as follows. For the large, diversified economy, real exchange rate devaluation brought about by nominal devaluation is possible but not necessary (Kenen), while for the small, undiversified economy, it is necessary but not possible (McKinnon). On balance, I would give more weight to the McKinnon argument: the smaller the economy, the less likely it is to be an optimum currency area.

Empirical work by Bayoumi and Eichengreen (1993) and others has sought to determine whether asymmetric shocks have been more or less common in the potential member countries of EMU than in the different regions of the United States. Of course there are big measurement problems. It seems that asymmetric shocks have been quite severe in the United States, which suggests that even the world's largest economy might not be an optimum currency area. Some cost is thus incurred because US regions do not have separate exchange rates. Asymmetric shocks within a European core group, consisting of Germany, France, the Netherlands, Belgium, and Denmark, have been low, suggesting that this region could well form a monetary union. But this empirical work does not embrace the German reunification period. Britain, Italy, and Spain have suffered asymmetric shocks—i.e. shocks that have differed considerably from the average in the EMS group and that have involved noticeable real depreciations or appreciations.

I have still to deal with the effects of different policy preferences among the member countries of the union. But it is useful to summarize at this point. When a monetary union is established, a cost is incurred—the cost of losing the exchange rate instrument—if two conditions are fulfilled. First, there must be Keynesian effects, that is, some degree of nominal wage rigidity downwards and real wage flexibility. Second, there must be a reasonable expectation of asymmetric shocks. On balance, it seems that short-run Keynesian effects—possibly lasting for some time—are usual. Furthermore, asymmetric shocks are always possible and quite likely, especially if countries preserve political and fiscal independence. In other words, there will always be need for real exchange rate changes and these will be brought about more readily by nominal exchange rate changes than through wage–price flexibility. But the Keynesian effects are only short run, and in some cases may be very brief. Furthermore, this cost of monetary union must be set against the benefits noted earlier.

V. DIFFERENT POLICY PREFERENCES

Suppose that there is a recession which affects the member countries of a monetary union much the same. The shock is thus symmetric. A union-wide monetary expansion would stimulate the economy in the short term but might raise inflationary expectations, and then increase inflation later. There is always an inflation risk, especially if the lags between the need for expansionary action, its recognition, its implementation, and then its effects, are allowed for. Different countries within the union may assess these risks differently on the basis of their historical experiences, and hence would choose different points on the trade-off between reduced unemployment now and higher inflation later. When it loses its monetary independence, each country can no longer pursue its own preferences. A single decision for the union as a whole has to be made by the union's central bank. It follows that, when policy tastes differ, monetary union imposes a cost even if shocks are symmetric. This argument applies to the policy response to adverse shocks of all kinds, whether resulting from a union-wide terms-of-trade deterioration or a recession.

This kind of problem can be found within countries now. Policy views differ, and these differences might be reflected in different regional attitudes. In Europe historical memories matter, like the German memory of hyperinflation and the British one of high unemployment. Different policy preferences, especially between Germany and the other countries, played a role in the failure in 1992 to maintain fixed rates within the EMS. In addition, social conditions may vary, so that some countries more than others can risk a short-term increase in unemployment for the sake of keeping inflation down in the long term. Perhaps, as the European Union becomes more integrated in many respects and memories of different experiences fade, this particular problem or cost of monetary union will also fade away.

VI. INFLATION: THE PHILLIPS CURVE AND CREDIBILITY

In Chapter 5, I introduced the distinction between the pro-equilibrium and the anti-equilibrium role of the exchange rate. I come back to this distinction now. Consider the effects of an adverse shock which reduces demand. If the nominal exchange rate were fixed, nominal wages, and prices of non-tradables, would slowly fall (at least relative to growing productivity) so that the real exchange rate would depreciate and equilibrium would be reached eventually. But during the process—while absorption reduction maintained external balance and switching was inadequate—excessive unemployment would result. The role of exchange rate depreciation is to help an economy reach the new equilibrium more quickly. As I have stressed in Chapter 3, this role depends on nominal wages being sluggish downwards and real wages being flexible.

Hence, adjustment of the nominal exchange rate has a pro-equilibrium role. Focusing on the need for the real wage to fall in response to an adverse shock, the role of monetary expansion and devaluation is to bring about a more rapid and smooth movement to a new equilibrium real-wage level. If the real wage needs to fall, it will fall more quickly, and so a temporary period of excess unemployment will be avoided.

(1) *The Phillips Curve and the Anti-Equilibrium Role of Monetary Policy*

I now come to the important case where monetary policy and the exchange rate fulfil an anti-equilibrium role. These policies are used to reduce the real-wage level and the level of unemployment below their equilibrium levels. Such an effort cannot succeed permanently and will eventually just leave a country with more inflation. But it may have a temporary effect. I explain the difference between these two roles with the help of a diagram in Appendix 8.1.

The argument that I now present has to be severely qualified in the light of recent thinking and an impressive literature about credibility and expectations, and I shall introduce these qualifications shortly. But the basic argument is still relevant. Conceptually, countries have short-run Phillips curves, even if these are in practice difficult to measure. The higher the rate of inflation and (in a flexible rate regime) the more the exchange rate depreciates, the lower the real wages and the greater the level of output. The details of this idea I shall not pursue here. These effects are clearly short term: the Phillips curves are expectations-augmented, meaning that the higher the actual rate of inflation, the higher will be inflationary expectations, and thus the lower the level of employment for any given rate of inflation later.

If one focuses on the real wage level as the principal determinant of employment, and thus abstracts from many other factors, the essential argument is that unexpected inflation reduces the real-wage level below its equilibrium level. It fulfils an anti-equilibrium role. It can only do this for a limited period: eventually, as expectations adjust, nominal wages will adjust to restore the equilibrium level of real wages, and thus the equilibrium level of output that goes with it. Nevertheless, in the short run there is a trade-off between inflation and unemployment. In addition, there is an intertemporal trade-off, so that the higher the rate of inflation that is chosen today, the worse the trade-off will be in later periods.

Let us now apply this idea to the monetary integration issue. Different countries have different Phillips curves and governments have different policy tastes, so that they will wish to choose different rates of inflation. Some, like Germany, will choose low rates of inflation, even at the cost of high short-run unemployment, while others—like pre-Thatcher Britain, and possibly also post-Thatcher Britain—will choose somewhat higher rates of inflation for the sake of lower unemployment and (as it is usually put in Britain), "going for growth" today, even though this is at the cost of a worse trade-off and thus more inflation, and possibly less employment later. In a monetary union, countries would no longer have this freedom of choice. The monetary policy of the union's central bank would determine the outcome for all of them. Possibly some countries, like Germany, would end up with more inflation than they would have chosen themselves, while others, like Britain, would end up with less inflation and, in the short run, more unemployment.

If one concedes that the government of each country acting independently would have chosen optimally in the national interest, a cost is then incurred when countries are deprived of the ability to conduct independent monetary policies. Short-term trade-offs do differ among countries. In addition, as I have already discussed, there are differences in policy tastes which have historical origins, and one should expect that such differences are manifest in the desire to practice anti-equilibrium monetary policies.

(2) *Credibility and Expectations*

The argument that an anti-equilibrium monetary policy can succeed in the short run in reducing real wages and unemployment below the equilibrium or natural level hinges on there being some lags in the adjustment of nominal wages to prices. If the expansionary monetary policy were fully expected, nominal wages would adjust quickly and no employment gain—not even a short-run one—would result. This is an extreme view which is not supported by the evidence. But let us grant it now in order to isolate an important consideration.

No employment gain will result, but inflationary expectations will have increased. To avoid growing unemployment, the money supply would have to increase just to keep up with the wage increases that have resulted from inflationary expectations. Not only wages but also prices would rise in anticipation of the monetary expansion. If it is widely expected that a government or central bank will try to stimulate the economy through monetary policy, inflation will be expected, and this expectation will then negate the desired outcome. The only outcome will be inflation. If a government then attempts to reduce inflation by slowing up the rate of money growth, it could only achieve this *without* causing unemployment if, at the same time or earlier, it succeeded in reducing inflationary expectations. Hence, its anti-inflationary intention must be credible. Granting this line of thought, the heart of the problem becomes: how can an anti-inflation commitment be made credible?

Germany's commitment is credible because the Bundesbank is, for historical and other reasons, firmly committed to a low inflation policy, and because the German public has an aversion to inflation. Most important, Germany has a post-war record of low inflation, and the Bundesbank has not tried to stimulate the

German economy at the cost of increasing inflation—at least not for any length of time. Hence, the Bundesbank has an excellent anti-inflation reputation. By contrast, the Italian reputation is not so good, and this was also true of France until the mid-1980s. Hence, commitments or promises by their governments to follow low-inflation policies would not be credible, especially in the case of Italy. The crucial question is whether an anti-inflation commitment of a European central bank would be credible.

Such a commitment by a new monetary union's central bank could not be based on its own history—that is, on a history of low inflation and independence from short-term political pressures. It can only be based on institutional arrangements of some kind. French and Italian support for EMU seems to hinge on the belief that a European central bank would be more effectively committed to the anti-inflation objective than their own central banks could be. In the case of Italy, particularly, it is a matter of the central bank being more remote from Italian political pressures than the Banca d'Italia. On the other hand, it is less likely that the European central bank would be as firmly committed to the anti-inflation objective as the Bundesbank, so that Germany has little or nothing to gain in this respect, and possibly something to lose. Other countries may still wish the European central bank to take short-term cyclical conditions into account to a limited extent, even while providing a fundamental German-like anti-inflation credibility. It is in the German interest to ensure that the union's central bank is as much like the Bundesbank—and controlled by persons of the same views—as possible.

Two conclusions emerge from this discussion. The first is an old-fashioned one. The short-term Phillips curve issue is relevant, though less than was believed in the early 1970s. Countries may indeed lose through having to concede short-term monetary and exchange rate policy to the union's central bank, given that policy tastes and circumstances (notably the reactions of wages) differ. The second conclusion follows from more recent thinking. There is a strong case for having a credible low-inflation monetary policy, and in this respect the monetary union may represent an improvement for some of its members (like Italy) but a deterioration for others (like Germany), the outcome depending on the constitution of the union's central bank and on the kind of persons appointed to its policy-making positions.

(3) *The Loss of Seigniorage*

I have supposed here that inflation is caused by demand-expanding policies designed to increase output and reduce unemployment or—when there are inflationary expectations—by policies that prevent declines in output and employment that would otherwise take place. But, as I have already noted in Chapter 5, another reason for inflation is that countries sometimes monetize budget deficits directly or indirectly, so that deficits lead to continuous monetary expansion. The resultant inflation generates the inflation tax.

A country may derive a significant amount of revenue (seigniorage) from the inflation tax, and the monetary union may deprive it of this revenue. Then its government faces a problem. Normally inflation is only a tax of last resort. Usually it reflects political weakness. While the inflation tax may be convenient politically, it is not necessarily desirable. In any case, if the European central bank follows a non-inflationary policy, a country such as Greece or Portugal would have to make fiscal adjustments. Other taxes would have to be increased or government expenditures would have to be reduced. In these two countries, like many developing countries, revenue from the inflation tax in the form of seigniorage has been significant (about 2 per cent of GDP). Forgoing the revenue from the inflation tax would present a political problem for the governments of these countries. But the issue is not really important in Europe: in other potential participants in EMU—even Italy—seigniorage from the inflation tax is not now a significant source of revenue.

VII. LABOR MOBILITY

The theory of optimum currency areas, pioneered by Robert Mundell (1961), provides the foundation for analysis of the economic effects of monetary integration. Optimum currency area theory asks: which countries or regions are best suited to combine in a monetary union? Thus, it is concerned with the first-best. Monetary integration theory, as explained here, asks a second-best question: would particular countries benefit by forming a monetary union? They may not form an optimum currency area, but the question is whether the currency area resulting from the monetary union is an improvement on the existing situation, where each country is a separate currency area. To establish *optimum* currency areas, the countries might have to be broken up into regions, or they might have to join with countries not included in the monetary integration proposal.

Mundell's focus was on labor mobility. Essentially he argued that countries or regions between which mobility is high would form optimum currency areas, and thus should establish monetary unions. The point is that the potential loss to a member country from forgoing the independent exchange rate instrument is modified when unemployed workers can readily migrate to other parts of the monetary union. When demand shifts away from France to Germany, for example, and yet real wages in France do not fall, the resultant unemployment in France is reduced when Frenchmen can and do readily migrate to Germany. At the same time, it must be remembered that migration itself imposes costs, and these costs (increased by language differences) rationally inhibit migration even when there are no legal restrictions.

Labor mobility is low within European countries, and even lower between them. One cannot expect regional unemployment problems, let alone national ones, to be solved by labor mobility. If labor mobility really were the principal criterion, EMU should certainly not be established, and many countries—notably Britain and Italy—should be broken up into separate regions each with its own exchange rate and central bank. For this reason labor mobility cannot be a significant criterion. Labor mobility is no substitute for wage flexibility. Labor mobility is much higher in the United States than in Europe and helps to explain why unemployment is relatively low in the United States—a large area of monetary integration with great regional product specialization. But it is not the only explanation: nominal and real wage flexibility are also greater in the United States than in Europe.

VIII. IS CAPITAL MOBILITY HELPFUL?

Does capital mobility reduce the costs of forming an exchange rate union? This was argued by Ingram (1973). At that time capital movements were not free within Europe, by contrast with the United States. He argued that capital mobility within the United

States helped to smooth adjustment to regional shocks there, and would do the same in Europe once monetary integration—which includes capital mobility—was brought about. A region that suffers a current account deficit can finance it by borrowing, and thus is not forced into an immediate crisis as would happen if it did not have adequate reserves and could not borrow.

The weakness of the argument is that borrowing—whether by private agents or by governments—is financing and not adjustment. If a country or region suffers an adverse shock expected to be permanent or long lasting, real wages and real spending need to fall. That is adjustment. Given the Keynesian conditions of nominal wage rigidity and real wage flexibility, devaluation is a way of bringing this about, or helping to do so. If the exchange rate is not available as an instrument of policy, adjustment is more difficult and slower. Financing the deficit just shifts the costs of forgoing the exchange rate instrument to the future.

Yet it is true that the ability to finance a deficit can ease the process of adjustment even though it does not actually bring about adjustment itself. Even with a fixed exchange rate, adjustment will eventually take place if demand for labor falls, since eventually nominal wages will fall, at least relative to trend. Adjustment will just take more time. Hence, the problem is temporary, though it may well be quite prolonged. Financing helps to tide a country over the adjustment period. It is, of course, important that the incentive to adjust is not reduced as a result of financing. Such adjustment is required if an adverse shock is believed to be permanent. In addition, borrowing—like the use of reserves in the absence of monetary union—can tide a country or region over temporary shocks, such as a recession. Thus capital mobility is certainly helpful in making possible a monetary union where members are subject to asymmetric shocks. But it does not deal with the need for wages to adjust in response to an adverse shock that is expected to be permanent or long lasting.

IX. FISCAL POLICY: INTEGRATED INCOME TAX AND
BENEFITS

Can fiscal transfers solve the central problem of monetary union? Suppose there were a common income tax and unemployment benefit system in EMU. If demand shifted from France to

Germany, French incomes would fall and German incomes would rise, while unemployment would rise in France and fall in Germany. An automatic redistribution from Germany to France would then take place, and this would mitigate the effects of the adverse shock in France. Such a common system could thus be helpful during the adjustment period.

The same comments can be made about fiscal transfers as about capital mobility. While capital mobility allows for financing rather than adjustment, fiscal transfers through a common income tax and social welfare system represent aid rather than adjustment. Both will actually reduce the incentive to adjust in the adversely affected country—that is, to lower nominal wage demands so as to reduce real wages. The most one can say is that financing and aid allow more time for adjustment, and this is necessary because, in the monetary union, adjustment will indeed take more time since the exchange rate instrument is not available to help it along.

If common income tax and unemployment benefit systems were established in the European Union to ease the operation of the monetary union, the transfers between nations that would take place would be very substantial, and would not just mitigate the effects of asymmetric shocks. There would probably be long-term transfers on a large scale from wealthy countries, notably Germany, to others. This is unlikely to be acceptable. The massive transfers that the Federal German government made to East Germany after reunification certainly made the unification process, including monetary union, easier, but surely do not provide a model for transfers to other countries. One can certainly conceive of a monetary union without an integrated income tax and benefits system. Temporary problems can be dealt with by financing, whether through private or public borrowing. This opportunity exists even in the absence of a monetary union, though a union may indeed increase the need. Hence, I now turn to the role of borrowing by governments.

X. FISCAL POLICY: SHOULD DEFICITS BE CENTRALLY CONTROLLED?

Would the budget deficit policies of the various national governments in EMU have to be centrally controlled or limited in some way? This has been a controversial issue in European discussions. I begin with the argument against such central control or limits. It seems to me to outweigh the arguments in favor.

Fiscal policy is distinct from monetary policy. The presumption is surely that the member governments of the monetary union can still run budget deficits or surpluses as they please. They can finance their deficits on the capital market of the union and, indeed, the world. The more they borrow, the more interest rates are likely to rise against them, at least if there is any default risk at all. If they borrow unwisely, the consequences will be borne either by their own future taxpayers or by creditors. This is no different from the situation now of any government in the world. In this view a government is really not so different from a large company. In the United States and several other federations, the central government or the central bank does not control the borrowing of the component states.

Thus there is a strong presumption that the governments of the countries that form the monetary union should retain budgetary freedom. The presumption is strengthened by the general case for decentralization of decision-making and—in the European Union case—by the explicit commitment to the principle of subsidiarity, namely, that the Commission and the central authorities only take on those duties that cannot be performed satisfactorily by national or regional governments. It would be a radical step to take away from national governments not only the monetary but also the fiscal policy instruments.

One other argument for independent national fiscal policies is powerful. When a country is deprived of the monetary policy instrument for short-term demand management, the need for the fiscal policy instrument becomes all the greater. If one grants that nominal wages are not flexible downwards in the short term, and that in a time of recession or adverse shock some deliberate demand management is appropriate, there must be a case for independent fiscal policies.

I am assuming here that governments can be trusted to manage demand sensibly. There is a case for government borrowing when shocks are adverse and time for adjustment is needed, or when the shocks are believed to be temporary. This must be balanced by budget surpluses, designed to reduce debt, in good times. At the minimum, the built-in fiscal stabilizers (the rise and fall of tax revenue and unemployment benefits with the state of the economy) must be allowed to work. Of course, fiscal policy is never very flexible and has to take into account the effects on long-term public debt accumulation. Hence, it is certainly an imperfect substitute for an independent monetary policy.

Now let me turn to the arguments on the other side. Fiscal and monetary policies affect each other, and mutually determine interest rates and the exchange rate of the monetary union relative to outside currencies. In the EMU case there will be four large economies, the fiscal policy of each of which could have a significant influence on the overall demand, interest rate, and exchange rate situation of the union. Extreme shifts in fiscal policies by Germany or France could create difficulties and disturbances in the same way as the US fiscal policy shift in the 1980s created difficulties for the world economy. There is clearly a need for co-ordination between the single central bank and the various fiscal authorities in the form of information exchange, consultation, and attempts to mutually influence policies. Monetary management designed to stabilize domestic demand, keep inflation down, or influence the external exchange rate in some way, must take the fiscal situations of the member countries into account. For example, a tight monetary policy raises interest rates and intensifies the fiscal problem of debtor countries. But these short-term demand management issues do not provide a case for the imposition of central control of fiscal deficits.

In the Delors Report (1989) and the report of the Commission of the European Communities (1990) on EMU, a much more important moral hazard argument in favor of central control of national budget deficits was advanced. This is worth exploring in detail.

A government that builds up a large public debt, and has difficulty paying interest and repaying its debt, might apply pressure on the union's central bank to bail it out. It is not hard to imagine a situation where Italy threatens to default, and thus threatens the solvency of financial institutions that hold its debt, and threatens perhaps the credit of all EMU governments, and where the attempt to continue to fully service its debt would create a political crisis. A bail-out could take various forms. The central bank might directly buy debt from the Italian government, hence monetizing the debt in the familiar way. Alternatively, it might increase its share of Italian debt when it engages in normal open market operations, thus buying the debt that the private sector is unloading, and so keeping up its price.

If several really large economies—say, Germany and France—ran large budget deficits, this would tend to raise the structure of interest rates of all debt, and not just that of these countries. To prevent such interest rate increases, the central bank might engage in an open market purchase of bonds of all its member countries. In that case the expansionary fiscal policies would have led to a more expansionary monetary policy in the union, and hence to more inflation. Of course, the central bank need not have reacted in this way. It could have engaged in a contractionary monetary policy, which would have raised interest rates further but offset the expansionary effects of the fiscal policies. This was how the Bundesbank reacted to the German fiscal expansion that resulted from German unification.

The concern of the Delors and European Commission reports was that governments would be more ready to run deficits if they could expect to be bailed out directly or indirectly. Hence, some controls must be imposed on them. In effect, the central bank would be providing them with insurance, so that there would be a moral hazard problem that could only be dealt with by controls.

An alternative solution to this potential problem is that the central bank of the EMU is made independent of political pressure, and that a specific no-bail-out rule is imposed on it. This solution is widely accepted. No government or financial institution should have any expectation of being bailed out. Such a rule can be readily applied to prevent purchases by the central bank of debt direct from governments. In the case of normal open market purchases, it would be necessary to ensure that certain specified proportions of the debt of different countries are bought. But general monetary expansion to offset the interest rate effects of budget deficits can be prevented only by a commitment of the central bank to a low-inflation target.

APPENDIX 8.1

Pro- and Anti-Equilibrium Exchange Rate Policy

The aim here is to display the difference between a pro-equilibrium and an anti-equilibrium exchange rate policy. In Fig. 8.1 the vertical axis shows the income real wage, W/P, and the horizontal axis the level of employment. W is the nominal wage and P is the price level facing wage-earners, being an average of exportable, importable, and non-tradable prices, with weights determined by the consumption basket of wage-earners.

EE is the labor-market equilibrium curve. It traces out the real wage desired in the labor market at various levels of employment. It can be

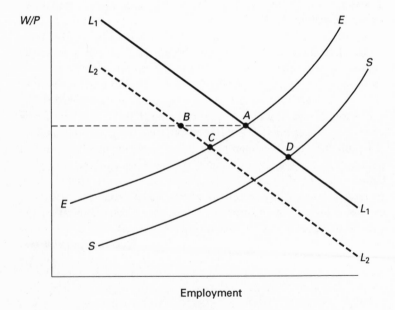

Employment

FIG. 8.1. Pro- and Anti-Equilibrium Exchange Rate Policy

thought of as determined by trade unions and all other factors, competitive and monopolistic, determining labor-market equilibrium. If it were horizontal, there would be complete real-wage rigidity; but that assumption is not made here. *SS* is the usual labor supply curve determined by individual workers: the higher the real wage, the more labor supply is on offer. *SS* traces out the full-employment level of employment (where any unemployment is voluntary) at various real-wage levels. When the labor market is in equilibrium (on *EE*), involuntary unemployment is given by the horizontal distance between the two curves.

L_1L_1 is the initial demand-for-labor curve. It shows how employment rises as the real wage falls, and is drawn for a given production function and given terms of trade. A decline in the terms of trade, or any other event that reduces the demand for labor at a given income real wage (or lowers the real wage compatible with given employment) is represented by a downward shift of the curve, say to L_2L_2. Initially equilibrium is at *A*. I shall assume that the product market is always in equilibrium, so that the economy is always on the relevant demand-for-labor curve, even though the labor market may be temporarily out of equilibrium.

We now tell three stories.

In Story I the exchange rate is fixed by means of an appropriate monetary policy. Thus it is not possible to use monetary policy to maintain employment. There is an adverse terms-of-trade shock that shifts the demand-for-labor curve from L_1L_1 to L_2L_2. The price level would rise if the terms-of-trade deterioration took the form of a rise in import prices, and would fall if it were caused by a decline in export prices and some exportables are consumed by wage earners. Here I assume that, on balance, the terms-of-trade deterioration keeps *P* constant. At first the nominal wage also does not change, so that *W/P* stays constant and employment falls to *B*. The labor market is now out of equilibrium. Gradually—perhaps very gradually—*W* falls until labor-market equilibrium is restored at *C*.

This story can be made more realistic in various ways. World inflation may be positive, so that *P* is steadily rising, and equilibrium may then be restored through *W* rising less, rather than *W* having to fall absolutely. Furthermore, the decline in the terms of trade may directly raise *P* (if it has raised import prices) and so bring about some reduction in the real wage. It is also possible that the downward shift of the demand-for-labor curve is caused not by a terms-of-trade shock but by a shift in output from non-tradables to tradables—required by a need to improve the current account—when non-tradables are labor-intensive. The main point is that, with a fixed nominal exchange rate, there may be a prolonged period of unemployment and loss of output before labor-market equilibrium is restored.

In Story II there is a monetary expansion and the exchange rate is depreciated when the adverse shock takes place. Hence P rises, the income real wage falls, and equilibrium can immediately move to C. This is a pro-equilibrium monetary and exchange rate policy. There is no need for nominal wages to fall (or their rate of increase to decline). The temporary, but possibly prolonged, stage of high unemployment (at B) is avoided.

In Story III there is no adverse shock, so that the demand-for-labor curve stays at L_1L_1. But the government wishes to raise employment and output above its equilibrium or natural level, as indicated by the EE curve. Monetary expansion, and thus depreciation of the exchange rate, cause P to rise. But W is slow to adjust, so that the real wage falls and employment increases, say, to D. The labor market is again in disequilibrium. Gradually W rises with the aim of restoring labor-market equilibrium. If monetary expansion and thus depreciation continue, P may rise as W rises, so that employment can stay to the right of A.

The more expectations in the labor market adjust to the inflationary policy, the more difficult it will be to keep wages from rising faster than prices as unions and others in the labor market seek to restore the real wage to the desired level. Increasing inflation will be needed to prevent it. In the extreme case, where the inflationary policy is fully expected well in advance, any rise in P will be associated with—or even anticipated by—a rise in W, so that employment cannot be increased above the level indicated by A. In any case, this anti-equilibrium policy is inflationary. If pursued frequently or systematically, it will not be successful in keeping employment above equilibrium for any length of time, if at all. It will just lead to a high rate of inflation and continuous depreciation.

REFERENCES

All the issues of this chapter are discussed in more detail in de Grauwe (1992), in Gros and Thygesen (1992), and in Eichengreen (1992a), the latter being particularly useful in surveying relevant empirical material. See also Commission of the European Communities (1990). Eichengreen (1992b) discusses whether Europe is an optimum currency area.

The classic article that pioneered optimum currency area theory is Mundell (1961), other important contributions being McKinnon (1963) and Kenen (1969). The literature was surveyed in Ishiyama (1975) and Tower and Willett (1976). Corden (1972) analyzed the pros and cons of monetary integration inspired by the proposal for a gradual move to European monetary union in the Werner Report (1970).

The argument about credibility and expectations is based primarily on Barro and Gordon (1983a, 1983b) and is expounded in de Grauwe (1992). See also Giavazzi and Pagano (1988) who apply it to the EMS.

9

Maastricht and the Transition to Monetary Union

THE previous chapter compared a monetary union with a flexible exchange rate regime, but did not discuss the transition from the latter to the former. Much of the debate and negotiations in Europe has always been about the transition process, and I turn to that here. I begin with some history, then outline four conceivable transition processes, and finally elaborate on the central problem created by the Maastricht Treaty, namely the plan to have an intermediate Stage Two in the monetary integration process.

I. FROM WERNER TO MAASTRICHT

The Werner Report (1970) proposed the establishment in stages by 1980 of an economic and monetary union by the then members of the European Community. There was to be a single currency or, alternatively, the irrevocable fixing of exchange rates with complete elimination of margins of fluctuation, the complete liberalization of capital movements, and a common central banking system. The first stage required the narrowing of exchange margins. So that is how it all began. The initiative was political; above all, the integration process was to be kept moving. There was also dissatisfaction with various aspects of the international monetary system. These Werner proposals were accepted by the member governments of the European Community.

Some exchange margins were indeed narrowed from April 1972 as part of the "snake in the tunnel scheme", but at various times countries left the snake and allowed their currencies to depreciate. The snake was the forerunner of the EMS. Once world floating began in 1973, the member currencies floated together relative to outside currencies. But, by 1974, France,

Italy, and Britain had all left the snake, so it became a system built around the DM.

Thus by 1974 the Werner process—a concerted gradual movement towards exchange rate union—came to a dead stop. The explanation can be found in the world inflation and the subsequent policy reactions of 1973 to 1975. Once world inflation had got going, and the initial policy reactions differed between countries, it was inevitable that rates of inflation would diverge—unless indeed countries with the high inflation rates were willing to accept sudden and large unemployment as the cost of getting back to equilibrium. Nominal exchange rates thus had to diverge sharply so as to avoid excessive divergences in real exchange rates. By 1974 it seemed that the prospect of European monetary integration was dead, only an emasculated snake surviving.

The European Monetary System was conceived in 1978. I discussed the motives in Chapter 7. Essentially it represented an improvement on the snake. It included France and Italy, and also provided more short-term financial resources for supporting exchange rates within the margins. Given that the EMS in its first stage allowed for frequent realignments, it cannot really be said to have been a big step, or any step, towards monetary integration.

In 1988 monetary union proposals were revived and then matters moved surprisingly rapidly. There were various political and economic motives, varying indeed between countries. Certainly there was a political desire to keep the integration process moving, a concern to lock Germany into the Community, an Italian belief that Italy would be able to reduce inflation more readily as part of a monetary union than on its own, and a strong belief that a single market—which was planned to be established by 1992—required a monetary union. Finally—possibly most important of all—there was the view that the ending of exchange controls by France and Italy, that was necessitated by the single market program, would threaten the stability of the EMS system. We know that it has indeed done so, though with a lag. Capital mobility would compel a choice between reverting to floating and moving to a complete monetary union.

Two landmarks followed, namely the Delors Report (1989) and the Maastricht Treaty of 1991, the latter heavily influenced by the former. The Delors Report was written by a committee headed by the number one Eurocrat, Jacques Delors, and filled with central bankers. Like the Werner Report, it proposed monetary integration in three stages. Exchange rates would be locked irrevocably in the third stage, and a European System of Central Banks would be set up. Official reserves would be pooled and managed by this system. This report also recommended binding rules for budget deficits.

The Maastricht Treaty of 1991 covered much more than monetary union. But it is the monetary union aspect that concerns us here. It involved a commitment to a gradual, three-stage process, with actual locking of exchange rates and a single money coming about in the third stage. Essentially it accepted the Delors Report's recommendations. Realignments would still be possible in Stage Two, and the European Central Bank (ECB) would only take over in Stage Three. The ECB would be independent from day-to-day political control, and would be committed to price stability as its principal objective. Important convergence conditions about inflation, exchange rates, budget deficits, and debt were set up which would have to be fulfilled during Stage Two before Stage Three could be achieved and before countries could actually join in.

The Treaty had to be ratified by all twelve signatory countries before being implemented, but this did not mean that a monetary union had to include all the members. Some might not fulfil the convergence conditions, but the others could eventually go ahead. Britain obtained a special dispensation giving it the right not to participate.

II. FOUR KINDS OF TRANSITION

There are four main ways of moving from a flexible exchange rate regime to a monetary union.

First, monetary union might be brought about all at once without a lengthy transition period and, above all, without various preconditions having to be fulfilled. The best example of this is German monetary unification that took place in 1990. There are so many problems with a lengthy transition period—particularly the uncertainties that it generates—that the case for choosing the all-at-once option is very strong.

Second, there is the gradual but concerted step-by-step approach. The countries all move together. This was the Werner approach. Apart from the many problems of gradualism, the special problem here is that the convoy will move at the pace of the slowest ship, which may be no movement at all. This disadvantage could be seen in the preliminary Maastricht step, which required ratification of the Treaty by all twelve countries. Any one country—such as Denmark or Britain—could hold up the whole process.

Third, there is the gradual approach where the various steps are not concerted. Countries join when they are ready, whether politically or economically. This was the approach of the snake and, in essence, is also the approach laid down in the Maastricht Treaty. This approach is clearly much more realistic and allows for the possibility that a core group consisting of Germany, France, and the Benelux countries, perhaps with Denmark, the Irish Republic, and Austria, form a monetary union before the others join in.

Finally, there is the parallel currency approach which is certainly a non-starter but which was proposed in the 1970s by a group of academics and in 1990 by Britain as an alternative to EMU. It involves establishing a new currency in addition to existing currencies, but not with fixed parities. The currency would either be managed so that it maintained constant purchasing power (the original academic proposal), or that it was never devalued relative to any other currency (the British proposal), hence being the strongest currency. The idea was that currency competition would gradually drive out the other, more inflationary currencies, so that market forces would bring about the single currency result. This is actually an improbable outcome, but in any case this approach—even if it could be implemented—has been dismissed by all but the British, and is truly only of academic interest. Hence, I shall not discuss it further.

III. ALL AT ONCE OR STEP BY STEP: THE CONVERGENCE CONDITIONS

Let us imagine an all-at-once story. This, of course, is purely imaginary. A firm, early date could be fixed for monetary union. From that date the union's central bank (the ECB) would take over control of monetary policy. The exchange rates of the various member currencies relative to the union currency (the ECU) would have to be fixed at the date of the agreement. The rates might be based on those existing at the time, or changes might be negotiated.

After formation of the union different currencies might continue in use, but each currency would be legal tender (or required to be accepted for large payments) in all countries. In that case, the ECU would be introduced as a parallel currency but, of course, at a fixed rate. The supply of the national currencies would be solely determined by the ECB. Given the overall monetary conditions which the ECB determined, an increase in demand for one currency relative to another would be met by changing the relative supplies. This would happen automatically as a result of intervention to maintain the parities. Gradually the use of national currencies would be phased out, and thus a complete exchange rate union established. This would involve a conversion phase where cash machines, computer programs, and so on, are adjusted appropriately. The ending of national currencies should happen as quickly as possible to avoid any doubts developing about the irrevocability of the fixed parities. But the doubts should be minimal because the commitment of the ECB to the parities would be embodied in its constitution.

The labor-market reaction to the establishment of EMU is crucial. If it is made absolutely clear to the public in all member countries that an ECB committed constitutionally to low inflation is taking over monetary control, labor markets should adjust their inflationary expectations immediately. A principal task of political leaders and central bank governors would be to bring this changed perception about. There would be a complete failure of the transition if they did not do this. There is a switch in monetary policy regime and, if this is understood, there should be no relation between inflationary expectations before the switch and afterwards. Hence, there should be no need for an extended transition period to allow the labor market to adjust.

The Maastricht Treaty includes various complicated convergence conditions, especially conditions about inflation and inflationary expectations, the latter measured by interest rates. The convergence conditions are summarized in Appendix 9.1. Inflation rates and interest rates of the high-inflation countries have to converge towards those of the low-inflation countries before Stage Three is started and hence EMU is attained. Yet these conditions are not really necessary. They create unnecessary obstacles to the monetary integration process, and hence uncertainties. There are two reasons that these conditions were inserted into the treaty.

Tight convergence conditions on inflation were favored by the representatives of Italy and Germany, both heavily influenced by their central bankers (who were members of the Delors Committee). For the Italians such conditions were meant to impose anti-inflationary discipline on their own politicians and the public, and reduce inflationary expectations, something which Italy, on past experience, was expected to have difficulty in achieving, whether during a transition period or if the move to monetary union were never completed. Lower inflation was desired by Italy's representatives for its own sake and not just as a prelude to monetary union, and the convergence conditions were meant to help. The Germans, by contrast, were concerned not with their own inflation but with that of their partners. In the German view, reduced inflation by Germany's partners during the transition would be more likely to ensure that they would not press the ECB to pursue inflationary policies. The Germans wanted countries like Italy, Spain, and Britain to develop non-inflationary habits so that they would readily accept low-inflation policies once EMU was established.

As it turned out, the convergence conditions—which also concerned budget deficits and debt ratios—were so tough that, by 1993, very few countries fulfilled them. Notably, of the core countries, Germany had a budget deficit that exceeded the maximum of 3 per cent set by the Maastricht Treaty, while Belgium had no hope of attaining a public debt-to-GDP ratio of 60 per cent (it was over 100 per cent). The four southern European countries did not fulfil any of the conditions.

In my view, the decision to have a lengthy transition period with very demanding convergence conditions was heavily motivated by the ambiguity of the commitment to monetary union. Some of the national central bankers and politicians who were responsible for or agreed to the Delors Report and the Maastricht Treaty must have been unclear about what they wanted to achieve.

The Bundesbank, and possibly the German government, were reluctant to give up control over German monetary policy—

rightly seeing little prospect of improvement if the ECB took the place of the Bundesbank—and yet German politicians wanted EMU for other reasons. Most important, they must have been aware that many citizens, especially in the key countries of Germany and France, were not ready for so drastic a step as monetary union. All the evidence indicates that the German people were not ready to give up the Deutschmark, while the French were not willing to hand over full control over monetary policy to an independent ECB constructed as a clone of the Bundesbank and dominated by Germans. The British wanted to be part of any process that took place but definitely did not want EMU. Both the Thatcher and the Major governments were quite clear on the latter point.

One guesses that it was hoped all these matters would gradually sort themselves out, and would become easier if convergence, especially in inflation rates, took place. Sometimes I feel that governments and central bankers of several countries—all but the Benelux countries—sleepwalked into Maastricht. Particularly under pressure from the Germans, they set up convergence conditions which would make the establishment of EMU very difficult. It is true that some discretion in the fulfilment of the convergence conditions was allowed and the conditions might well be modified. But discretion, of course, will increase uncertainties.

IV. NARROWING EXCHANGE RATE MARGINS AND FIXING CENTRAL RATES: AN UNREALISTIC APPROACH

The idea that an exchange rate union should be approached gradually, by gradually narrowing margins and by fixing bilateral central exchange rates even before the union is consummated, is appealing. Yet it is unrealistic. The general idea, widely accepted up to September 1992, was that exchange rate stability, leading eventually to fixed rates (moving within narrow margins), should first be attained by harmonization of macroeconomic policies. This was Act II of the ERM. Then a fixed exchange rate commitment would actually be made. This next stage is embodied in the Maastricht Treaty through the requirement that a country will only be accepted as being ready for Stage Three—i.e. to join EMU—if its exchange rate has stayed within the narrow ERM margin, and has not been realigned, for two years.

Monetary union would be the rather undramatic end result— the coronation or culmination of the process. There must thus first be a pseudo-union before there is a complete union. But, to put it mildly, this idea has problems. Suppose a government is serious about fulfilling the Maastricht conditions and joining EMU. It will then have to keep its central rate fixed for two years in advance and stay within the narrow margins. It would be making a commitment to vary its domestic interest rates to any extent necessary to maintain the exchange rate during that preliminary stage. The credibility of the commitment would thus be crucial. But achieving credibility cannot be relied upon. The exchange rate arrangement during this stage is exactly what I have defined as a pseudo-union in Chapter 8.

Wages and non-tradable prices may not have fully adjusted to the fixed exchange rate relative to the prospective union partners. Real appreciation may thus continue for some time. Perhaps an adverse exogenous shock takes place which would have led to devaluation in the absence of the commitment. The market will then be alert to any doubts about the government's commitment to joining EMU at the proclaimed date. A speculative crisis is surely possible until the move from pseudo to actual exchange rate union has been made. This is exactly the story of 1992 and 1993.

It was thus unrealistic to require a lengthy (two-year) pseudo-union period to precede establishment of a complete union. Hence, it is hard to believe that the Maastricht preconditions on exchange rate stability can be fulfilled. It was even more unwise for Britain, Italy, and Spain to anticipate the Maastricht requirement by avoiding realignments before the required two-year period. Even a requirement or intention to gradually narrow margins and avoid realignments (as in the Werner program) is subject to the same criticism.

The desire to impose a preliminary fixed exchange rate commitment is understandable. It is unlikely to be generally achieved or sustained, for the reasons just given, but perhaps it is worth presenting a rather subtle argument in favor. The aim is to avoid the end-game problem. In the absence of the fixed exchange rate commitment, countries might try to devalue just before entering EMU. This raises the question of whether it is in the interests of a country to enter a monetary union with as much depreciation or appreciation as possible, or whether there is some optimum exchange rate for entry.

One view is that, if countries are free to alter exchange rates at the last moment, hence determining the parity of their existing currency relative to the union currency (the ECU), they may engage in competitive devaluations. This view assumes that there is some nominal wage sluggishness downwards (the Keynesian case), and that governments are more concerned with ensuring the competitiveness of their countries in the union than with the decline in real wages that devaluation would normally lead to. If the exchange rate at entry happened to be too depreciated, yielding real wages that were thought too low by unions and employers, a rise in nominal wages could easily rectify the matter. On the other hand, if the exchange rate upon entry were too appreciated, yielding excessive unemployment, the required decline in nominal wages would be much slower. Hence, it is better to risk excessive depreciation rather than excessive appreciation, and the bias on this account will be to depreciation. One could thus expect a tendency to competitive depreciation before exchange rates are finally fixed.

The two-year fixed exchange rate requirement of the Maastricht treaty would not wholly avoid this problem. In theory there could still be some incentive to devalue before the two-year period begins. But such a tendency must be inhibited by the likelihood that early devaluations would affect the credibility of the subsequent period of pseudo-exchange rate union to which I have referred. This is borne out by the fact that central rates in the ERM were actually fixed well in advance of the two-year period, with no attempts at deliberate devaluations through realignments.

One should also take into account the effect on the real values of assets and liabilities of the choice of parities upon entry into the union (or whenever exchange rates are fixed). Governments have an interest in reducing the real value of their domestic currency-denominated debts, and can do so by devaluation before entry. On the other hand, private citizens and companies have an interest in raising the real value of their net holdings of domestic-currency denominated assets. A large part of their assets are the liabilities of other private agents, and the interests of different persons and companies will differ depending on whether their net domestic-currency denominated assets are positive or negative.

Once the union is established, the initial base money is a net asset for the country as a whole, and the more appreciated the exchange rate for the purpose of determining the monetary union conversion rate, the better for those whose assets are dominated by holdings of base money.

This consideration was important in the case of German monetary union. The principal assets held by East Germans before reunification were currency and bank deposits. The more favorable the rate for the Ostmark, the better for them. In the German case the adverse effect on competitiveness of a very favorable exchange rate was irrelevant since increases in nominal wages—which resulted from trade union integration and a desire for real wages to get closer to West German levels—ensured in any case an uncompetitive economy. If the Ostmark had been given a less favorable exchange rate—that is, had been less appreciated—nominal wages in the East would simply have risen further.

To come back to the main point, a pseudo-union always has a credibility problem and invites crises. This is the main objection to a gradual rather than a sudden transition, and to the whole concept of a preliminary Stage II period in the Maastricht program. This problem does not rule out an attempt at co-ordination of macroeconomic policies designed to lead to some convergence of inflation rates, presumably towards German levels, as a prelude to monetary union. Such an attempt would be designed to stabilize exchange rates as far as possible, even while still allowing realignments in response to shocks and market pressures.

The Maastricht procedure will be successful only if there is a very strong political commitment to EMU, strong enough to assure markets that, whatever happens, monetary policy will support the fixed central rate and narrow margins during the Stage Two period. In 1993 such a commitment certainly did not exist. Of course, the more favorable the fundamentals, the better. These fundamentals include relative inflation rates and indications that real exchange rates are appropriate for the longer run, taking into account likely long-term capital flows. It is very important to bear in mind that the fundamentals also include the levels of unemployment and excess capacity, and indications of whether these are perceived in the countries as being structural or caused by lack of demand. If substantial unemployment is perceived as Keynesian—caused by lack of demand—there will always be some temptation to break with the exchange rate commitment. In 1993 France had unemployment of over 11 per cent and even though the government affirmed its strong commitment to maintenance of the *franc fort* policy within the ERM, the market did not perceive it as fully credible, and so forced the widening of the margins and some franc depreciation.

The Convergence Criteria of the Maastricht Treaty

Following is a very rough paraphrase of the criteria set out in the Treaty, determining whether a member state of the European Union is eligible to join EMU.

1. For two years before entry, the country's exchange rate must have stayed within the normal EMS band of 2.25 per cent, and it must not have devalued its bilateral central rate against any other member state's currency for the same period.
2. Its average rate of consumer price inflation must not have exceeded by more than 1.5 percentage points the rates observed in the three member countries with the best inflation performance over the year before. Furthermore (also as an indicator of inflation convergence), the average long-term interest rate shall not have exceeded by more than 2 percentage points those of the same three best performing member states.
3. While various allowances can be made for temporary fiscal deficits and for an excessive debt ratio that is diminishing, the specified indicators of fiscal problems are whether the general government deficit exceeds 3 per cent of GDP and whether the ratio of government debt to GDP exceeds 60 per cent.

REFERENCES

Kenen (1992) analyzes carefully the Maastricht Treaty, its proposals for a European central bank, convergence conditions, and the three proposed stages. The agreement is summarized in International Monetary Fund (1992, 52–5). The history of monetary integration proposals and transition issues are discussed in de Grauwe (1992), Gros and Thygesen (1992), and Eichengreen (1992a). On the parallel currency proposal, see also de Grauwe (1992).

The Managed-Floating,
High-Capital-Mobility Non-System

10

The International Macro-System

THIS chapter assesses the international macro-system that has emerged since the breakdown of Bretton Woods. The essential feature is that it is unplanned and uncoordinated, and might be better described as a non-system. It certainly was not the outcome of any plan or grand international conference. While there were many individual decisions by governments—notably by the US Nixon Administration in 1971—that contributed to the breakdown and the evolution of the new non-system, there was nothing very deliberate about the system that has emerged since March 1973, when generalized floating began. In January 1976 the members of the International Monetary Fund met to amend the Articles of Agreement of the Fund to bring them into conformity with the realities of the new system. The new Articles provided "principles for the guidance of members' exchange rate policies" and for "surveillance" of such policies by the IMF. But, for all practical purposes, countries could do what they liked.

It is not always understood that an international system that is not centrally planned or is not systematically coordinated through international negotiations or a system of rules can nevertheless reach an equilibrium, and that this equilibrium may be preferable to one that is planned by a political or bureaucratic process. At the same time, such a system may not be optimal; it might be improved by some degree of coordination or acceptance of rules. But I shall come back to this issue below. At this point it should just be noted that there are two overriding features of the current situation. The first is the very high and still growing international capital mobility. The second is the decentralized nature of the system—which, indeed, makes it a non-system. Both of these features have shaped the current account "imbalances" that have emerged and the exchange rate regimes and practices of various countries. I shall first discuss current account developments and the nature of the international equilibrium that is attained, and then exchange rate regimes.

I. CURRENT ACCOUNT IMBALANCES AND THE NON-SYSTEM

The principal feature of the present system is that it is a form of international *laissez-faire*. Not only does it allow free play to the private market, but it allows free play to governments and their central banks to conduct their macroeconomic policies as they wish and to operate in the market as they choose. This, of course, is subject to the limitations accepted by the members of the European Monetary System. Leaving this aside, countries are free to borrow and lend, and to intervene as they wish in the foreign exchange market. The essential feature of the present system is decentralization and the absence of uniform, world-wide rules of any real significance.

Focusing now on current accounts, this apparently anarchic system naturally establishes an equilibrium. Indeed, this should not be surprising, since general equilibrium theory tells us that, given reasonable assumptions, decentralized decision-making with markets does tend to lead to an equilibrium. Looking at one small country on its own, its private sector savings and investment decisions combined with its fiscal policy will determine its current account balance, and hence its net lending or borrowing abroad. If the country has some effect on the world capital market, the more it borrows or the less it lends, the higher will be world interest rates.

If each country, including the United States, had a current account target, the targets might not add up for the world as a whole. There might be excess demand for or supply of funds. In principle the system can equilibrate in two ways. The first is the $n - 1$ way and the second is the market way.

In the first way, every country except one large one—obviously the United States—has a current account target, and the United States is the residual borrower or lender. The Bretton Woods equilibrium has sometimes been described in these terms, though it was never fully like this. Most countries did not have clear current account targets, and the United States was not entirely passive. But the way such a system would work is like this. Countries other than the United States manage their fiscal, monetary, and exchange rate policies so as to get the current account balances they want. The United States does not intervene in the foreign exchange market, and follows fiscal and monetary policies that are focused purely on domestic considerations. The US current account imbalance thus comes out as a residual.

In the waning days of Bretton Woods there was much discussion of the so-called $n - 1$ problem. The common view was that a satisfactory system with current account objectives should be symmetrical, and not give a special privilege, or impose a special burden, on the United States. Yet a symmetrical system, with current account targets and no residual borrower or lender, would not equilibrate unless some centralized rules or cooperative processes were introduced. Current account targets of all the countries had to be compatible. The same applied to the exchange rate system. All countries could not have independent exchange rate targets. If they all independently fixed their exchange rates to the dollar, the United States would have to accept the exchange rate implications for itself. It could not devalue relative to everyone else.

In the current system the major countries do not have current account targets. There is thus no $n - 1$ problem. Essentially, with respect to current accounts, the system is equilibrated in the market. The mechanism of adjustment is primarily through effects on world interest rates. We have a system where a price (interest rate) adjustment mechanism in the capital market equilibrates the system just as the market for apples is equilibrated by changes in the price of apples.

Let me spell this out. What happens if there is a fiscal expansion in one large country, say the United States? How are other countries affected? (I shall simplify here, as this is dealt with in more detail in the next chapter.) A fiscal expansion in the United States financed by the sale of bonds on the open market (and not through monetization of a deficit) will lead to more borrowing by the United States on the world capital market and thus raise world interest rates. The higher interest rates will have crowded out some US private investment, so that the US current account will not change to the same extent as the fiscal balance. Now comes the key transmission mechanism. Interest rates also rise abroad. I shall use Germany as representing all non-US countries.

The higher interest rate crowds out some private investment in

Germany, and possibly also raises savings there. Hence, Germany develops a current account surplus to match the US deficit. Essentially the increase in the US fiscal deficit has been financed by a diversion of US and German private savings away from financing private investment both in the United States and Germany. The world interest rate will rise until the reduction in world investment combined with any increase in world savings is equal to the increased demand for the world's savings coming from the US government. In each country market forces lead to a crowding out of private investment by US public borrowing.

At the same time, of course, German fiscal policy might react. A German fiscal expansion would raise world interest rates further but reduce the current account imbalance that results—more of the US fiscal imbalance having to be financed by crowding out in the United States. This is a policy reaction one might expect if Germany wanted to prevent the current account surplus and associated real depreciation. On the other hand, a German fiscal contraction would moderate the rise in world interest rates but increase the German current account surplus and US current account deficit.

One could imagine a situation where all governments pursue fiscal policies that ignore their current account and exchange rate implications. To a considerable extent, this has actually been so. Governments are influenced by concerns about long-term public debt accumulation, by short-term demand management objectives, and by various political considerations which (as in the United States) make all changes, especially fiscal contractions, difficult. Private sector savings and investment decisions then have to adjust so as to equilibrate the world capital market. Other things being equal, world interest rates would rise if major countries all engaged in fiscal expansion. Current account effects will come out as by-products.

It is also possible that market forces influence government borrowing decisions: the higher the real interest rate, the greater the incentive to reduce borrowing. Thus, if governments respond to market forces, they will *not* aim to keep fiscal balances constant when the US government increases its borrowing, but will seek to have lower deficits or greater surpluses.

Put in the most general terms, the world capital market reconciles the desires of different countries to buy and sell financial claims, the potential transactors including central banks that are intervening in the foreign-exchange market. The system equilibrates provided that at least some of the demands for or supplies of financial claims are responsive to interest rates. Given some elasticity, price changes in this market reconcile targets that initially seem incompatible.

There are, of course, countries that are concerned with their current accounts, especially those developing countries that have limited borrowing capacity and are compelled to adhere to what I have called the Old View of the current account. Many other countries have some concern about their current accounts, and allow this to influence their fiscal and exchange rate policies to a limited extent: but they do not actually have or enforce current account targets, and, in practice, subscribe to the New View. While concerns about the US current account are frequently expressed, the United States is a country that in practice treats the current account outcome as a residual—as probably it should. Its fiscal and monetary policies are dominated by purely domestic considerations.

II. IS THE NON-SYSTEM OPTIMAL?

The fact that the system equilibrates does not necessarily mean that it is optimal. But such a decentralized system may come closer to optimality than one where net current account imbalances (and possibly also exchange rates) are internationally planned or negotiated, or are subject to rules. Furthermore, the appearance of anarchy is deceptive. There is a logic. I come now to an argument which I first advanced in Corden (1983) and which has sometimes been criticized or misunderstood. It can be argued that the decentralized system which I have described is efficient for the same reasons that one usually regards a market system as efficient. Decentralized decision-making is more efficient and flexible than the alternative central planning approach. Individual governments are normally better judges than an international organization or committee of what would be an appropriate short-term trade-off point to choose between current unemployment and future inflation, what the efficacy of various policy instruments is likely to be, how much the public sector should run into debt, and what political scope there is for various policy adjustments. The current *laissez-faire* international macro-system is simply a market system which coordinates the decentralized decisions reached by private *and public* actors and is likely to be as efficient in this as the market system is within the domestic economy. In particular, it coordinates the various independently determined monetary and fiscal policies.

When the United States runs a current account deficit and Japan a surplus, the United States is a net seller of financial claims in exchange for goods, and Japan is a buyer of claims in exchange for goods. The United States has an export surplus in claims and Japan in goods. If the United States wants to sell pieces of paper and buy goods, and Japan is willing to buy the pieces of paper in exchange for goods, that is just normal trade, and yields gains from trade. It seems reasonable to presume that the various agents that trade in goods and in claims know what they are doing and are the best judges of what is good for them.

Of course, the agents may make mistakes: it may be unwise for Japanese financial institutions to buy dollar-denominated claims the real value of which might be depreciated by US inflation—though the interest rate should compensate for this risk—and it might be unwise for the US government to sell claims that will oblige it in later years to raise taxes unduly. But the presumption is surely that each agent, including the two governments, is a better judge of how much it should buy and sell at various prices than would be an international agency or than would result from an international agreement or *ad hoc* negotiation. There is surely no presumption that the current account imbalance—which is the quantity of trade in goods and services in exchange for financial claims—is any indication of the degree of possible non-optimality.

We have thus a simple market paradigm—extended to include public actors, notably finance ministries and central banks—as a useful reference point for analyzing the current non-system. But it is only a reference point. The outcome is not necessarily optimal. This is the qualification that has to be remembered. We know that markets do not inevitably lead to optimal results. There are various domestic distortions. There are income distribution considerations, externalities, and oligopolistic (strategic) interactions. In an environment with a limited number of very large actors, the possibility of oligopoly and the need for the ideas of game theory are relevant. I shall come to these in Chapter 13.

Indeed, the issue here is the same as that discussed earlier with regard to the Old View and the New View of the current account. The New View provides the right reference point, but needs to be qualified. Similarly, this market approach provides the right reference point, but is certainly subject to qualifications as a guide to the optimal system or outcome. I shall now discuss some of the optimality issues with regard to an important case, namely the long-standing Japanese current account surplus.

III. THE JAPANESE SURPLUS: HOW UNDESIRABLE FOR JAPAN?

Japan has a long history of current account surpluses. In 1992 its surplus was $118 billion which can be compared with the US deficit that year of $66 billion. The second largest surplus was that of Switzerland, with $16 billion. Large Japanese surpluses emerged already in 1971 and 1972, and again in 1978 and 1979. In both episodes, as also later, they were associated with very large bilateral trade surpluses with the United States, so that a popular and political concern in the United States with these imbalances goes back a long way. Typically, after each oil shock Japan went into deficit, but quickly its exports increased—generating strong resentments from competitors—and surpluses were restored.

From 1983, and especially from 1986, Japanese current account surpluses became really large, a change that matched the increase in US deficits caused by the US fiscal expansion. The peak imbalance year from the point of view of the United States was 1987. In that year the US current account deficit was $167 billion, the Japanese surplus was $87 billion, and the German surplus $46 billion. The only other countries with substantial surpluses were Taiwan and Korea (totaling about $30 billion together).

In assessing all this, it is very relevant that the Japanese surplus in relation to GDP has not been dramatically high—3.6 per cent in 1987 and 3.2 per cent in 1992. We are talking about an essentially marginal excess of national savings over national investment. The Japanese surplus reflects an excess of private savings over private investment combined, since 1986, with a modest fiscal surplus, which was 0.5 per cent of GDP in 1987 (general government fiscal balance) and 1.5 per cent in 1992, though somewhat higher (reaching 3 per cent) in between. Japan has had by far the highest savings and the highest investment ratios of any OECD country. In 1992 Japanese savings (private and public) were 34 per cent of GDP, of which 31 per cent of GDP went into investment in Japan (also private and public) and only 3 per cent into foreign investment, as reflected in the current account.

From their own point of view, did the Japanese save too much or invest too little at home? This raises the same issues as I discussed in Chapter 6 with regard to current account deficits. When the problem in so many countries, notably the United States and Britain, is that private savings are very low and government's contingent obligations very high, so that future tax increases will be needed, one should be reluctant to urge any people to save less. Surely prudence is a virtue, at least leaving aside the need for short-term demand management at a time of recession!

To a great extent, the high private savings ratio of Japan has been explained by demographic trends: a radical aging of the Japanese population can be expected in a few years, and the Japanese are very wisely saving for their old age. Dissaving in future years is likely to reduce the Japanese current account surplus. Turning to investment, should Japan have invested even more at home even though it has an exceptionally high domestic investment ratio? It is at least arguable—and apparent to many visitors—that there has been underinvestment in public infrastructure, so that a larger deficit in the Japanese government's capital budget would have been appropriate. Indeed, an increase in public investment was set in train in 1992 and 1993. But, even here, the answer is not clear. Higher public borrowing, even though it is borrowing the savings of Japan's own citizens, will increase the public debt and create future tax obligations. This would be no problem if the increased public investment raised Japanese taxable GDP sufficiently, but this is not inevitable.

Surprisingly, one can actually think of a reason why the Japanese current account surplus might have been too low. It is surely optimal for a high savings economy to maintain a diversified portfolio—to invest both at home and abroad—so as to cover itself against adverse shocks affecting Japan which might severely reduce the profitability of investments in Japan. Indeed, seen in this light, investing only 10 per cent of an annual increment of financial wealth in the world outside Japan, and 90 per cent in Japan (the 1992 proportion, when the savings ratio was 34 per cent and the current account ratio 3 per cent), seems an unbalanced allocation. Surely more should go to the outside world, and hence the current account should be greater. This will, of course, seem a perverse conclusion in view of the endless litany of complaints in the United States about the Japanese surplus.

This argument implies that there is a bias on the part of Japanese banks and institutions to prefer lending to domestic borrowers rather than investing abroad. The Japanese lenders are better informed and feel more confident in their judgments about domestic investments. No doubt exchange risk and the bad experience resulting from dollar devaluation since 1985 have played a role here. Essentially, international capital mobility is imperfect for these reasons, a general conclusion fitting in with the views of Feldstein and Horioka (1980) who noted that, in general, there was a high cross-country correlation between savings and investment ratios: countries that had high savings ratios also had high investment ratios, while low investment ratios went with low savings ratios.

Looking to the future, will Japan's current account surplus relative to GDP decline or increase? There are two sides to the answer. On the one hand, Japan's demographic trends—the aging of the population—suggest that the current account surplus will decline. On the other hand, as international capital mobility becomes less and less imperfect, current account imbalances should increase. More of Japan's savings will be invested abroad, to get closer to what would be an optimal portfolio allocation if information about domestic and foreign investments were of the same quality and there were no or reduced exchange rate risk. Of course, this could be partly offset by increased foreign investments in Japan, as foreign savers also diversify their portfolios. But, since Japanese savings are a higher proportion of world savings than Japanese domestic output is of world output, the net effect of increased capital mobility would be an increase in the Japanese current account surplus. As so often, opposing factors are at work.

IV. THE JAPANESE SURPLUS AND THE US DEFICIT: HOW
UNDESIRABLE FOR THE WORLD?

In the next chapter I shall discuss in detail the effects of a fiscal expansion by one country on other countries. Here I shall be rather sketchy to focus on some basic points. Would the world benefit if Japan took steps to reduce its current account surplus? The obvious way of doing so would be for Japan to engage in a fiscal expansion, and indeed such a policy has been continually urged by the US government on the Japanese in the belief that a reduced Japanese surplus would be beneficial for the United States, helping to reduce its own current account deficit.

One might wonder how a Japanese fiscal expansion could reduce a US current account deficit even when there is no change in US policy. In simplified form, the mechanism is as follows.

Reduced Japanese lending abroad raises world interest rates. This reduces US private investment, and hence US absorption. The reduced capital outflow from Japan appreciates the yen, hence depreciates the dollar and switches expenditure away from Japanese towards US goods. The combination of reduced US absorption owing to higher interest rates and dollar depreciation improves the US current account. There will be opposing effects on US internal balance. The main point is that the US savings–investment balance is altered by a reduction in domestic investment.

One's immediate question is: why should it be desirable for the United States to face higher interest rates and hence reduce investment? Surely the United States benefits when high Japanese savings keep down world interest rates and allow the United States (a net borrower) to borrow more cheaply. The future US taxpayer will certainly not benefit from higher interest rates which increase the public debt (for a given primary fiscal deficit), and increase debt service costs in the future. As I noted above, the United States has been selling financial claims and the Japanese have been buying them. Japan has been a net exporter of goods and services (hence having a current account surplus) while, in return, the United States has been a net exporter of financial claims. Hence, the United States will not benefit when Japanese demand for claims contracts, so that the price of claims falls. Can it ever be to the benefit of a seller to encourage a buyer to restrict supply?

There is, of course, an answer. A reduction in the Japanese surplus would involve Japanese real appreciation and reduce profits and employment in Japan's export and import-competing industries, while it would have a favorable effect on US producers of tradables. This is a familiar point from discussion of exchange rate protection motives in earlier chapters. The distributional effects are crucial, and the US dislike of its deficits and of Japanese surpluses is no doubt explained by a concern with competitiveness—with the ability of US tradable producers to compete with Japan at home and in Japan. For the same reason, the Japanese want to avoid real appreciation—and may intervene in the foreign exchange market for this purpose—because of an exchange rate protection motive, and this may then lead them to pursue more fiscally contractionary policies than otherwise. Similarly, with the same motive, the United States welcomes any Japanese and German action that will depreciate the dollar and—being unable to bring about sufficient fiscal contraction itself—seeks fiscal expansion from others, notably Japan.

What were the international implications of high Japanese private savings and fiscal consolidation (reduction of fiscal deficits) during the 1980s? If one ignores the sectional interests of US industries that compete with Japanese producers, one must surely conclude that the effects have been beneficial. At the time the US national savings ratio declined sharply, owing both to a decline in the private savings ratio and to the shift into fiscal deficit. High Japanese savings kept world interest rates lower than otherwise. Hence, the indebted developing countries benefited. Private investment, and hence growth rates, were higher than otherwise. In addition, all OECD governments were net debtors and their budgetary problems were eased by lower interest rates. Creditors the world over would, of course, have benefited from even higher interest rates.

This discussion must be related to the earlier analysis of whether the current account matters. To a partial extent, the Japanese surplus was a mirror image of the US deficit. From 1983 to 1990, the US deficit was higher than the Japanese surplus, but from 1991 to 1993 it was lower. Mostly they tended to move together. Can one conclude that the Japanese surplus was beneficial for the world, including the United States, while the US deficit was not, when they were mirror images of each other?

This question poses an apparent paradox which can be easily resolved.

To answer the question, the New View of the current account is appropriate. The United States and the rest of the world (ROW) benefited from the lower interest rates that high Japanese savings, relatively lower domestic private investment, and fiscal consolidation in Japan produced. If these lower interest rates increase private investment in the United States and thus increase the US current account deficit, as is likely, it is a current account outcome that is beneficial for the United States. The essential point is that capital imports into the United States have become cheaper—the price of private bonds and equities that the United States sells will have risen—and this is beneficial.

On the other hand, the US current account may also—and did—go into deficit because of the increased US budget deficit. From the US point of view—and certainly from the point of view of future taxpayers or potential future recipients of government expenditures and social transfers—the fiscal policy decisions that led to the budget deficit were unwise. The movement of the US current account into deficit was simply a by-product of the unwise fiscal policy decisions.

When the US current account goes into deficit because private investment has increased in response to a decline in world interest rates, it is a symptom of a desirable development; when it goes into deficit because of an unwise US fiscal expansion, it is a symptom of an undesirable development. As for the rest of the world (ROW), it is probably, on balance, damaged by a US fiscal expansion (and the current account deficit that goes with it) because such expansion raises world interest rates.

It follows that a reduction of the Japanese current account surplus and US current account deficit resulting from Japanese fiscal expansion would have an adverse effect on the United States and ROW because world interest rates would rise and private investment would fall. As aggregate borrowers and debtors, they lose. By contrast, if the two current account imbalances were reduced as a result of US fiscal contraction, the effects would be favorable for the United States and ROW because world interest rates would fall and private investment would rise. In addition, the United States would benefit insofar as the fiscal expansion represented an unwise or non-optimal intertemporal decision for present and future American taxpayers and beneficiaries from transfers.

I have disregarded the interests of Japan itself here. The higher are world interest rates, the better for Japan's savers. And since Japan is a net saver in the world economy, Japan as a whole gains from a US fiscal expansion that raises world interest rates. On the other hand, its borrowers, including the government and private corporations, lose. I have also ignored the sectionally adverse effects of a Japanese surplus on US and ROW producers of tradables who compete with Japanese producers, whether in Japan or elsewhere. It is their interests that have dominated public discussion. I have looked only at the overall effects in the United States and ROW, including effects on growth.

From the point of view of the special interests of US and ROW industries competing with Japanese producers, anything that reduces the Japanese surplus is beneficial. It is clearly this concern that explains the hostility to or concern with the Japanese surplus. When Japan exports more goods and imports more financial assets, the adverse effect on competing tradable producers is very apparent, and leads to pressures for protection or to do something about the surplus. On the other hand, producers of non-tradables and sellers of financial assets will gain. But the American gainers—such as borrowers in the housing market or firms supplying investment goods—are unlikely to attribute their gains to an increased Japanese willingness to save or to invest less at home.

The United States and Japan have generated the biggest aggregate current account imbalances of all countries since 1983. But this does not mean that the issues just discussed are relevant only for these countries. Germany had large surpluses from 1985 to 1990. After the two oil shocks, oil exporters generated large surpluses and a group of mainly middle-income developing countries ran into large deficits. For example, in 1981 the total surplus of oil exporters was $33.5 billion and the deficit of "countries with recent debt-servicing difficulties" (as defined by the IMF) was $84 billion. The United States had a surplus of $7 billion and Japan of $4.8 billion in that year. But for the world as a whole, the calculated deficit added up to $69 billion—and in 1992 it was $106 billion—so that one should not treat any of these figures with great respect.

V. THE EXCHANGE RATE SYSTEM

I turn now to the exchange rate system that has emerged since the breakdown of Bretton Woods. Is it also a non-system, and does it also have a logic?

It may seem strange to discuss exchange rates separately from the current account issue. There is, of course, a tendency for current account movements to be associated with real exchange rate movements. A country that moves from current account balance into deficit is also, other things being equal, likely to experience a real appreciation. This was certainly the message of the basic model of Chapter 2. Even within the framework of that model, there are qualifications. For example, differential productivity changes may cause the equilibrium real exchange rate to change even for a given current account. But there are three further qualifications when relating current accounts and exchange rates.

First, nominal exchange rates do not need to be correlated with real exchange rate changes. In the floating rate regime since 1973, nominal and real exchange rates of the dollar have indeed moved closely together. But in a fixed nominal rate regime, there can still be changes in the real exchange rate, brought about by appropriate variations in the prices of non-tradables. A country can move into current account deficit and import capital both in a fixed and a floating rate regime. In both cases the real exchange rate will initially appreciate. Second, changes in the current account tend to follow real exchange rate changes with a considerable lag. For example, the sharp depreciation of the dollar that began in 1985 and was completed in 1987 only bore fruit in a reduced US current account deficit in 1988; from 1985 to 1987 the deficit relative to GDP kept on rising. Third, superimposed on movements in nominal exchange rates that reflect current fundamentals, notably monetary and fiscal policies, are short-term exchange rate fluctuations reflecting expectations. These have little or no immediate effect on current accounts.

From March 1973, the principal G-7 currencies have floated, and the relationship between them can be described as a managed floating regime. I am referring here to the dollar, yen, Deutschmark, sterling, and Canadian dollar rates. For a brief period, 1990 to 1992, sterling was in the ERM, and I ignore this episode now. I discussed the adventures of the French franc and the Italian lira in the ERM in Chapter 7, and will also ignore them. The many other countries have a variety of exchange rate regimes, which are difficult to describe briefly. There are managed floating regimes, pegged rates that are frequently adjusted (flexible pegs), exchange rates that are adjusted regularly in line with the rate of inflation (crawling pegs), pegged rates that are infrequently adjusted (fixed-but-adjustable rates), and fixed rates. Rates are usually pegged to a currency basket, but sometimes to the dollar or the franc. The main point is that countries are free to choose their exchange rate regimes. The general tendency since 1973, and especially since 1980 or so, has been to move from fixed-but-adjustable rates to very flexible (i.e. frequently adjusted) pegged rates or to managed floating rates.

Focusing on the five main currencies since March 1973, they make up a managed floating non-system. Each country has been completely free to conduct its monetary policy as it wished, and flexible exchange rates could accommodate differential inflation rates. Countries intervened intermittently in the foreign exchange market, usually to moderate sharp movements without reversing them or even changing the direction of the movement. This was "leaning against the wind". These interventions were often made unilaterally, but sometimes (mostly since 1985) several central banks intervened together to achieve an agreed result. Thus there was intermittent *ad hoc* coordination.

No formal exchange rate commitments have been made by the five governments concerned. Thus it has been a regime of complete freedom for governments, but because they have intervened, it has been a managed rather than a free floating rate regime. Furthermore, it must always be borne in mind that the principal way in which governments influence exchange rates in a world of high capital mobility is through their monetary policies, and not (other than in the very short run) through their direct foreign exchange interventions.

With every country having complete freedom in the pursuit of its monetary policies, and being able to intervene in the foreign exchange market as much or as little as it likes, it can also conduct short-term demand management as it pleases. But it must be prepared to accept the exchange rate consequences. For example, in a recession, the United States can expand the money supply and lower domestic interest rates, but it must then accept the dollar depreciation that is likely to result and that, indeed, may happen when the monetary expansion is anticipated, even before it actually takes place. It must also be borne in mind that, because of very high international capital mobility, actual exchange rate outcomes have depended heavily on market expectations.

Since March 1973, the five governments have never had well defined exchange rate targets. Thus, a question of incompatibility of targets—the $n - 1$ problem—has never arisen. Mostly, the governments have pursued their monetary and fiscal policies taking into account primarily domestic objectives, and the exchange rate outcomes have been by-products. Fundamentally, this is the logic of the system. Each government of a country makes its own decisions about the short-term trade-off between inflation and unemployment and what would be an appropriate short-term demand management policy. But sometimes governments have had limited exchange rate objectives, and this has influenced their monetary policies and their exchange rate interventions. For some periods (notably 1981–4), the United States had no exchange rate objective at all, hence resolving any $n - 1$ problem—though its own monetary and fiscal policies combined with market expectations actually dominated the exchange rate outcome, overshadowing the interventions of the Bank of Japan and the Bundesbank. At other times, mostly from 1985, there was consultation about intervention, and sometimes coordinated intervention in pursuit of agreed objectives. I discuss intervention and coordination further in Chapters 12 and 13.

The exchange rate system that has evolved is the result of increasing international capital mobility. In the presence of various shocks and the expectations these generate, it was not possible to maintain a fixed-but-adjustable regime, so that the Bretton Woods system broke down. Speculative capital movements generated by expectations overwhelmed the system.

As long as there is a possibility of devaluation—as long as the commitment to a fixed exchange rate is not seen as immutable—capital movements can destabilize a fixed exchange rate system. They would not actually do so if domestic monetary policies were consistently conservative and there were no shocks that were expected to create an incentive for devaluation. But such shocks do happen. Hence in the new non-system that followed Bretton

Woods, exchange rate commitments by governments have been given up, and as a result the market perceives great uncertainty about the levels of future exchange rates. This is an important feature—perhaps the greatest weakness—of the present system. It explains why de Grauwe (1989) has described it as "The System without Commitments".

One might expect that future exchange rates would be influenced or even determined by future fundamentals, notably monetary policies, but there is always great uncertainty about these. This, in turn, is the reason that current exchange rates, reflecting fluctuations in expectations, fluctuate so much, and sometimes appear to respond to quite irrational motives. In turn, these fluctuations have given rise to dissatisfaction with the floating rate system. As I have already noted, such dissatisfaction motivated the establishment of the EMS and the plans for the EMU. There is a hankering—unrealistic in my view—for the restoration of the certainties of a fixed rate regime. But I leave all these issues to later chapters.

VI. DOES THE DOLLAR HAVE A SPECIAL ROLE?

In the Bretton Woods system the dollar had a special role. The details I shall not pursue here. The question is whether this really changed when the Bretton Woods system broke down. Can one really say that the current non-system is symmetrical with regard to the dollar and the United States? There are, of course, no international rules affecting exchange rates and macroeconomic policies to which the United States has agreed to adhere, so its government and central bank do have complete freedom, subject to domestic considerations, as do other governments. But is the symmetry not just *de jure* but also *de facto*?

The United States has been able to finance large current account deficits on the international capital market, especially since 1983. But that is no special privilege. The United States is unique only in being a large economy. Other industrial countries have also been able to run large deficits in relation to their GDPs and finance them on the world capital market. For the whole period 1985–92, the US current account deficit was 2.7 per cent of GDP. But the deficits of Canada for the same period averaged 2.9 per cent of GDP, and of Australia 4.7 per cent. In 1992 the current account deficits relative to GDP of Finland, Canada, Australia, and Spain were, respectively, 4.7 per cent, 4 per cent, 3.7 per cent, and 3.2 per cent, while that of the United States, still the largest deficit absolutely in the world, was 1 per cent.

The United States government is able to borrow wholly in terms of its own currency, while other governments also issue bonds denominated in their own currency but in addition are obliged to borrow on the international capital market in dollars. The United States thus appears to have the special privilege of being able to inflate away the real value of its public debt. But, of course, expectation of such an intention would raise nominal interest rates that the US government has to pay, so that the privilege only applies to surprise inflation. Is this a significant privilege? Arguably, there are few surprises in the world's most open society and governmental system, and the domestic resistance to inflation (as evidenced by the electoral reaction—the defeat of President Carter—in 1980) is such that a significant, deliberately engineered, increase in inflation is probably not an available instrument of policy.

Coming to the exchange rate regime, can one say that the United States is passive while other countries determine their exchange rates? I have already discussed this. With regard to actual exchange market intervention, the United States was mostly passive from 1973 to 1980, and wholly so from 1981 to 1984. Since 1985 the United States has taken part in, and indeed initiated, episodes of coordinated intervention. But this only refers to actual intervention in the foreign exchange market. Much more important is US monetary policy. The dollar has been greatly influenced by US monetary policy, and the exchange rate results have not always been welcomed by other countries, notably Germany and Japan, the currencies of which appreciated as a result of US monetary expansions, especially after the 1987 stock market crash and during the US recession of 1991.

In practice, the US authorities have felt completely free to manage monetary policy in the light of domestic conditions as they perceived them, but taking account of possible exchange rate effects if they chose to do so. Hence, the United States has not been passive. The dollar has also been influenced by US fiscal policy and, above all, by market expectations, as I shall discuss in the next two chapters.

Finally, the dollar has remained special as a medium of exchange, unit of account, and store of value, both in the official and the private sector. As McKinnon (1993) points out, this is essentially because of economies of scale. The use of the dollar for all these purposes, rather than the yen or the DM, is explained by historical factors, by the relative size of US trade and capital movements, and by the depth of US financial markets. A record of political stability and relatively low inflation is clearly required. The general use of one particular currency is a convenience for everyone. It yields some modest seigniorage for the United States, since it increases the demand for dollar base money.

The dollar is the dominant vehicle currency for interbank clearing, is generally used for official intervention (except in the EMS, where the DM fills this role), is mostly used for invoicing trade, including trade not involving the United States, and is still the main form in which foreign exchange reserves are held (about 64 per cent of foreign exchange reserves in 1992). Claims in Euro-currency markets are also mainly in dollars. In 1992, 83 per cent of foreign exchange transactions had the dollar on one side. But the DM was catching up, from 27 per cent in 1983 to 38 per cent in 1992, the last a particularly high figure because of the EMS turmoil. In 1992, 13 per cent of official foreign exchange reserves were held in DM, making it the second most important reserve currency.

APPENDIX 10.1

The Current Account Imbalance and the World Interest Rate

Fig. 10.1 assumes a two-country world, Japan and the United States. Hence the US current account deficit is equal to the Japanese surplus. Many simplifying assumptions are made to illustrate some key points of this chapter. The vertical axis above 0 shows the world interest rate and the horizontal axis the US deficit. The vertical axis below 0 shows the dollar real exchange rate, a movement downward being a real depreciation.

Curve UU shows the potential US demand for funds (US supply of financial claims) on the world capital market at various interest rates. The lower the interest rate, the greater US private investment, and hence the greater the demand for funds. Curve JJ shows the potential Japanese supply of funds (demand for financial claims). The lower the interest rate, the greater Japanese private investment (and also, possibly, the less private savings), and hence the less the supply of funds.

UU and JJ also take into account the bond-financing of government deficits. An increased Japanese budget deficit would shift JJ to the left, and a reduced US budget deficit would shift UU to the left.

Curve RR shows the US real exchange rate for any given current account balance, assuming a given level of real income (or employment) in the United States. (The latter assumption will be maintained initially.) The greater the current account deficit, the more appreciated is the real exchange rate.

We start at A and A'. Japanese fiscal expansion (without a US policy change) would bring equilibrium to B and B', hence reducing the imbalance and depreciating the dollar real exchange rate. A US fiscal contraction (without a Japanese policy change) could bring equilibrium to C, and again to B', hence having the same effect on the imbalance and the real exchange rate. The two policies differ by their effects on the interest rate.

The RR curve is meant to trace out an equilibrium relationship (which can be derived from Fig. 2.1) when the real exchange rate has its full switching effect (which may be very little in the short run but high in equilibrium) and when income and employment are at the natural or

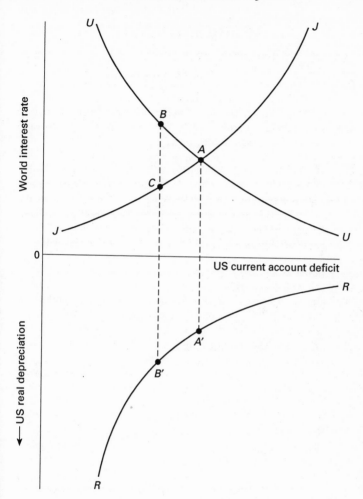

FIG. 10.1. Current Account Deficit and World Interest Rate

internal balance level. If real income were above that (as it might be in the short run), a point below *RR*, with more dollar real depreciation for a given US current account deficit, would be reached.

REFERENCES

De Grauwe (1989) gives an excellent description of the current exchange rate "system without commitments". See also Black (1985) and McKinnon (1993) for historical perspectives.

The argument that the international non-system has a logic and that the principles of welfare economics apply to it was advanced in Corden (1983). I developed it further in Corden (1986) when discussing the logic of policy coordination. Corden (1984) gives an exposition of the normative theory of trade policy which can be applied directly to trade in financial assets, and which is the underlying theory in this chapter.

Exchange rate arrangements of developing countries are described in Aghevli et al. (1991) and in Little et al. (1993). Trends in national savings are analyzed in Aghevli et al. (1990) and Japanese savings behavior, in particular, in Hayashi (1986).

On the role of the dollar as an international currency, see Kenen (1983) and McKinnon (1993). Figures cited come from the Bank for International Settlements, published in Group of Ten (1993), and the *Annual Report* of the IMF. On broader issues of the international use of currencies, see Black (1990) and Tavlas (1991).

Current account figures all come from the IMF's *World Economic Outlook*, October 1993.

11

The International Transmission of Disturbances

In a flexible exchange rate regime, countries can have monetary independence. Allowing for lags and problems of short-term economic management, every country can choose its own inflation rate. But this does not mean that disturbances—even monetary disturbances—are not transmitted between countries. Events since 1974 have certainly borne this out. In a world of flexible exchange rates there are still *real* links between countries, the mechanisms of transmission being (1) the capital market and (2) the terms of trade. For example, a monetary disturbance in one country will have effects on output in that country—and thus have *real* and not just nominal effects—and, in turn, may affect the terms of trade, and thus have real effects on another country. In turn, the other country's monetary policy stance, while independent in principle, may respond to the change in its terms of trade. Similarly, the effects of a fiscal expansion will be transmitted internationally.

The purpose of this chapter is to present a systematic analysis of the transmission of policy disturbances from one large country (the United States) to other countries (represented here by Germany) when the exchange rate is floating. While effects of expectations on the exchange rate will be ignored (to be discussed in the next chapter), the analysis is short term in the sense that it allows for Keynesian effects of demand on output. The starting-point will be the Mundell–Fleming model which is indeed based on Keynesian assumptions. The two policy disturbances to be considered are a fiscal expansion in the United States and a monetary expansion. Of course, the analysis can readily be applied to contractions.

I shall consider, first, the original policies in the United States and their effects in the United States; second—and most important—the process of transmission to Germany; and third, the monetary policy and labor-market reactions in Germany. I shall give particular attention to several possible labor-market reactions, including the case where real wages in Germany are (more or less) rigid as a result of formal or informal indexation.

The issue of how policy changes in major countries—notably the United States, Japan, and Germany—are transmitted to other countries has been prominent in international debate for the whole twenty-year period since 1973 when the floating rate regime began. During the whole of the 1980s the effects of the US budget deficit on the international economy were continually discussed, and it is this episode—especially the period from 1981 to 1984 when the dollar appreciated so sharply—that inspired this kind of analysis. At the same time, Germany, Japan, and most other developed countries apart from the United States were reducing their budget deficits (fiscal consolidation), and the effects of these policies can be analyzed in the same way. As a result of German unification in 1990, Germany radically shifted its fiscal stance, moving into large budget deficit and, again, generating the kinds of effects that are analyzed in this chapter. Furthermore, there have been many episodes of monetary expansions and contractions by the major countries, and no doubt more can be expected. Such episodes always have international repercussions. Notable expansionary episodes were in 1973, 1978–9, and 1988–9, while the outstanding episode of a monetary contraction not just by the United States but also by all the other major industrial countries other than France was that of 1979 to 1982.

I. HOW US FISCAL EXPANSION AFFECTS GERMANY: THE MUNDELL–FLEMING STORY

I shall now assume that there is a fiscal expansion in the United States which causes the budget to go into deficit. I shall tell at first a very simple Mundell–Fleming story. But this is only a beginning, though very necessary for more complex analysis. The money supply is kept unchanged and the deficit is bond-financed. There is slack in the US economy and, at least in the short run, extra demand would increase output and incomes without prices rising very much, if at all. This is the Keynesian assumption.

Initially I shall assume that the fiscal deficit has no direct effect on private savings, a matter to be reconsidered later.

The international effects of the US fiscal expansion can be divided into two parts: first, the spending effect, and second, the capital market effect. To consider the first on its own, it can be assumed initially that there is no international capital mobility because of firmly enforced exchange controls. It is thus possible for the interest rate in the United States to rise relative to that in Germany without capital flowing in.

The deficit will increase spending on US goods and on imports. The extra spending will result not only directly from higher government expenditure, or from tax reductions that have raised the disposable income of the private sector, but also from the multiplier process that higher demand for US goods initiates. But there will also be a counteracting effect: the US interest rate will rise, and this will crowd out some domestic investment and reduce spending. Thus there is both an expansionary and a deflationary force at work. I shall now assume, as in the simple model, that there will be a net increase in total spending and, at a constant exchange rate, also on imports. Yet the current account has to stay in balance, given the two assumptions made so far, namely, a floating exchange rate and hence absence of foreign exchange intervention, and absence of international capital movements owing to exchange controls. Hence, the exchange rate will depreciate until the whole of the net increase in spending has been diverted on to US goods. Thus US output will increase further.

The next step is to allow for international capital mobility. Owing to the higher US interest rate, capital will flow from Germany to the United States, appreciating the US dollar. It will also raise the German interest rate and moderate the crowding-out effect in the United States. Thus, combining the spending and the capital mobility effects, the dollar might depreciate or appreciate. But, if capital mobility is high, a net appreciation is likely. The effect of a fiscal expansion on interest rates and on capital movements will be very quick, while increased spending may take place with a lag, so that the immediate effect will certainly be to appreciate the exchange rate. Of course, this may be offset by the effect of a fiscal expansion on exchange rate expectations, but that is a complication which will be dealt with in the next chapter.

How would this US fiscal expansion affect Germany? This is the question which was much discussed in the 1980s, the concern, of course, being with the effects on many other countries, and not just Germany (which represents here the whole of the non-US world). To begin with, would the net effect on Germany be demand expansionary or contractionary? And how would it affect the current account, as well as various relative prices? It is clear that there are three effects on Germany at work. First, the direct spending effect—before the exchange rate alters—is expansionary. German exports would rise on that account. Second, the rise in the German interest rate resulting from capital outflow reduces German investment spending and thus is contractionary. With perfect capital mobility there would be a single world interest rate, and the US fiscal expansion will have increased it. Third, the depreciation of the DM, which is the mirror image of the dollar appreciation, is expansionary. It switches US and German demand away from US goods towards German goods.

If we adhered to the simple Mundell–Fleming model, we would now make the assumption that the German money supply in real terms is kept constant. (In the *IS-LM* diagram, the *LM* curve does not move.) In that case the net effect would be expansionary. This is shown diagrammatically in Appendix 11.1. To put the mechanism (awkwardly) in words, the exchange rate would have to keep on depreciating until the German interest rate had risen to the new, higher world rate that has been brought about by the US fiscal expansion. The higher interest rate would reduce the demand for money, which has to be compensated by an increased demand for money resulting from higher incomes in Germany.

We thus get the result in this Mundell–Fleming model that the fiscal expansion in the United States is expansionary in Germany, a case of positive transmission. It is worth stressing that this would be true even if the initial spending effect (before capital mobility) were low or zero. (See Fig. 11.1.) The key point is that, with a given real money supply, a rise in the world interest rate is expansionary. This outcome appears, at first sight, a paradox, because the rise in the interest rate reduces investment. But the expansion is caused by the switching effect of the DM depreciation, which outweighs in this model the direct contractionary effect of the rise in the interest rate.

II. THE MONETARY POLICY REACTION IN GERMANY

The next step is to consider the monetary policy reaction in Germany to the changes that have been brought about in Germany by the US fiscal expansion. The assumption that the real money supply of Germany is held constant is surely a weakness in the model. So we must go beyond the standard model to consider alternative possibilities.

First, one might assume the nominal money supply to be held constant, though I would not regard this as realistic either. In that case the real money supply would fall: the reason is that the depreciation would raise the domestic price level owing to the higher DM prices of imports, and in addition, insofar as there is a net expansion at all, prices of German-produced goods would rise somewhat. Hence the net expansion in Germany would be reduced and there could actually be a net contraction.

Second, one might assume that the German monetary authorities would want to moderate the rise in the interest rate. I am assuming here that Germany's impact on the world capital market is large enough to affect the world interest rate. Hence, the German authorities would increase the money supply, hence moderating the rise in the world interest rate and depreciating the DM further. The net effect would be even more expansionary than when the real money supply in Germany was held constant.

It is the third possibility that seems to me the most plausible. The German authorities would seek to manage their monetary policy so as to maintain what they think of as internal balance—i.e. a level of demand for German goods that trades off the benefits of reducing unemployment against the dangers of inflation. This, of course, implies a Phillips curve concept, and I shall discuss this in detail later in this chapter. At this point it can simply be supposed that the initial level of demand, yielding the initial level of German real incomes, is the one the authorities want to maintain. In other words, they will vary the money supply so as to avoid any net expansionary or contractionary effect of the US fiscal expansion. If the initial effect is expansionary, as suggested by the Mundell–Fleming model, a German monetary contraction would then be called for. The benefit of studying the effects on Germany of a US fiscal expansion under the assumption that the German money supply is held constant is then limited: it only tells us in which direction the money supply will have to be adjusted to maintain German internal balance.

Let us now suppose that the internal balance policy does indeed represent the German policy reaction. What, then, is the net effect on the German current account? Here the answer is very simple if we use the savings-and-investment approach. There is no particular reason why German savings would change, since incomes will have been kept constant by the internal balance policy. But the higher interest rate will have crowded out some investment. Hence, assuming internal balance initially, the German current account will have gone into surplus. The evidence is not clear that savings are interest-elastic, but if the higher interest rate had increased savings, the current account surplus would be all the greater. This outcome is to be expected. If Germany is to finance some part of the US fiscal deficit, Germany has to run a current account surplus. This is generated, essentially, by the higher interest rate, which crowds out some German investment.

It is worth listing the sectoral and broader effects in Germany of the US fiscal expansion, given the pursuit of an internal balance policy in Germany, though we shall look at these effects in more detail later. First, there has been a real depreciation, which benefits producers of tradables and hurts producers of non-tradables, probably reducing real wages. Second, the higher interest rate has benefited lenders and hurt borrowers, being, on balance, beneficial for Germany, as it is a net lender. And third, investment has been reduced, which will both reduce the relative price of investment goods and also have long-term adverse effects on growth.

III. THE TRANSMISSION OF US MONETARY EXPANSION

Exactly the same analysis can be used to analyze the effects of a US monetary expansion. It would be boring to pursue this in detail here. Yet it is important to consider the effects of monetary policy shocks, since sharp variations in monetary policies by the three major economies are always possible. While the 1981–5 period provides an excellent example of a fiscal policy shock emanating from the United States, and 1991–2 a similar example of such a shock coming from Germany, examples of sharp monetary policy shifts, whether expansion or contraction, are more common, and very likely to recur in the future.

To put it briefly, a US monetary expansion would reduce the US interest rate, increase US investment, and thus have a spending effect which would raise output and incomes in the US as well as increasing imports. The dollar would depreciate both because of the spending effect and because of the reduction in the interest rate (which leads to capital outflow). In Germany there would again be three effects: the spending effect would be expansionary, as in the case of fiscal expansion; the decline in the interest rate would also be expansionary, since it would lead to an increase in investment; but the DM appreciation would be contractionary, since it would switch US and German demand away from German goods. As shown in Appendix 11.1, with a given real money supply in Germany, the exchange rate effect would outweigh the other two effects, and the net result would be a German contraction. Superficially that seems a surprising result: a US monetary expansion contracts demand and hence incomes in Germany, a case of negative transmission. But, of course, a monetary expansion in Germany could compensate for this effect, so that internal balance could be maintained. It would depreciate the DM somewhat (partially reversing the earlier appreciation) and lower the world interest rate further. If such an internal balance policy were pursued, finally Germany would end up with the same level of incomes and savings, but a lower interest rate, more investment, a current account deficit, and, on balance, a net real appreciation. The interest rate, current account, and exchange rate effects would be the opposite from those resulting from a US fiscal expansion, even though in both cases there was an initial positive spending effect.

V. GAINERS AND LOSERS FROM US FOREIGN BORROWING

In a world of capital mobility and flexible exchange rates the essential feature of a fiscal expansion by a major economy—i.e. the United States—is that it leads to a rise in the world interest rate, appreciation of the real exchange rate of the expanding country, and crowding out of investment both at home and abroad. The United States goes into current account deficit, or the deficit increases, and this is matched by a German current account surplus. Part of the US fiscal deficit is thus financed by borrowing from Germany. That is the story so far. I shall now assume that appropriate monetary contractions in the United States and in Germany have avoided net expansionary effects in both countries. Hence both countries have maintained internal balance. But there is more to say.

It is particularly interesting to discuss who the gainers and losers are in Germany and whether Germany might be an overall gainer or loser. Of course, the term "Germany" represents here all countries other than the United States. In the 1980s Europeans were full of complaints about the US fiscal deficit, focusing on the adverse effects on them. Were they justified? Did the US fiscal expansion really have an unfavorable effect on other countries? At the same time, US politicians and commentators complained about the Japanese current account surplus, and pressure was put on Japan to slow up or reverse its process of fiscal consolidation so as to reduce its current account surplus. The analytical issue is the same in this case: would other countries gain or lose—or more specifically, who would gain or lose—from a Japanese fiscal expansion or avoidance of contraction?

The effects of US fiscal expansion on Germany are complex. The DM depreciation is likely to worsen the German terms of trade. That is an overall loss to Germany. It is likely to affect German producers of non-tradables adversely, and specifically will reduce real wages in non-tradables (relative to what would have happened to them otherwise), while raising them in tradables. Overall, German real wages may well fall. With lower investment at home, owing to the higher interest rate, the investment goods industries will be adversely affected, and since the building and construction industry is a producer of non-tradable investment goods as well as of highly interest-elastic private housing, it would lose.

Borrowers will lose from the higher interest rate while lenders will gain, and these lenders will include wage-earners or retired wage-earners. Since Germany as a whole has been a net lender, in this respect there will be an overall gain to Germany. Since much of Germany's international lending has been at floating interest rates, or has been short term, there will also be a gain as a result of its net creditor position. Reduced domestic investment will lower the rate of growth of the gross domestic product. The crucial point is that more of German savings are lent to the United States to finance the US fiscal deficit, so that less is left to invest at home. By lowering the long-term capital–labor ratio (relative to what would have happened otherwise), the reduction of German investment will also tend to reduce German real wages. But, insofar as wage-earners are also savers, they may be compensated by the fruits of the extra lending to the United States at the higher interest rates.

It is worth noting here that the developing countries that were big net debtors at floating interest rates during the 1980s were very adversely affected by the high world real interest rates resulting from US fiscal expansion and monetary contraction. They were clearly losers from the diversion of world savings, at least marginally, towards the United States. On the other hand, they surely benefited from the fiscal deficit reduction policies of Japan and some European countries. As I discussed in the previous chapter, a concern with the interests of US export- and import-competing industries led the United States to press Japan to engage in fiscal expansion and hence reduce its trade surplus with the United States. But this advocacy was contrary to the interests of US borrowers—including the US government itself—and the developing countries.

VI. DYNAMICS OF THE US DEFICIT

The dynamics of the US fiscal deficit—and hence of the US–German current account imbalance—need also to be taken into account. Initially there is a real appreciation of the dollar which—together with the appropriate savings–investment balance—generates the non-interest current account deficit (the primary deficit) of the United States and surplus of Germany that I have described. But the US interest bill will build up. If the debt is growing faster than GDP, while the current account deficit as a proportion of GDP is constant at its new higher level, the primary deficit has to fall, and it would have to fall even more if the current account deficit were reduced and eventually turned into a surplus (as debt was being repaid). There must then be real depreciation of the dollar to generate the necessary rise in US exports and import replacement required for an improvement in the primary balance. In other words, the real exchange rate, having first appreciated as the United States went into fiscal deficit, must then gradually depreciate. Various effects would then be reversed: Germany's terms of trade would improve owing to real appreciation, producers of non-tradables and wage-earners in Germany would gain, while German tradable industries would tend to lose.

There is another reason, quite distinct from the one just discussed, why a US fiscal expansion would tend, in due course, to bring about depreciation of the dollar, at least in the absence of a counteracting monetary policy. As more and more dollar-denominated financial assets accumulate in international financial portfolios, hence raising the ratio of dollar-denominated to DM-denominated assets, portfolio balancing would require both depreciation of the dollar and increase in the interest rate on dollar assets relative to the interest rate on DM-denominated assets. The dollar depreciation would reduce the relative nominal value of US assets (raise the relative value of DM assets), and so help to restore balance in portfolios. This follows from portfolio balance models. Unless offset by monetary policies, depreciation would be continuous, at least as long as the international portfolio composition was changing.

VII. RICARDIAN EQUIVALENCE

Finally, one should take another look at the initial spending effect of the US fiscal deficit. Private savings and investment could be affected in various ways by the rise in government spending or by the tax cuts which gave rise to the fiscal deficit. For example, extra government investment in infrastructure might be complementary with private investment, so that private investment would actually rise on that account. Reductions in certain taxes may encourage private savings, while increased social welfare payments may reduce savings.

Note needs to be taken of the so-called Ricardian equivalence theorem, which has recently been amazingly popular with some macroeconomic theorists in the United States. The argument is that, as the US government goes into deficit, its citizens or residents should foresee that this will mean higher taxes in the future to pay for the accumulating interest bill and the eventual repayment of the debt. If they wished to smooth consumption levels over time, they would save more now in anticipation. Hence a rise in private savings would offset the reduction in government savings (or increase in dissavings). Of course, such a reaction would only result from a tax cut, an increase in transfers, or an increase in government consumption spending. If the increase in the budget deficit were caused by higher public investment spending, it might not be necessary to save more in order to pay higher taxes later, because the higher investment might generate the extra output from which the debt service could be paid.

Conceivably there could be a complete offset: the increase in private savings might actually equal the increase in the budget deficit. In that case total national spending would not increase at all as a result of the change in fiscal policy. Furthermore, the interest rate would not rise since extra private savings would fully finance the fiscal deficit. For example, if the fiscal deficit had resulted from an income tax cut, the whole of the increase in disposable income would be saved. That is an extreme case; people may not show so much foresight or be so concerned about a future tax burden which their heirs, and not they themselves, will partly or wholly bear. Indeed, they are unlikely to have the empirical knowledge required to determine how much extra private savings are needed. But perhaps—just conceivably—there is some tendency in that direction: to some extent private savings might increase when taxes are reduced even before real incomes rise—if they do. Some economists believe that there is indeed empirical support for such a Ricardian result. In any case, it appeals to them because it implies rational behavior. Incidentally, David Ricardo should not really be blamed for the idea, since he thought such rational behavior improbable.

From 1980, and, even more, 1982, the US fiscal deficit relative to GDP rose sharply and stayed high after that, beginning to fall in 1987. Thus we have a laboratory experiment for the theory. Yet the US private savings ratio actually fell, or at least did not rise. Hence, this episode did not give support to the Ricardian equivalence theorem. It is likely that the low concern for the future—and the confidence that something, such as high productivity growth, will turn up—influenced both the elected rulers of the United States and the savings behavior of the private sector. Hence there was both public and private profligacy, rather than that the profligacy of the former was offset by the prudence of the latter.

VIII. WAGES BEHAVIOR AND THE TERMS OF TRADE[1]

So far we have assumed in this chapter that nominal wages are sticky (the Keynesian case). They may also be flexible so as to equilibrate the labor market (the neo-classical case). Now we allow for a tendency to real-wage rigidity—a concept already introduced in Chapter 3. This complication is particularly important when constructing models designed to apply to European countries where trade unions are strong and where there is usually some degree of formal or informal wage indexation, partial or complete. The main point is simply that a rise in prices would lead, possibly after a lag, to an increase in nominal wages which would compensate partly or wholly for the rise in prices. In the extreme case, a demand expansion which raises the general price level may not succeed in reducing real wages at all and hence may not be able to increase employment.

I shall now assume that real-wage rigidity applies in Germany. This is an extreme assumption and provides the basis for the more realistic Phillips curve model to be discussed later. The distinction, already made in Chapter 3, must again be made between the product real wage and the income real wage. This time we disregard taxes; it can be assumed that they stay unchanged.

Assume that there is a single composite product produced in Germany, with price (in DM) of P_h. Some of it is consumed at home and some of it is exported. Hence, this time we do not make the distinction between tradables and non-tradables. German wage-earners consume this product as well as imports, the latter having a DM price of P_m. A depreciation will raise P_m. A change in the price ratio P_h/P_m represents a change in the terms of trade. The weighted average price level based on these two prices is P. The nominal wage is W and the product real wage is W/P_h. It is the real wage in terms of Germany's own product. This is the wage that German employers will perceive when they make employment decisions. An increase in the product real wage will reduce employment. The income real wage is W/P, and it is this wage that will be rigid if there is complete wage indexation: a rise in P will stimulate a rise in W, usually after a short lag, such that W/P does not fall.

[1] See also Appendix 11.2.

(1) *US Fiscal Expansion*

Let there be a US fiscal expansion that causes the DM to depreciate. Hence P_m will rise, hence P will rise, and so W will rise, the income real wage staying constant because of complete wage indexation. For given P_h, the product real wage, W/P_h will have to rise as a result. In other words, the rise in import prices brought about by depreciation induces nominal wages to rise, and this, in turn, raises the product real wages facing employers, and causes them to reduce employment. Of course, P_h could rise, but then there would have to be more nominal depreciation, and hence a greater rise in P_m and so W.

Finally, there has to be a real depreciation in Germany in the form of a rise in P_m/P_h. The outflow of capital from Germany caused by the US fiscal expansion requires a German real depreciation to generate the necessary switching of demand. In this model (with a single composite product produced at home) a real depreciation is the same as a terms-of-trade deterioration.

We saw earlier that the initial impact of the depreciation, assuming a constant real money supply, would be expansionary for Germany. This was the switching effect. Hence demand for German goods would increase, the conclusion following from the Keynesian Mundell–Fleming model where output depends on demand. It was then assumed that the initial level of demand represented the internal balance level, above which inflationary tendencies would develop. It was thus plausible to assume that a reduction in the money supply would reduce demand back to this internal balance level. Now we can define the internal balance level of demand and output more precisely, departing from the Keynesian assumption. There is a constraint on the level of output. Given the product real wage, the internal balance level of demand defines the maximum level of output possible without a wage–price spiral. If demand were less, output would also be less (a Keynesian effect), but an increase in real demand *above* internal balance could not be sustained: an initial rise in prices would lead to a rise in nominal wages, followed by a further rise in prices, a further wage increase, and so on, until real demand had returned to the internal balance level.

The product real wage (which depends on the income real wage and the terms of trade) thus determines employment, provided demand is adequate. It determines the maximum level of output possible without a continued rise in wages and prices. It thus determines the internal balance level of demand. But, as noted above, the DM depreciation (or terms-of-trade deterioration) caused by the US fiscal expansion will raise the product real wage. Thus it will reduce income, output, and employment at the internal balance level.

This is a very significant result. If we assume, as seems plausible, that the German monetary authorities aim to maintain internal balance, and thus avoid a wage–price spiral, they will have to respond to a real depreciation by reducing real demand and hence output. The net effect of the US fiscal expansion on Germany is then contractionary. There is negative transmission. This conclusion hinges on the reaction of wages to depreciation, and is to be contrasted with the conclusion reached earlier that, with Keynesian assumptions and a constant real money supply, there is positive transmission.

(2) *US Monetary Expansion*

The whole analysis also applies to the effects on Germany of a US monetary expansion, provided that in the United States such an expansion still has real effects, increasing real spending and reducing the interest rate. In other words, there must not be real wage rigidity in the United States, surely a realistic assumption. If there were real wage rigidity, there would be no changes in output, the real money supply, and the interest rate, and hence no real transmission to Germany. Only the nominal exchange rate (the dollar) would depreciate.

Given, then, a monetary expansion in the United States that does have real effects there, the US interest rate will fall, hence the DM will appreciate, and the first impact will be contractionary in Germany (as described earlier), essentially because of the switching effect of the appreciation. But a German monetary expansion could restore internal balance. This time (with real wage rigidity in Germany), the internal balance level of demand will actually increase because the product real wage will fall. Hence, output can rise above its initial level. A rise in output requires a fall in the product real wage W/P_h, which is now possible even though the income real wage W/P cannot fall owing to the reaction of nominal wages. The reason is that P_m has fallen owing to the appreciation. Finally there has been positive transmission, at least if monetary policy maintains internal balance.

(3) *Effect on the Phillips Curve*

To summarize, we have assumed here that the maximum level of output and employment—called the internal balance level—is determined by the production function and the product real wage. The product real wage, in turn, is determined by the rigid income real wage and the terms of trade. An improvement in the German terms of trade (caused by appreciation) allows the product real wage to fall and a deterioration (caused by depreciation) allows the product real wage to rise. It might be added that, if the rigid income real wage were determined in after-tax terms, the internal balance level of output would also depend on tax rates levied on wage incomes.

One might modify the approach just presented and assume that a lower income real wage is possible, though only temporarily, and only at the cost of continuous and possibly accelerating inflation. This Phillips curve argument is expounded more fully in Appendix 11.2. Inflation caused by monetary expansion, especially accelerating inflation, may reduce the income (and product) real wage because wages tend to lag behind prices. Inflation, resulting from increased nominal demand, can thus increase employment temporarily, especially if the demand expansion is unexpected. It does so by reducing the income real wage as nominal wages lag behind prices in an inflationary process. This makes possible a lower product real wage and hence higher employment. There is then an employment–inflation trade-off: the higher the rate of inflation, the greater employment and output. This yields a kind of short-term Phillips curve. The German terms-of-trade improvement resulting from a US monetary expansion shifts the Phillips curve in a favorable direction. An increase in demand brought about by German monetary expansion can through this mechanism always increase employment, at least for a short time, but the better the terms of trade, the less inflation is required for any given increase in employment. Similarly, a US fiscal expansion, which depreciates the DM and thus worsens the US terms of trade, will shift the German Phillips curve in an unfavorable direction.

IX. THE LOCOMOTIVE THEORY

During the recession and low-growth period of 1975 to 1978, a so-called "locomotive theory" was sponsored by OECD and by some US officials who argued that expansion in one country depended to some extent on expansion by others. In particular, Germany and Japan were urged to stimulate their economies so as to allow economic recovery elsewhere. When the United States did embark on a prolonged expansion, it was argued that it was doing duty as a locomotive for the rest of the world. This idea surfaced again during the recession of 1992 and 1993, with Germany and Japan again being urged to expand. A first reaction might be that this view was based on fixed exchange-rate thinking even though exchange rates between the major countries were either floating or, at least, were by no means firmly fixed. Surely, in a flexible exchange rate regime, each country is free to pursue its own expansionary or contractionary policies, taking into account its domestic situation and influenced by whatever is its government's current economic philosophy. But the preceding analysis provides some rationale for the locomotive theory.

The main argument can be put as follows: a unilateral monetary expansion by Germany would lead to DM depreciation, worsening Germany's terms of trade and lowering her real wage rates. The attempt by German wage-earners to restore their real wages would then set up an inflationary process which would eventually force a reversal of the original expansion. But if other countries expanded at the same time, raising demand for German goods, the initial German depreciation could be avoided, and hence the German terms of trade would not need to fall. Sustained joint expansion is then possible; unilateral expansion is not. In terms of an OECD concept which followed the locomotive theory, countries need to move "in convoy".

The argument can also be put in Phillips-curve terms. It is assumed that economic expansion by the United States will shift the German Phillips curve in a favorable direction. It was shown above that this must be so when the US expansion is brought about by monetary expansion, at least provided the expansion has *real* effects on output in the United States, not just raising prices. In the case of a US fiscal expansion, it would be true only if capital mobility were low, the spending effect of the US expansion outweighing the capital market effect, so that the dollar would depreciate. Given this favorable effect, while Germany could choose any point on its curve, it will find it optimal to choose a point with less unemployment than before because it will now be possible to combine this with a lower inflation rate. Economic expansion in the United States will then have encouraged expansion in Germany. Expansion in Germany would have been possible without US expansion—since Germany is assumed to have monetary independence—but at greater cost in terms of inflation.

The mechanism by which expansion in one country affects another country's Phillips curve favorably is through the terms of trade. A US monetary expansion appreciates the DM and improves the German terms of trade in the way described earlier. The terms of trade improvement reduces wages pressure. For a given rate of inflation of German-produced goods it is possible to have a lower product real wage than before, and hence more employment.

It has to be underlined that a crucial assumption in this argument is that a monetary expansion in the United States does have real effects, at least in the short run. But it is possible that the short run is so brief that a short-run monetary expansion would be hardly worthwhile, once the effects on inflationary expectations are taken into account. The evidence from the United States during the administration of President Carter shows that it is possible to obtain big increases in output as a result of demand expansion policies, but that, after a lag, there are inflationary effects that force a reversal of policies. Similarly, the monetary policy-induced recession of 1980–2 shows that contractionary demand policies can have severe real effects, but that, after a lag, the rate of inflation will decline, in that case quite drastically. Thus the historical evidence suggests that in the United States there has been something like a non-vertical short-term Phillips curve, and that the short term has been long enough to be very noticeable.

APPENDIX 11.1

Transmission Effects on Germany of US Expansion

US fiscal expansion

Fig. 11.1 shows the effects of a US fiscal expansion on Germany under various assumptions. The diagram refers to Germany. At first it is assumed that the price level of German-produced goods is constant. The starting-point is at *A*, with the German *IS* curve at IS_0. German output (income) is at its internal balance level, Y_0. At this stage it is assumed that the real-money supply stays constant (the *LM* curve does not shift).

The spending effect of the US expansion

It increases the demand for German goods, hence shifts the German *IS* curve from IS_0 to IS_1, and so brings equilibrium to *B*. This assumes that

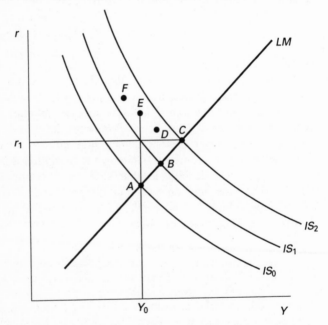

FIG. 11.1. Effects of US Fiscal Expansion on Germany

the exchange rate stays unchanged. There is clearly positive transmission: the US expansion brings about a German expansion (rise in Y).

Capital flows out and exchange rate depreciates
The next step is to allow the exchange rate to alter and to introduce capital mobility. The higher world interest rate resulting from the US fiscal expansion is represented by r_1. Capital flows out as long as the German interest rate is below the new world rate. Hence, the exchange rate depreciates until r is equal to r_1. The depreciation shifts the *IS* curve to IS_2, hence bringing equilibrium from B to C. If the spending effect had been stronger, B might have been above C (IS_1 being above IS_2) and a DM appreciation would have been required. There would still have been positive transmission of US fiscal expansion, since IS_2 would still be above IS_0 and hence C would still be to the right of A. The story up to this point represents the simple Mundell–Fleming model.

Real-money supply falls
A further step is to allow the *LM* curve to move and thus the real money supply to change. If the nominal money supply is fixed and the average price level rises because of the rise in import prices (in terms of DM) caused by the depreciation, the real-money supply must fall, so that the *LM* curve will move to the left. The reduction in the German real money supply will tend to raise the world interest rate further. Thus the new equilibrium will move to a point such as D, which reverses some of the expansion. This reduction in the real money supply will bring about some appreciation (so that D is on an *IS* curve that is below IS_2). If the German nominal money supply were reduced sufficiently to restore the original level of real demand (at Y_0), equilibrium would move to E. (It is possible that D was the same as or to the left of E, so that no change or a rise in the nominal money supply might have been needed to achieve this.) If the internal balance level of output had not changed, E would thus represent the new internal balance equilibrium for Germany, given the US fiscal expansion. The reduction in the German real-money supply would have raised the world interest rate above r_1.

The wage reaction
The depreciation lowers the real income wage for a given product wage and thus for given employment. If the real income wage is rigid (or partially so), the real product wage will have to rise, and thus output and employment will have to fall. Hence, to preserve internal balance, the level of demand will have to fall. In other words, the internal balance point will move to a point such as F. The *LM* curve will move to the left until F is reached. This result could be brought about by a reduction in

the nominal money supply designed to avoid temporary inflation, or by temporary inflation that raises the price level until the required reduction in the real-money supply and thus in real demand has been brought about. Positions to the right of F cannot be sustained and F (or any point to the left) becomes the new equilibrium. There has thus been *negative* transmission.

US monetary expansion

Fig. 11.2 shows the effects of a US monetary expansion on Germany. Again, the diagram refers to Germany and the starting-point is at A, with the IS curve at IS_0. The increase in US spending on its own would bring Germany to B (shifting the IS curve up to IS_1). This time the world interest rate facing Germany falls relative to the initial interest rate: a US monetary expansion lowers the interest rate, by contrast with a US fiscal expansion, which would have raised it. Appreciation of the DM resulting from capital market transmission therefore brings equilibrium right down to C (shifting the IS curve down to IS_2). This is the Mundell–Fleming

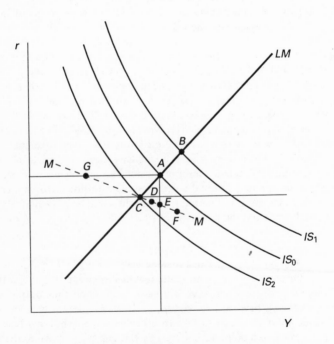

FIG. 11.2. Effects of US Monetary Expansion on Germany

story, which leads to *negative* transmission, with equilibrium finally moving from A to C. Again, it is assumed that the real-money supply is held constant.

Appreciation lowers the average price level and thus raises the real-money supply (shifts the LM curve to the right), and, when that effect is introduced, a point such as D is reached. Restoration of real demand to its original level, brought about by an appropriate increase in the real-money supply, would achieve point E. (Again, D might be the same as or to the right of E.) This time, because of appreciation, the real income wage is raised for given employment so that, given wage rigidity, the product real wage can fall. Hence, employment will rise, provided demand is adequate. Internal balance thus requires real demand to increase: the internal balance point moves to F, this being brought about by an increase in the nominal money supply (and hence real-money supply) that shifts the LM curve sufficiently to the right. Allowing for the labor-market effect, there is thus *positive* transmission.

If the aim of German monetary policy had been to reverse the decline in the interest rate, the money supply would have had to be reduced (the LM curve shifting to the left) so as to get to point G. The MM curve (which goes through G, C, D, E and F) traces out the effects of changing the German money supply, given the US monetary expansion. A movement down the curve (German monetary expansion) both lowers the world interest rate and depreciates the DM. A similar curve could be drawn in Fig. 11.1.

APPENDIX 11.2

The Terms of Trade, Wages, and Output

Real wage rigidity

W is the nominal wage, P is the average price level facing consumers, so that W/P is the income real wage, R. The target income real wage is $R^\star$, and it is initially assumed that it is attained very quickly by increases in W (though decreases in W are ruled out).

The price of the home-produced product is P_h so that the product real wage is W/P_h, called Q here. The Keynesian assumption is made that a reduction in demand would not lower the product price P_h below its initial level. Hence output Y depends on demand D, up to a maximum determined (for a given production function) by the product real wage. Thus,

$$Y = Y(D) \qquad Y' > 0 \tag{1}$$
$$Y_{max} = Z(Q) \qquad Z' < 0 \tag{1a}$$

Next we link the income real wage R and the product real wage Q. The price of imports is P_m. The consumer price, P, is a weighted average of P_h and P. Hence

$$P = \Theta P_h + (1 - \Theta)P_m$$

Therefore

$$W/P = (W/P_h) \left[\frac{1}{\Theta + (1 - \Theta)P_m/P_h} \right] \tag{2}$$

$W/P \equiv R$, $W/P_h \equiv Q$, and $P_h/P_m \equiv T$, the terms of trade, a rise being an improvement (and resulting from appreciation).

Hence,

$$Q = R \left(\Theta + \frac{1 - \Theta}{T} \right) \tag{3}$$

This tells us that the product real wage, Q, depends positively on the income real wage and negatively on the terms of trade, that is,

$$Q = Q(R,T) \qquad Q_1 > 0, Q_2 < 0 \tag{4}$$

Finally,
$$R = R^\star \tag{5}$$

From (1a), (4), and (5),

$$Y_{max} = Z(R^\star, T) \quad Z_1 < 0, Z_2 > 0 \qquad (6)$$

Thus, given real-wage rigidity, maximum (internal balance) output is higher, the lower the target income real wage and the better the terms of trade.

The discussion here and in the text of the real-wage rigidity case (before the Phillips curve is introduced) may be clarified with the help of Fig. 11.3.

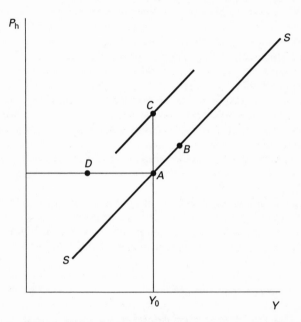

FIG. 11.3. Effects of Appreciation and Depreciation with Real-Wage Rigidity

The vertical axis shows the price of domestic German output, P_h, and the horizontal axis its quantity, Y. SS is the supply curve drawn for a given W. The starting-point—before the US monetary or fiscal expansion—is at A. This is the initial internal balance point, where output is Y_0. If demand fell below A, output would be demand constrained, and thus decline to a point such as D, the Keynesian short-run assumption being that P_h would not fall. Now consider the effects of an increase in demand. *If* the nominal wage, W, stayed constant, and hence the supply curve stayed unchanged, an increase in nominal demand would lead to higher output at B. But P_h would rise, and thus it would involve a fall in the product real wage, Q, and hence in the income real wage, R. If, after a lag, the nominal wage rose to compensate for the temporary fall in the income real wage, R, the supply curve would move to the left, P_h would rise, W would rise more, and so on, until the original level of real demand at C was attained. Thus, points A and C represent the maximum level of output possible, at least if a temporary wage–price spiral is to be avoided.

Now consider the effects of an appreciation of the DM (caused by US monetary expansion). It would reduce demand for German goods owing to the familiar switching effect. As noted above, the Keynesian assumption is made that a reduction in demand would not lower the product price P_h below its initial level. Hence the reduction in demand would lead to a point such as D. A German monetary expansion could certainly bring demand back to A. But it could actually go further. The appreciation has lowered P_m, so some rise in P_h is possible without W starting to rise. A constant income real wage is compatible with a rise in P_h. It is thus possible to get to a point such as B, a case of positive transmission. The movement from A to B can thus be described as follows. First there is an appreciation which reduces demand for German goods to D. Then there is an expansion of domestic demand, which eventually raises P_h and which also partly reverses the appreciation, finally bringing demand and output to B.

As one might expect, the effects of a depreciation of the DM (caused by US fiscal expansion) are exactly the opposite. It would increase demand and output for German goods initially, at least if W were given, bringing the economy to a point such as B. This is the switching effect. But the product real wage, Q , will have fallen at B. Hence, to avoid a wage–price-depreciation spiral, demand must be reduced by German monetary contraction. The depreciation will have raised P_m, and, given that P_h cannot (by assumption) be reduced below its initial level, W will have to rise to compensate for the rise in P_m. Hence, the supply curve will shift to the left and the new internal balance equilibrium will be at a point such as D, a case of negative transmission.

Phillips curve

Now we come to our version of the Phillips curve. We assume now that the income real wage depends on the rate of inflation. Actual inflation is $\hat{p}$ and expected inflation is $\hat{p}^e$. If $\hat{p} = \hat{p}^e$, then $R = R^\star$ (the target income real wage). Unexpected inflation causes prices to rise ahead of wages, so that, in the short run,

$$R = R^\star + \alpha \, (\hat{p}^e - \hat{p}) \tag{7}$$

If we hold $\hat{p}^e$ constant in the short run (of course, it will change adaptively in response to errors), then

$$R = R(\hat{p}, R^\star) \quad R_1 < 0, R_2 > 0 \tag{8}$$

The higher inflation, the lower the income real wage. From $(1a)$, (4), and (8),

$$Y_{max} = Z(\hat{p}, R^\star, T) \quad Z_1 > 0, Z_2 < 0, Z_3 > 0 \tag{9}$$

Thus, maximum output (which is actual output now) rises as $\hat{p}$ rises and as T rises. The product real wage, Q, determines output (with a given production function), and the income real wage, R, falls as a result of inflation. In addition, output rises with the terms of trade. The terms of trade deteriorate when P_m rises ahead of P_h. A rise in the target real wage, $R^\star$, reduces output.

In Fig. 11.4, the curve T_0 shows how output rises with inflation for given initial terms of trade, and T_1 shows the relationship for improved terms of trade. A movement upwards along a curve represents a decline in R (since higher inflation reduces the income real wage), and

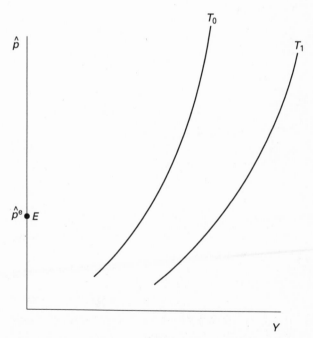

FIG. 11.4. The Terms of Trade and the Phillips Curve

a movement to the right a decline in Q (since a decline in the product real wage raises output). At E, $\hat{p} = \hat{p}^e$. At that point, $R = R^\star$, while above it $R < R^\star$. A US monetary expansion—which improves the German terms of trade—shifts the curve to the right (from T_0 to T_1) and thus makes possible a higher level of German output at any given inflation rate. Similarly, a US fiscal expansion will shift the curve to the left because it worsens the German terms of trade. If the income real wage were rigid—so that an increase in the rate of inflation could not reduce it—the T curve would be vertical. This would also be the result if changes in the inflation rate were always expected.

REFERENCES

The analysis of capital market transmission was pioneered by Mundell (1964)—which is the original reference for the two-country Mundell–Fleming model. Important articles on the international transmission of disturbances are Hamada and Sakurai (1978) and Mussa (1979). For a detailed analysis of positive and negative transmission through the terms of trade, see Corden and Turnovsky (1983) and Corden (1985).

Wage effects are introduced into the Mundell–Fleming model in Argy and Salop (1979). See also Dornbusch (1983) and Branson and Buiter (1983).

International economic linkages are surveyed in Larsen *et al.* (1983), and the interaction of monetary policies is analyzed in a simulation model with a similar focus to that here, in Artus (1984). Empirical work on international interdependencies is reported in Bryant *et al.* (1988).

The portfolio balance model can be found in every textbook of international finance, and is employed in numerous articles. It is primarily owed to William Branson. See especially Branson (1979) and Allen and Kenen (1980).

The modern revival of the Ricardian equivalence theorem is owed to Barro (1974). It is expounded, with supporting evidence, in Barro (1989). Critical evaluations can be found in Bernheim (1987) and Gramlich (1989).

12

What Determines Exchange Rates in a Floating Rate Regime?

WHAT makes exchange rates move in a floating rate regime? The previous chapter ignored expectations. But if one wants to understand why exchange rates move the way they do, one must certainly give expectations at least equal pride of place with current monetary and fiscal policies.

I. EXPECTATIONS AND FUNDAMENTALS

At any point in time, the exchange rate in a floating rate regime with high capital mobility depends both on current variables—such as current monetary and fiscal policies—and on expectations about future exchange rates. In fact, short-run fluctuations in exchange rates can be explained to a great extent by fluctuations in expectations.[1] The expectations themselves are more difficult to explain. Our discussion so far has managed to bypass these effects of expectations by making the static expectations assumption.

To some extent the expectations depend on assessments of the future consequences of the current fundamentals as well as on expectations about future fundamentals based on current assessments of political and economic prospects. For example, an increased fiscal deficit, while leading to a current appreciation, is likely to lead to later depreciation for reasons discussed in Chapter 11. The interest payments to be made to foreigners are likely to build up and eventually a primary (non-interest) deficit will have to turn into a surplus. In addition there is the portfolio balancing effect as the supply of domestic-currency-denominated

---

[1] See Appendix 12.1 for the simple interest parity relationship, showing how the current exchange rate depends on the interest rate differential and expectations.

assets rises relative to foreign assets. Furthermore, eventually the deficit may be monetized.

These expectations of later depreciation based on rational expectations will then bring about some current depreciation unless this tendency is offset by a sufficient increase in the domestic relative to the foreign interest rate.

There are many rational expectations models along these lines, notably the Dornbusch (1976) overshooting model. In that model a monetary expansion leads to a depreciation so great initially that some appreciation will have to follow, and the expectation of appreciation makes it possible to maintain temporarily an interest rate below the world rate.

An alternative, or supplementary, view is that expectations in the foreign exchange market are not rational. People follow various fads or the crowd (which still raises the question of who leads the crowd). They make use of charts that assume regularities from the past, or they have oversimplified or fallacious models in mind. In other words, they do not make an attempt at rational expectations, bearing in mind, of course, the costs of collecting information. Quite a strong argument can be made for this approach. It is plausible that when there is so much uncertainty people will grasp at any simplification, given that they really want to know and cannot admit to themselves or their employers that it is unlikely they could do better than a random walk. Uncertainties come both from uncertainties about future government policies—fiscal and monetary policies of the home government and relevant foreign governments—and about the various parameters and functional relations in the complex model of the economy on which reliable forecasts must be based.

With so much uncertainty, quite sensible people would give up trying to understand or predict the various fundamentals since even if one could reasonably predict some of them, one would still be very unsure about other fundamentals and about the full exchange rate implications. Hence, the past exchange rate, either in real or nominal terms, or some past trend or cycle detectable from charts, might provide as good a prediction as any. The market might respond to news about changing fads and fashions, but not necessarily to news about fundamentals. This second view—termed by de Grauwe (1989) "near-rational"—is plausible within limits. Small changes in expected fundamentals might well be ignored by the market. On the other hand, news of likely big changes is unlikely to be ignored.

II. THE DOLLAR 1980-5

Modern thinking about floating exchange rates has been greatly influenced by the extraordinary gyrations in the dollar during the 1980s. Beginning in 1981 and ending in February 1985, there was a huge appreciation, both nominal and real. On a trade-weighed basis the real appreciation was about 50 per cent. Then, in 1985, the dollar suddenly and rapidly depreciated, and around 1987 it was back where it started. Surely fundamentals did not change that much. If 1980 or perhaps 1988 were the norm, the dollar must have been misaligned in between. As a result, discussions about the need for reform of the exchange rate system flourished in the mid-1980s.

The literature aimed at understanding what happened during this period is very interesting, and I shall draw on it here, particularly the writings of Jeffrey Frankel and his colleagues. It is clear that changing expectations played a major role and that it is difficult, if not impossible, to describe expectations as rational.

The period of appreciation can be divided into three parts, namely 1981-2, 1982-4, and June 1984 to February 1985.

The first stage is on first sight not difficult to explain—and was readily explained at the time—in terms of the Mundell–Fleming and the Dornbusch models. Appreciation was about 20 per cent. There was fiscal expansion and monetary contraction in the United States, both very sharp. The Federal budget deficit changed from 2.3 per cent of GDP in 1980 to 4 per cent in 1982. It increased further in later years, reaching a peak of nearly 6 per cent in 1985. Some of the 1982 deficit was explained by the recession in that year, but nevertheless the US fiscal impulse was positive. At the same time, the fiscal impulse was negative in Germany and, to a lesser extent, Japan. Monetary policy was also tight in the other major countries (except France), but it tightened much more in the United States than in Germany and Japan.

In addition US real interest rates exceeded those in Japan and Germany by about 2 per cent. This could be explained in three possible ways. In terms of the Dornbusch model, appreciation overshot, so that some depreciation came to be expected. In terms of a static expectations model with lagged adjustments, the US interest rate would rise relative to those of other countries, and gradually they would be equalized by capital flows, these flows being the cause of the appreciation. Finally, a portfolio balance model would also yield an interest rate differential of this kind.

The appreciation actually started in 1981 before the US Federal deficit started rising. This can be explained both by the monetary contraction that began in October 1979 and by the announcement effect of the Economic Recovery Tax Act of early 1981. In any case, there is no shortage—and even an excess—of explanations of the first stage of the appreciation of the dollar. The heart of the explanation is the Mundell–Fleming model which benefited from a real boost at this time.

The second stage is a little more puzzling. The fiscal expansion in the United States continued while, at the same time, there was some fiscal contraction in Germany and Japan. But there was a sharp reversal in US monetary policy in the United States late in 1982 provoked by the recession, and probably also the debt crisis. US monetary policy became very expansionary. The annual growth rate of M2 (a measure of money which includes currency, checking accounts, and a number of short-term financial assets) rose from about 6 per cent in 1979–82 to 13 per cent in 1983–4. But monetary policy in the other countries did not become expansionary. In view of this, it is surprising that the real interest differential (the excess of US interest rates over those in Germany and Japan) increased further and the dollar appreciated further. An explanation based on fundamentals would have to give a heavy weight to the continued US fiscal expansion. It has been suggested that there may have been a gradual adjustment and a learning process at work as the market came to understand the implications of the differences in fiscal policies between the United States and other countries. Conceivably this effect outweighed the effects of the US monetary expansion.

Things got really out of hand in the last stage (beginning in mid-1984), which definitely could not be explained in terms of any models based on fundamentals or expectations of them. The dollar appreciated another 20 per cent, even though the interest rate differential actually *declined*. Fiscal and monetary policies could not explain this episode. No longer could one argue that higher interest rates were drawing funds into the United States and hence appreciating the dollar. It seemed that something irrational had taken over. This episode was usually described as a "speculative bubble".

Concerning expectations, there were really two distinct puzzles. First, the continuous interest differential and the forward discount in the market suggested that all the time from 1982 some depreciation was expected. This has been confirmed by an analysis of surveys of exchange rate forecasts at the time. Operators in the market expected depreciation, but, year after year, the expectations turned out wrong, at least until 1985. People expected the dollar to depreciate, but kept on buying or holding dollars and so appreciating it further. This meant that in the *very* short term, say a day or a week, the dollar was actually expected to appreciate. When we talk of expectations as reflected in the forward discount or surveys of forecasts, we are referring to a longer period than that. The continued appreciation did not change the direction of these expectations. Second, the extent of depreciation expected, as indicated by the interest rate differential, was far less than would eventually be needed if one bears in mind the accumulation of foreign debt, and the eventual need for a non-interest current account deficit to turn into a surplus.

Eventually the bubble burst, namely in February 1985, and from then on the dollar depreciated, as the fundamentals had indicated it should have done a long time earlier. The timing of the bursting of the bubble was probably explained by the change in the administration of the US Treasury, from Donald Regan to James Baker. The latter was known to favor some intervention to bring the dollar down.

This and earlier bubble episodes have given rise to a good deal of theorizing. One suggestion is that there can be "rational bubbles". Everyone knows that *eventually* the exchange rate must depreciate, but it is not known when, and, meanwhile, there is money to be made by buying the currency, and so appreciating it further, in the belief that it will appreciate further. The hope is that the ship can be jumped before it sinks. It is possible to show that in some circumstances this can be rational, especially for risk-neutral or risk-loving folk. The short-term expectations of appreciation—which ignore the fundamentals—are thus self-fulfilling.

Another, quite convincing, suggestion, owed to Frankel and Froot (1986, 1990), is that there are two different approaches on the foreign exchange market, possibly pursued by different people, or even the same people at different times. One is to predict on the basis of fundamentals, such as future monetary and fiscal policies, and considerations mentioned above, which would have suggested well before 1985 that the dollar would and should depreciate. The other is to predict by extrapolating the past, ignoring current and future fundamentals, but using charts of various kinds. Thus there are "fundamentalists" and "chartists", and the latter kept on pushing the dollar up during 1984. They acquired more and more weight in the market—convincing more and more portfolio managers—as their predictions turned out correct (in the short term!) while the predictions of the fundamentalists did not come true.

III. EXCHANGE RATE BEHAVIOR: THE EMPIRICAL EVIDENCE

A vast amount of econometric research has looked for some regularities in exchange rate behavior in a floating rate regime, analyzing movements in the dollar in the 1970s and 1980s. The results are rather depressing. It is clear that fundamentals matter in the longer run—and sometimes even in the short run—but often the prospects for the fundamentals are unclear, so that expectations are dominated by uncertainty.

Econometric tests of various popular, oversimplified theories have shown that none of them on their own could explain exchange rate behavior. They might explain particular episodes, but they do not allow one to make firm predictions because different theories seem to provide explanations at different times. This applies to the monetary theory of exchange rate determination, to the purchasing power parity theory (which suggests that real exchange rates would tend to stay constant), to the portfolio balance model (which suggests that exchange rates and interest rate differentials should be explained by the variability of relative asset supplies), to the Dornbusch overshooting model, and even to the Mundell–Fleming model.

The behavior of the dollar in 1980–2 did give strong support to the Mundell–Fleming model. But de Grauwe (1989) has looked closely at other medium- and longer-run swings in real exchange rates—looking at the bilateral dollar–yen, dollar–DM, and DM–yen rates while adjusting for productivity differentials—to see whether relative fiscal and monetary policies (ignoring expectations) could explain exchange rate movements in the 1970s and 1980s. The answer is negative.

For example, the dollar continued appreciating after 1982 even though US monetary policy became relatively expansionary. Of course, as I observed earlier, this episode might be explained by the lagged learning effect of the US fiscal expansion. But such a slow learning process is not in the simple model. From 1976 to 1978 the yen appreciated in real terms relative to the DM. Japanese and German monetary policies were much the same, but Japanese fiscal policy was considerably more expansionary. This episode appears to endorse the Mundell–Fleming model, but at that time there were strict capital controls in Japan, so that one would expect yen depreciation.

Models with static expectations are thus inadequate on their own in explaining exchange rate movements. Actual nominal and real exchange rate movements have been much affected by, and sometimes dominated by, changing expectations. From an analysis of surveys of exchange rate expectations, Frankel and Froot (1987) have concluded that expectations tend to be regressive, and hence stabilizing. For example, when the spot exchange rate appreciates, the expectation is of some depreciation, and indeed more than takes place subsequently. This result may have been heavily influenced by the 1981–5 dollar episode, which I have already described, when there was continued appreciation, and yet there also was a consistent forward discount in the market. In the period 1981–5 recorded expectations were in the right direction—i.e. depreciation was expected—if a longer view was taken, but in the short term not only did they turn out wrong (until the February 1985 turning-point) but they cannot have reflected very short-term expectations.

Where does the research in this field leave us? Here one can quote some authorities. Frankel and Meese (1987) wrote: "No set of macroeconomic variables that has been proposed is capable of explaining a high percentage of variations in the exchange rate." In a classic survey, Levich (1985) concluded that "the major foreign exchange markets exhibit behavior that is characteristic of other asset markets. Exchange rates react quickly to news; rates are volatile and difficult to forecast. Both spot and forward rates can be modelled as anticipatory prices, but the exact parameters of the models are unknown." De Grauwe (1989) concluded that "in an uncertain environment, economic agents may prefer to use backward looking rules for most of the time". And he went on to express skepticism about the ability of economists to predict exchange rates from fundamentals. "We should reduce our ambitions in this field. Movements of the real exchange rate are, within certain bounds, unexplainable."

A reasonable conclusion is that the various fundamentals analyzed in this book, notably fiscal and monetary policies, but also current accounts, relative productivity changes, and so on, do matter, particularly in the longer run. But in the short run, expectations dominate, and these are hard to analyze or understand. Yet, all is surely not lost. For example, if clear signals emerged that the monetary authority will engage in an inflationary policy relative to those of other countries, one should surely expect the currency of this country to depreciate in a floating rate regime. Furthermore, much of the empirical work published since 1984 seems to have been dominated by the unusual experience of the dollar from 1981 to 1987. Since 1988 or so, there has been rather more stability in the major markets, apart from the EMS crises.

IV. OFFICIAL INTERVENTION: DOES IT MATTER?

So far I have ignored the role of official intervention in the foreign exchange market. Governments buy and sell foreign exchange with the aim of influencing the exchange rate. But do they really make a difference when they do so? More specifically, to what extent have interventions by the German, Japanese, and US monetary authorities affected the movements of the dollar, yen, and DM since floating began in 1973?

All three authorities have intervened a great deal since floating began. This can be seen readily by noting how their foreign exchange reserves have moved. In the 1970s all of them intervened. During the first Reagan administration from 1981 to early 1985, the United States avoided intervention, but Germany and Japan did intervene. Since the Plaza Agreement of September 1985, there have been a number of episodes of concerted intervention, when they have all intervened together with a common aim, sometimes to depreciate the dollar, at other times to prevent too much depreciation and thus to stabilize it.

Intervention is of two kinds, non-sterilized and sterilized. In the case of non-sterilized intervention, the money base is allowed to change as a result of intervention. For example, when the Bank of Japan buys dollars, the Japanese money supply rises. Thus non-sterilized intervention is a form of monetary policy. In this example it would lower, or potentially lower, the interest rate and hence depreciate the exchange rate, for the same reason that a monetary expansion brought about by a domestic open market operation does so.

In the case of sterilized intervention, the potential effect on the money supply is prevented by an offsetting operation, for example an open market sale of bonds designed to prevent the money supply from rising. US intervention has always been sterilized, but Japanese and German intervention has often been at least partly unsterilized. There have been some offsetting operations, but they have not fully offset the direct monetary effects of intervention.

Suppose there is a monetary expansion in the United States which tends to depreciate the dollar. Japan and Germany then intervene in order to lean against the wind: they wish to moderate the decline in the dollar, without necessarily expecting to prevent its decline completely. This kind of leaning against the wind intervention has been quite common. If the intervention is not fully sterilized, the Japanese and German money supplies will increase. In this way US monetary expansion is transmitted to the other two countries through a mechanism which is essentially the same as that which operates in a fixed rate regime. This was the way in which a US monetary expansion was transmitted to other countries under the Bretton Woods regime. As McKinnon (1982) has noted, since 1973 exchange rates have floated and yet a similar transmission mechanism has tended to operate as in the Bretton Woods fixed rate regime. Whenever the dollar depreciated, Japan and Germany intervened, thus increasing their money supplies. Hence, US monetary expansion—which caused the dollar depreciation—led also to monetary expansion in other countries. Similarly, dollar appreciation led to some monetary contraction. Of course, movements of the dollar have not only depended on current US monetary policy—a lesson that surely emerges from our discussion above—and much intervention has actually been sterilized.

The really interesting and much analyzed question is whether sterilized intervention can affect exchange rates. In this case monetary policy, as indicated by changes in the money base, does not change as a result of intervention. Leaving aside expectations, at first sight the portfolio balance model appears to be the right one to use here. When the Bank of Japan engages in sterilized intervention designed to moderate or prevent dollar depreciation, it buys F (foreign bonds) and sells B (domestic bonds), while the Japanese money supply stays constant. The market will have to adjust to less F and more B. In this model such an operation will raise the Japanese interest rate and depreciate the yen (or appreciate the dollar). The essence of the model is that B and F are assumed to be imperfect substitutes. The more substitutable they are, the less a given quantity of intervention will succeed in changing the exchange rate.

The trouble is that the amount of intervention that usually takes place is very small relative to the vast stock of financial assets in the market, and one should not really expect a particular intervention episode—even a concerted intervention by the monetary authorities of all three countries—to have a significant effect. Such an episode is very different from a prolonged process of fiscal deficit in one country where, say, the supply of dollar-denominated assets steadily rises over a long period relative to yen-denominated assets, in which case the message of the portfolio balance approach may still be relevant.

All the empirical work suggests that sterilized intervention does not have any significant effects through this channel. It has not been possible to detect clear exchange rate responses to modest changes in relative stocks of assets. Possibly the degree of substitutability between foreign and domestic bonds is rather high, though it is surely not perfect. The amounts of intervention have certainly been relatively small even when they have been concerted.

One might then wonder why countries have engaged in concerted sterilized intervention since 1985. Furthermore, it does appear that announcements of intervention have affected exchange rates. Indeed, one can identify exchange rate turning-points with episodes of intervention. The current state of thought on this subject is that the key lies in the signaling role of intervention. Sterilized intervention, especially when it is concerted, affects expectations. The basic argument is the following.

Short-term changes in the exchange rate are determined by expectations. These depend, above all, on expectations of future monetary policies and the extent to which they are likely to be directed to an exchange rate objective. If concerted intervention is designed to depreciate the dollar, it is a signal that the authorities wish to depreciate the dollar. Possibly they have a target. In some episodes from 1987, the proclaimed aim was to stabilize the dollar. Operators in the market then deduce that an appropriate monetary policy to bring about the aim will be followed. Of course, non-sterilized intervention would do so automatically, but in practice sterilization has separated the intervention decisions from the monetary policy decisions.

If the market finds subsequently that monetary policy does not fit in with the expectations that were generated by the intervention episode, the exchange rate will quickly react. Thus there have been episodes where the proclaimed exchange rate aim was not achieved. For example, after the stock market crash of October 1987, the authorities wanted to stabilize the dollar, but in fact it depreciated substantially. This outcome can be explained by a relatively expansionary US monetary policy.

Research on this subject—as on every aspect of the topic discussed in this chapter—is ongoing and by no means conclusive. The most recent works by Catte *et al.* (1992) and Dominguez and Frankel (1993) suggest that sterilized intervention is effective in the short run. One might ask why announcements of monetary policy intentions are not sufficient to signal policy intentions. Why is it necessary actually to engage in sterilized intervention? Various answers have been suggested, though none of them seems satisfactory.

It has been suggested that if the Japanese government, for example, buys more dollar bonds in exchange for yen bonds, it has a greater interest than before in dollar appreciation. Hence, it is more likely to pursue an appropriate monetary policy designed to appreciate the dollar. But this is surely a trivial consideration in its monetary policy stance.

Another suggestion is that intervention involving a publicly proclaimed exchange rate target gives a clearer signal to the market about the exchange rate that is intended to be achieved by monetary policy than a general statement about future monetary policy. But why not just proclaim the exchange rate target? Furthermore, some concerted interventions have not been associated with publicly stated targets. Perhaps the reluctance to go public can be explained by the fear of failure to achieve the target, and hence the fear of criticism.

It seems plausible that a general commitment to stabilizing exchange rates by means of intervention backed up by monetary policy has actually helped to stabilize the dollar–yen–DM rates since 1987. They have by no means been fully stabilized because monetary policies have not been fully dedicated to this objective. Sometimes—as after the stock market crash—domestic considerations have dominated. As Fig. 1.1 shows, the trend of the dollar was downward from 1987 to 1993, but the movement was not precipitous at any time, and this may be explained by monetary policies combined with fairly stable expectations. The main conclusion must be that the dominating policy instrument for the short and medium term is monetary policy and not sterilized intervention, but that the latter often has a short-term effect on expectations.

APPENDIX 12.1

Expectations and the Exchange Rate

The following is a modified version of the familiar open interest parity condition. It represents an equilibrium condition. It provides the basis for Fig. 7.1 and for the discussion in Appendix 7.1, and is explained more fully in textbooks.

$$r = \left[r^\star + \frac{E-e}{e} \right] + S$$

E is the expected exchange rate over the relevant period, say a year, e is the spot exchange rate, hence $(E-e)/e$ is the expected depreciation, while S is the so-called risk factor. The expression in square brackets is the return on foreign assets F, in terms of domestic currency, while r is the return on domestic assets B. A positive S means that in equilibrium the return on domestic assets must be higher than the return on foreign assets. S could also be negative, and if B and F were perfect substitutes, it would be zero. If S were zero, there would be uncovered interest parity.

Suppose that $r^\star$ and S are constant. Also, suppose that monetary policy keeps r constant. An expected depreciation—i.e. a rise in E—will then require a rise in the spot exchange rate e to the same extent. Fluctuations in E will cause fluctuations in e. Alternatively, suppose that the money supply rather than the rate of interest were kept constant. In that case there must be a positive relationship between r and e. (A rise in r would reduce the demand for money, which would have to be compensated by a rise in e, which raises the demand for money because it raises the price level.) A rise in E would still lead to a rise in e, but, as r would also have to rise, e would rise less than in the previous case where r was kept constant by an increase in the money supply.

Monetary policy might be committed to keeping e constant—i.e. to fixing the exchange rate. In that case r might have to rise very much when E rises. Fluctuations in E would be fully reflected in fluctuations in r. Stabilization of e would be attained at the expense of destabilization of r, a point already introduced in Chapter 7.

Finally, a change in S with E given could obviously affect e and r, depending on monetary policy. The assumption of static expectations (maintained in Chapter 11) is that always $E = e$, so that $r = r^\star + S$. Any increase in the spot exchange rate would be expected to last, so that E would rise to the same extent. An increased supply of domestic bonds, B, would raise S, and thus raise r or e, or both, this being part of the portfolio balancing effect.

REFERENCES

This has been an exceptionally brief chapter on a subject that has indeed dominated the literature in international finance since the 1970s. It is not possible to do it justice in a chapter of reasonable length, so that I have been very selective. But excellent expositions and surveys are available.

The best references on exchange rate determination and the exchange rate experiences of the dollar and other major currencies are de Grauwe (1989) and various papers by Frankel and his collaborators, mostly reprinted in Frankel (1993). See also Frankel and Meese (1987).

There is a vast literature in this field. For a recent comprehensive survey, see Taylor (1994). Earlier reviews are by Branson (1984), Mussa (1984)—which deals with the theory only—and Levich (1985), which contains a particularly thorough survey of empirical studies. A textbook on all aspects of floating exchange rates is MacDonald (1988).

Edison (1993) surveys the literature on the effectiveness of sterilized intervention. Catte *et al.* (1992) conclude, from detailed studies of seventeen episodes of concerted intervention between 1985 and 1991, that all were successful, at least temporarily, in moving the dollar in the desired direction. Dominguez and Frankel (1993) give a detailed account of intervention episodes and conclude that intervention has worked through the signaling effect, at least in the short run, especially when it is publicly announced. They use new data of daily intervention operations by the three major central banks.

The portfolio balance model of exchange rate determination can be found in Branson (1979), Allen and Kenen (1980), and in international finance textbooks.

13

Macroeconomic Policy Coordination

THERE are various levels of macroeconomic policy cooperation among countries, ranging from information exchange, to policy consultation, to bargaining to reach a cooperative result (true policy coordination), and then to rules-based and centralized decision-making arrangements. Proposals for the latter are the most ambitious. A large and sophisticated literature has discussed the third of these, namely policy coordination, though the actual practice of coordination seems to have yielded rather modest results. There has been a mountain of theory but (apart from a few exceptional episodes) a molehill of results. I shall now review each of these four levels in turn, especially the theory, practice, and possibilities of policy coordination.

I. INFORMATION EXCHANGE

The most modest level of cooperation on macroeconomic policy is exchange of information about the states of each other's economies and governments' policy intentions. This goes on all the time through numerous channels, notably under the auspices of the OECD and the IMF, and through regular contacts among central bankers at their monthly Basle meetings and otherwise. Information exchange, especially of macroeconomic forecasts, has been an important feature of the regular meetings of the finance ministers of the G-7 (the United States, Germany, Japan, Britain, Canada, France, and Italy), and of their civil service deputies.

Exchanging information must surely be good, since it is better to make decisions on good information than bad. With advance information of neighbors' changes in policies, countries can more readily make appropriate adjustments. Nevertheless, there have been times, as in 1980 and 1981, when policy switches of countries coincided, and it appears that they did not take full account of the total effect of the whole herd reversing direction together.

II. CONSULTATION: REACHING THE NASH EQUILIBRIUM

The next level involves a more subtle concept. I shall call this policy consultation. One country's policies will depend on the forecasts for other countries, and especially on what policy changes other countries are intending. This may not always be so. The United States may form its policies completely ignoring what will happen abroad. But other countries are unlikely to ignore economic prospects and intended policies in the United States and, in the case of European countries, prospects in Germany. If we consider a two-country model, country A will form its policies taking into account what country B intends to do, allowing for the reaction of country B to country A's own policies. And the same applies to country B.

Consider an example based on the locomotive theory expounded in Chapter 11. When there is a world recession, country A may engage in more monetary expansion (reflected in a lower short-term interest rate) if it also expects B to expand, than if B's policy is not expected to change, because a depreciation of A's exchange rate may then be modified or avoided, and vice versa. At a time of recession, when the two governments are both considering policy changes, there will then be a need for consultation where, in effect, each government indicates how it would react to policy changes of the other. The discussions may not appear to take that form, but implicitly the governments are acquainting each other with their mutual policy reactions. They will feel their way to a new equilibrium where both will be satisfied. In that new equilibrium country A will not wish to change its policy if country B does not, and country B, for the same reason, will not change its policy. This is a Nash equilibrium. Such an equilibrium is stable, though it will, of course, change if underlying conditions change.

III. MUTUAL POLICY ADJUSTMENT

The third level is true policy coordination. It involves mutual policy adjustment. Countries seek to modify each other's macroeconomic policies to take some account of each other's interests. This can achieve a result more favorable than the Nash equilibrium.[1] The aim is to bias each country's policies in a direction more favorable to its neighbors. The underlying theory is that, in the small numbers case, the Nash equilibrium is not Pareto-optimal. There exist sets of policies that would (in the two-country case) make both countries better off, even though neither country has an incentive to move its policies in that direction unless the other does also. Hence, a bargain must be struck and there must either be an enforcement mechanism or a concern with reputation that creates a high probability that the bargain will be adhered to.

The Nash equilibrium is not Pareto-optimal because there are international spillover effects or externalities. Any one country will not take these spillover effects into account in its policy decisions unless it is rewarded by the other country also taking into account the externalities it creates. But if they both take into account the interests of the other country, they both can benefit.

The following example is based on the locomotive theory. An economic expansion by country A may improve country B's terms of trade, so that country A loses some of the benefits from its expansion. Part of the benefit spills over to B. If A acted unilaterally (i.e. non-cooperatively), it would not take into account the benefit to B. It would thus expand less than if it took into account the benefit to B. The same applies to the other country. Both countries could be better off if they *both* expanded more. This simple idea—that the Nash equilibrium can be improved upon by coordination or bargaining because of international spillover effects—is the central theme of the theoretical literature on policy coordination. There are, of course, many practical problems about the coordination process. Useful results from international negotiations are difficult to achieve. But, presumably, it is the task of diplomacy to extract some benefits from the existence of potential mutual gains. As I shall stress in the rest of this chapter, the key issue (surprisingly ignored in the literature) is to explore various possible spillovers or externalities.

A further level of cooperation goes well beyond the mutual policy adjustment or policy coordination that I have just

---

[1] See Appendix 13.1 for a more formal exposition.

discussed. This consists of a rules-based arrangement where certain rules are agreed upon, and then countries must adhere to them, possibly induced by some enforcement mechanism. I shall discuss briefly various proposals of this kind at the end of this chapter. Here I am concerned with cooperation within the framework of the essentially *laissez-faire* floating rate system. Actual policy coordination at meetings of G-7 finance ministers and through other channels has been *ad hoc* and not rules-based. Rather, it has consisted primarily of information exchange and policy consultation, and (to a very limited extent) mutual policy adjustment. I shall now outline two policy coordination (mutual policy adjustment) models or theories, where the sole policy instrument of each country is its monetary policy, and then review coordinated foreign exchange market intervention, which is the main form in which actual coordination has taken place.

IV. THE LOCOMOTIVE THEORY RECONSIDERED

Theoretical discussions of monetary policy coordination have mostly been based on the assumptions of the locomotive theory, which was outlined at the end of Chapter 11 and which was advanced by US policy-makers at the Bonn summit in 1978, after the 1987 stock market crash, and, again, during the US recession in 1991.

If one country expands through monetary policy alone, or through a combination of monetary and fiscal policy that depreciates its currency, it must take the adverse effect of depreciation on its Phillips curve into account. At the same time its expansion will have a favorable effect on the other country, whose currency will appreciate, as a result. Monetary expansion worsens the terms of trade of the expanding country and thus has a favorable spillover effect on the other country, whose terms of trade improve. There is thus positive transmission of economic expansion.

Depreciation is likely to induce a rise in nominal wages which would negate at least part of the stimulating effect of the demand expansion. If other countries expanded at the same time, this adverse effect would be avoided, and the first country would thus choose to expand more. That is the essence of the locomotive theory. Unilateral monetary expansion will thus be less than joint expansion. Each country is a locomotive for the other. Alternatively, they should "move in convoy". The absence of coordination is deflationary in its effect.

This argument is straightforward and has frequently been modelled. It is relevant in a recession when all countries would like to expand demand but may hesitate to do so because unilateral expansion might sharply depreciate their currencies. Given that expansion is desirable for Keynesian reasons, there is then scope for coordination. At a minimum there needs to be consultation so that countries can know each other's intentions or possible reactions to others' policy changes. But beyond that, mutual gains can be realized when both expand together beyond the non-cooperative Nash equilibrium to reach or approach a Pareto-optimal solution.

There are at least four qualifications or objections to this simple argument.

The first is that, in this locomotive case, the concern is only with short-term Keynesian effects, given that the fundamental neo-classical factors—in particular real wages relative to productivity—determine employment in the medium and long run. Yet the processes of policy coordination, even in the modest form of mutual policy adjustments attained by negotiations, take time, during which the circumstances that gave rise to the negotiations will have changed. Specifically, the short-term Phillips curve will have changed.

The second possible objection concerns the inflationary bias of government policies. It will hardly be disputed that politicians' interests do not necessarily coincide with the national interest. It could be argued that politicians generally take a short-term view, aiming, above all, to win the next election. Since the favorable output and employment-increasing effects of expansionary policies tend to come ahead of the unfavorable inflationary consequences, the politicians will be predisposed to excessive expansion from the point of view of the true national interests. The *de*flationary bias of non-coordination may then simply offset the *in*flationary bias of the politicians, so that the net effect of coordination may not be favorable from the point of view of the true long-term national interest.

How much weight should one give to this argument? There are plenty of countries and historical episodes where one can find evidence for an inflationary bias in the political process. But the recession of 1981–2, which was induced by the considerable enthusiasm of major governments for halting inflation, gives no support at all for the generalization, nor do the policy reactions to the recessions of the early 1990s.

The line of thought which considers government policies in general to be too inflationary is reinforced by the following, more formal, argument. Inflation rates are determined to some extent by the anti-inflationary credibility of governments. The less is credibility, the higher will be inflationary expectations, and hence the less favorable the Phillips curve. It has been argued by Rogoff (1985) on the basis of the model of Barro and Gordon (1983*a*, 1983*b*) that governments' anti-inflationary credibility would be reduced if it were generally believed that, because of the habit of coordination, governments could avoid the adverse exchange rate effects of a short-term monetary expansion. If the habit of coordination developed, policies would become more expansionary, hence inflationary expectations would rise, and this would eventually negate the effects of expansionary policies.

The essential point is that Keynesian expansionary policies that may be desirable in the short run—and that would be pursued more vigorously with coordination—are likely to have an adverse effect in the medium and long run through raising inflationary expectations. It is thus a matter of trading off short-run gains against later losses. But in a deep or prolonged recession a heavy weight may justifiably be given to the short term; at other times, this would indeed be short-sighted.

Third, it is not always clear that transmission of monetary policy is positive. If the United States expands demand in a recession, commodity (raw materials) prices, including, above all, oil prices, will rise, or at least be maintained. Hence, the terms of trade of European countries and Japan may worsen or not improve as much as otherwise. Similarly, European and Japanese expansion may, on this account, have an adverse effect on the United States. Transmission will be positive to producers of basic commodities the prices of which are more flexible than those of manufactured goods, but will be negative to fellow members of the G-7.

A final point is that depreciation is not always seen as undesirable. After all, it improves the competitiveness of a country's tradable industries. We must recall the exchange rate protection motive. The Phillips curve effect, if any, is not always seen as important. Hence, during the 1980s there were periods when the United States administration (though not the Chairman of the Federal Reserve) appeared to welcome depreciation of the dollar because of its stimulating effect. Thus, depreciation did not necessarily inhibit monetary expansion.

V. TWO INSTRUMENTS AND THREE TARGETS: A COMMON EXCHANGE RATE OBJECTIVE

The assumptions of the locomotive theory may well explain motives for coordination in a general world recession, and the theory certainly explains US policy advocacy at certain times. But another model provides a closer description of actual motives and pressures at other times.[2]

We have again two countries, the United States and Germany, the latter representing all the European G-7 and Japan here. Again, each has one policy instrument, namely, monetary policy. For the moment I rule out sterilized intervention in the foreign exchange market as a separate policy instrument. At the simplest level, each country's monetary policy affects both its domestic economic conditions and the common exchange rate. I ignore here direct effects on foreign economic conditions, other than through the exchange rate. The two countries have a common exchange rate target, which may involve depreciation of the dollar, as at the Plaza Agreement of the G-7 finance ministers, or stabilization of the dollar, as at their Louvre Agreement. But each country has its own domestic target.

We start in an equilibrium where both countries were happy to stay, given that the other was. A change in economic conditions, or perhaps in government, causes the United States authorities to desire a demand expansion, though they do not want the exchange rate to change. Germany seeks no change at all. Hence, one of the three targets changes. For the United States it would be optimal to have a joint monetary expansion (joint decline in short-term interest rates), as this would keep the exchange rate constant, or moving in the agreed direction. On the other hand,

---

[2] This case is presented in detail, with diagrams, in Appendix 13.1.

for Germany it would be optimal to have no change in the previous policies. There will then be a new Nash equilibrium that will involve greater monetary expansion by the United States than by Germany, and some depreciation of the dollar. None of the three targets would be fully achieved in the new Nash equilibrium.

Cooperation involving information exchange and consultation will be needed for a smooth attainment of this new equilibrium. But it will not be Pareto-optimal. Both US contraction from the Nash equilibrium and German expansion would move the exchange rate closer to the common exchange rate target, and would be mutually beneficial. Each country creates a favorable spillover or externality for the other by adjusting its monetary policy so that the exchange rate outcome gets closer to the common target. This further move by both countries would be the outcome of coordination.

It was indeed a characteristic of the debates and negotiations of the 1980s that exchange rate targets were broadly agreed upon but that the United States often wanted expansion—using implicitly the locomotive theory as an argument—while Germany and Japan did not really want expansion at all, or not so much. German policy-makers, regarding high European unemployment as primarily structural in origin, were much less Keynesian in their thinking than the Americans. They had different theories or models in mind. This, of course, did not rule out Pareto-improving opportunities for both cooperation and coordination. It has been wrongly suggested that when the two parties have different models in mind, coordination is less likely to be beneficial. But it is not necessary for each party to have the same model. Even with different models there is scope for mutual policy adjustment.

Within the framework of the three-targets model I have just described (and as it is laid out more carefully in Appendix 13.1), different sub-models can explain the choice of targets by the governments of the two parties. Each government can make concessions to the desires of the other government, however unsoundly based it believes these desires to be. The result will be perceived as beneficial by both. Whether it actually turned out to be beneficial would depend on whether the models and relevant forecasts were correct. Furthermore, it is true that agreement on the model or (better) economic philosophy certainly makes negotiations more harmonious and pleasant.

VI. COORDINATION OF EXCHANGE-MARKET INTERVENTION

Let us now see what has actually happened since floating began. How much macroeconomic policy coordination has there actually been? If one were to summarize the nature of macroeconomic policy coordination among members of the G-7 or the G-3 (United States, Japan, Germany) that has actually taken place in the twenty years since 1973, one would have to say that it consisted primarily of concerted intervention in the foreign exchange market designed to achieve common exchange rate objectives. In addition, some agreements (or bargains), often rather imprecise or informal, were reached on desirable fiscal and monetary policies, and sometimes these probably did affect actual policies—though how much is usually unclear. These agreements reflected implicitly some of the issues I have discussed above. But the coordination story is dominated by exchange rate intervention episodes.

There were many concerted intervention episodes, the outstanding ones having been the dollar rescue in 1978, the effect of which lasted only a few months, the Plaza Agreement of September 1985, and the Louvre Accord of February 1987. The 1985 Plaza Agreement appeared to have a big effect in bringing the dollar down (though the downward movement had started already in February of that year). The 1987 Louvre Accord involved heavy intervention designed to halt a slide in the dollar. At the Louvre meeting a confidential target range was established, but it was already breached by April of that year. After that, there were various episodes of intervention, mostly designed to prevent a rise in the dollar by leaning against the wind. Clearly, close contact on intervention operations was maintained by the principal central banks or governments, but from 1989 it seemed that the coordination process itself had ceased and that there were sometimes marked differences in objectives.

Looking back on the heyday of coordinated intervention from 1985 to 1988, in 1985 the common objective was to bring the dollar down from its excessive 1984 level, and so stave off protectionist pressures in the US Congress. In other years the common objective was usually to stabilize the dollar or to lean against the wind of change. Thus stability was the principal common motive.

I have already discussed the role of foreign exchange market intervention in Chapter 12, and noted that its effectiveness is only short term and depends primarily on the signaling effect. This refers to sterilized intervention—and to a great extent intervention was indeed sterilized. Non-sterilized intervention is simply monetary policy. Only in the very short term and to a limited extent can sterilized intervention be regarded as an independent policy instrument that has some effect on exchange rates. If an exchange rate movement is purely a speculative bubble (as the rise in the dollar from June 1984 surely was), then sterilized intervention can make a difference quite independent of the relative monetary policies of the countries concerned. The market is looking for an anchor for its expectations, and the signal provided by intervention and its associated announcement may provide it. But, normally, intervention must soon be backed up by an appropriate adjustment in monetary policy to be effective.

The question that remains is why exchange market intervention was often coordinated. Of course, there have also been plenty of interventions by individual central banks on their own, notably by the Bundesbank and the Bank of Japan, usually leaning against the wind. Clearly, any one central bank can intervene provided it has the resources to do so. Nevertheless, it is accepted that coordination between central banks is desirable. There are two reasons.

First, intervention, like any economic activity, involves risks. There may be a high chance that it will be profitable, but there is also the risk of loss. After all, the central bank that intervenes is pitting its judgment against speculators who have every incentive to use their money profitably. Hence, central banks wish to spread the risk. Second, a central bank has limited resources of foreign currency, so it may not be able to achieve its objectives on its own, and, if this is known, credibility is lost, and the amount of intervention required to attain a given exchange rate target will increase. Clearly, this is not a problem if the Bundesbank wishes to depreciate the DM, in which case it will accumulate dollars, but it is a problem if it aims at appreciation. The problem will be solved if the Bundesbank has access to funds from the Federal Reserve.

VII. WHAT SCOPE FOR FISCAL POLICY COORDINATION?

Fiscal policies have international spillover effects through affecting real exchange rates, current accounts, and interest rates. Hence, one might expect that there is scope for coordination. In the 1980s there was certainly plenty of talk about it. But it is unrealistic to think that fiscal policies can be internationally coordinated to any significant extent. Hence, there is little point in pursuing coordination models where fiscal policies are the instruments.

In the United States, fiscal policy cannot be used for short-term demand management since the administration does not have control of it; it depends on agreement with Congress, which is inevitably slow to act. In the other G-7 countries, short-term management is possible, and does take place, but in Germany and Japan, and to a lesser extent other countries, it has been limited by medium- and long-term objectives of reducing the growth of public debt and restoring or maintaining fiscal discipline. The most one can expect is that fiscal policies might be slightly modified because of international pressure or bargains. The proclaimed aim has usually been to reduce current account imbalances. Possibly there have been one or two episodes of Japanese fiscal expansion that would not have taken place to the same extent if there had not been pressure from the United States. Also, Germany engaged in some fiscal expansion as a result of the 1978 Bonn summit. The US deficit as a proportion of GDP did fall from 1987, but the continual international pressure surely played no role in this trend.

VIII. THE STABILIZATION MOTIVE: AVOIDING SHOCKS

When there are international spillovers or externalities of national policies, there is potential scope for policy coordination in the form of mutual policy adjustment. So much can be agreed, and this simple proposition provides the basis for elaborate theories that have been constructed. But what are these spillovers, and when are they beneficial or harmful? That is a crucial issue.

When country A engages in monetary expansion or fiscal contraction that depreciates its real exchange rate and appreciates that of country B, is that beneficial or harmful for B? Sometimes

Europeans have complained about dollar depreciation and at other times about dollar appreciation. Similarly, when a country like the United States moves rather suddenly from fiscal balance into deficit, why should that be harmful, bearing in mind that another country, namely Japan, is criticized for not having a large enough fiscal deficit? Much of the academic literature rests on the assumptions of the locomotive theory, explained above, but this is only concerned with the short term and is only one possible model providing a framework for motivating coordination.

In my view, a consistent and legitimate motive has been stabilization of real variables. But the frequent mistake has been to focus only on real exchange rate stabilization. Departures from a period of stable exchange rates, whether appreciation or depreciation, have been disliked, and this has been associated with a dislike of sharp changes in current account balances. Yet disturbances of world interest rates, and of the terms of trade of commodity exporters, have also created problems. In general, a country has generated a negative spillover when it has imposed shocks on other countries to which the latter must then adjust. These shocks create redistributive effects in other countries, and the losers always complain. Furthermore, shocks create inevitable adjustment costs. Sometimes particular countries are clearly losers overall. The major examples of big shocks since 1973 have been the two oil shocks imposed by OPEC, the tight money (high interest rate) shock imposed by the central banks of the United States and some other G-7 countries in the early 1980s, leading to high real interest rates and sudden declines in the terms of trade of developing countries, the US fiscal policy shock owed to the Reagan Administration, and the German unification shock.

It follows that the best thing that countries can do for each other is to maintain stable and predictable policies. The theme of policy coordination should then be to encourage stable independent policies and thus avoid shocks, as far as possible.

Yet, for political and other reasons, shocks cannot be avoided. This is apparent when one reflects on the shocks I have just listed. Indeed, sometimes shocks are desirable for purely economic reasons, for example to squeeze accelerating inflation out of the economic system. But the impact of shocks can be moderated, and this could be a motive for policy coordination.

The country that is the source of the shocks needs to moderate the policies that gave rise to them, or to practice counteracting policies. But for other countries there is a question mark: what is to be stabilized? If there is a US fiscal expansion which appreciates the dollar and raises world interest rates, should Germany and Japan also engage in fiscal expansion (as was usually urged on them by US policy-makers) so as to moderate the dollar appreciation? Or should they engage in fiscal contraction (as they actually did, for their own domestic reasons) so as to moderate the effect on world interest rates? If a European locomotive, led by Germany, expands demand, depreciates the DM, and causes a commodity boom—possibly leading to an oil price explosion— should the United States follow with its own demand expansion, so moderating the DM depreciation (dollar appreciation), or should it contract so as to moderate or prevent the commodity boom?

Usually the focus has been on real exchange rate stabilization. This bias is explained by the remarkable swing in the dollar nominal and real exchange rate in the 1980s. But interest rates, terms of trade, and domestic demand conditions should surely not be completely sacrificed to a real exchange rate objective. The truth is that the source of the problem is the shock, which often has a political or ideological origin that cannot be negotiated away at meetings of finance ministers. Some instability and need for adjustment is then inevitable. It can be shifted around, being borne more or less by the real exchange rate—and hence the relative profitability of tradables and non-tradables—or by other variables, such as the interest rate.

IX. REFLECTIONS ON COORDINATION

If fiscal policies are generally not available for international coordination purposes, and if sterilized intervention has only a very short-term (though noticeable) effect, monetary policies become the main policy instruments. This certainly limits the discussion. It also puts the main coordination responsibility on central banks. Monetary policies do offer scope for coordination, above all, because they are flexible. But the effect on the real economy of monetary policy, and hence of coordination, cannot be longterm. For example, if US monetary policy had been used to prevent further dollar appreciation in 1983 or 1984, inflation in the

United States would have increased and any short-term real depreciation effect would eventually have been eroded.

What can one conclude? In general, real exchange rates should be allowed to vary in response to underlying conditions, such as fiscal policy variations, changes in private investment flows, and return flows of dividends and interest.

Monetary policy should be concerned primarily with domestic conditions, especially inflation. But when there is obviously a speculative bubble, as in the latter part of 1984, there is a role both for coordinated intervention in the foreign exchange market and for some adjustment of monetary policies. Monetary policies should not ignore exchange rate effects completely. Intervention and interest rate adjustments in 1985 were clearly justified. At certain times, such as a severe world recession, the message of the locomotive theory becomes relevant. Countries can expand demand unilaterally—and will always do so if domestic conditions convince their governments of the need—but it is helpful if the expansion is somewhat coordinated, and in that case the total world expansion is likely to be greater. In the short run, such additional expansion will be beneficial, though, in the medium and long term, inflation rates may well be higher as a result, as discussed earlier. Information exchange, consultation, and possibly coordination are needed to avoid excessive world booms and slumps that might result from unintentionally synchronized expansions or contractions. Finally, policies that raise world real interest rates have negative international spillover effects. If one thought optimistically that fiscal policies could be influenced by international discussions, they would thus provide the instruments for some coordination activities.

X. TARGET ZONES AND OTHER RULES-BASED SCHEMES

The highest level of macroeconomic policy cooperation among countries involves arrangements where countries negotiate certain rules and then independently adhere to them without further need for negotiations. Of course, legal interpretation of the rules will still be necessary—and will give rise to disputes—and there has to be some kind of enforcement mechanism. Elements of *ad hoc* negotiations may still creep into such a system. The Bretton Woods system was, broadly, of this kind, as (to a limited extent) is the GATT system of international trading rules. Authority can be handed over to a centralized international agency, as is proposed in the European Monetary Union.

Such a system has two advantages compared with *ad hoc* policy coordination. First, it may economize on negotiations, once-for-all negotiations to set up the rules replacing frequent or intermittent *ad hoc* negotiations. The more frequent the need for coordination negotiations under the *ad hoc* system—which depends, above all, on the frequency of shocks—the greater would be the advantage of rules. Second, a rules-based system introduces some certainty or predictability, which is helpful for private and public sector decision making. The disadvantage is the relative inflexibility such a system imposes. Of course, many contingencies can, in principle, be allowed for when the rules are constructed, but the more complicated the rules, the more difficult the enforcement problem and the less certainty there is.

Since the breakdown of the Bretton Woods system in 1973, various proposals for the re-establishment of some kind of new rules-based system, involving at the minimum the G-3 and sometimes a much larger group, have been made. I have noted that actual *ad hoc* policy coordination has been irregular and rather weak in its effects. Hence, one should not be surprised that these far more ambitious proposals have not been accepted. The preoccupation of the European members of the G-7 with EMS and EMU has also been a discouragement. In the absence of really severe shocks to the present non-system—shocks that domestic macroeconomic policies combined with some *ad hoc* policy coordination cannot readily cope with—it is highly unlikely that a new rules-based system will emerge in the near future. But I shall come back to reflections about the future in Chapter 16.

The various proposals have been influenced by three events. The first was simply the breakdown of the Bretton Woods system which did provide high nominal and considerable real exchange rate stability, and which coincided with a period of high worldwide growth. There was a hankering for a revival of its certainties. Second, and most important, the extreme movements of the dollar in the 1980s—associated with current account imbalances that many thought undesirable—stimulated advocacy of reform proposals. Real exchange rate movements seemed to lose contact with fundamentals—at least in 1984—and threatened to lead to a revival of US protectionism. The effects were certainly adverse for tradable-goods producers in appreciating countries, up to 1985 the United States, and later Japan. Hence, some concluded that the floating rate system needed some regulation or should be replaced completely. Finally, the European Monetary System was surprisingly successful, especially since 1983, in stabilizing intra-European exchange rates and yet ensuring adjustment, and from 1987 to 1992 it was even more surprisingly successful in producing an almost-fixed-rate system. To some it provided a model or laboratory experiment for a worldwide or G-7-wide system. Of course, this sub-system crashed in 1992.

Here I shall just select two proposals for discussion, one for the establishment of a fixed-rate regime, and the other for target zones. The first originated with Ronald McKinnon (1984) and involves the establishment by the G-3—the United States, Japan, and Germany—of a fixed exchange rate regime and a common monetary policy. There would not be a single central bank, so that countries would maintain control of their monetary policies, although they would have to coordinate them subject to rules designed to ensure fixed exchange rate relationships *and* low inflation for the G-3 area as a whole.

In other words, this is a proposal for a pseudo-exchange rate union, a concept that I discussed in Chapter 8. As long as there is not a single money and central bank in a world of capital mobility, the speculation problem will remain. Apart from that, all the familiar issues for and against monetary integration apply here. If Germany, France, Italy, and Britain find it difficult to establish a monetary union, one would expect that the United States, Japan, and Germany would find it even more difficult! The arguments need not be rehearsed again.

The target zone proposal originated with John Williamson (1983) and was modified and elaborated by Williamson and Miller (1987). In its modified form it is indeed very moderate or flexible. It is quite complicated and only the main features can be noted here.

Countries would use their monetary policies (interest rates) both to stabilize exchange rates within a target zone range—rather as in the European Exchange Rate Mechanism—and to maintain an agreed rate of growth of combined nominal demand. Thus continuous coordination of monetary policies would be needed. They would also use intervention in the exchange markets to keep exchange rates within the target zone. National fiscal policies would be adjusted to achieve national target rates of growth of nominal demand. Certain rules are suggested for the establishment of target rates of growth of nominal demand in each country, taking into account inflation, output, and current account effects. Exchange rates could fluctuate within the target zone, and wide limits (say, 10 per cent each side of the central rate) are suggested. Thus this proposal is really one for a floating rate regime with some limits to the extent to which rates can float away from the central rate. The proposed zones are much wider than those allowed by the ERM, as it was before August 1993.

The central exchange rate would be fixed as a result of a calculation of a fundamental equilibrium real exchange rate which would take into account normal capital flows, elasticities in international trade, and so on. Since the fundamental rate would be a real and not a nominal exchange rate, the central nominal rate would be adjusted in line with relative rates of inflation. In some ways the proposal is similar to the ERM, especially since the ERM margins were widened in 1993. But the system would depend on elaborate calculations of fundamental equilibrium exchange rates. It is hard to believe that agreement would be reached on such rates, especially as they would have to be changed as new information came in. Since the central rates could be altered, the zones would not provide any kind of discipline. The most they might do would be to avoid extreme short-term movements of exchange rates. Indeed, that seems to be the main purpose.

With regard to the use of fiscal policies for domestic purposes, there is hardly a need for centrally imposed rules, and it is inconceivable that such rules would be acceptable, or their implementation practical. As I have noted above, fiscal policy in the United States is not flexible and in all three countries is subject to various considerations, of which short-term demand management is only one. Hence, the blueprint that Williamson and Miller have put forward is not realistic, though it contains modifications and loopholes so that, if implemented, it might lead to a system not too far removed from the one that the G-7 seemed to be moving towards at the 1987 Louvre Accord. My own view is that it is not only politically impracticable to enforce such rules, but also unnecessary. Using monetary policies and sterilized intervention to avoid or modify extreme movements in exchange rates that appear to be speculative bubbles would be enough.

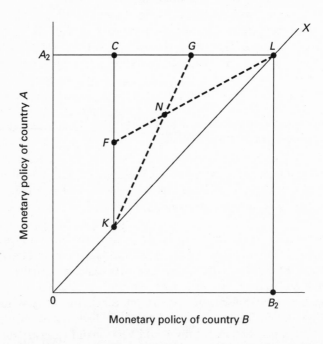

FIG. 13.1. Monetary Policy Interaction in a Two-Country Model: the Nash Equilibrium

APPENDIX 13.1

Coordination with Two Instruments and Three Targets: the Nash Equilibrium and a Pareto Improvement

Figs. 13.1 and 13.2 illustrate the two-instrument, three-target case discussed in the text. The main feature is that both countries view a change in the exchange rate (whether depreciation or appreciation) unfavorably, but are prepared to trade-off this common target against their domestic demand targets.

In Fig. 13.1 the vertical axis shows monetary policy in country A (the United States). A movement upwards is a monetary expansion. Similarly, the horizontal axis shows monetary policy in country B (Germany). A movement to the right is an expansion. (Indicators of monetary policy could either be short-term interest rates or some measure of the money supply.) The starting-point is K. Along OX the exchange rate stays constant. Above OX, A's currency depreciates relative to the exchange rate at K, owing to greater monetary expansion by A than by B.

Initially A and B are both content to stay at K. Then domestic conditions or the official economic philosophy change in A, and A wishes to expand domestic demand. But, also, it does not want the exchange rate to change. Thus, ideally, it wishes to reach L, which would be attained if it expanded to A_2 while B expanded to B_2. Both its targets would then be attained. On the other hand, B does not desire any change at all. Both its domestic and its exchange rate target would be attained at K.

What will happen in the absence of coordination? A might simply ignore the adverse exchange rate effect of unilateral expansion and move to A_2. If B is not aware in good time of A's policy change, equilibrium will move to C. Another possibility is that A realizes that B is not changing, and hence realizes that its unilateral monetary expansion will lead to depreciation. It will then expand less, to avoid some of the unfavorable effect of depreciation, and will choose a point such as F. Yet another possibility is that A moves to A_2, and then B reacts with some monetary expansion designed to moderate the adverse effects of appreciation. It will then choose a point such as G.

The Nash equilibrium N is derived by drawing two reaction curves, one for A (*FL*) and one for B (*KG*). A's curve shows how A would expand from F as B expanded, B's expansion modifying the depreciation resulting from A's expansion. In the movement from F to L, A would get closer to achieving both its targets, and so would become better off. Similarly, B's curve shows how B would react as A expanded. In the movement from K to G, B would become worse off. The Nash equilibrium is a compromise where none of the three targets is achieved.

One should not imagine that countries actually move along these reaction curves. Other than at N, this would imply continuous myopia, since each curve is drawn on the assumption that at each point one country assumes the other's policy to remain unchanged when actually policies are changing along the curve. The curves are needed to define the Nash equilibrium N, to which the countries might jump through consultation. This limited meaning of the reaction curves is often not understood.

Fig. 13.2 is the same diagram again, but this time indifference curves for both countries are drawn. These concentric curves map out points of equal welfare around the bliss points K (country B) and L (country A). At N an indifference curve belonging to A is tangential to the vertical line, which means that, given B's monetary policy, A is at a local optimum. Similarly at N, an indifference curve belonging to B is tangential to the horizontal line, so that B is also at a local optimum, given A's monetary policy. Hence neither country wants to change, knowing that the other country does not wish to change, and N is indeed an equilibrium. As explained in the text, the aim of consultation is to get smoothly from K to N.

Both A and B would be better off if they moved to any point in the shaded area (contained by the two indifference curves through N). Hence such a move would be a Pareto-improvement. This is the objective of policy coordination. Each country would move further from its domestic target: relative to N, A would have to contract and B to expand, this being mutual policy adjustment, but they would get closer to their common exchange rate target. Yet, neither country would have an incentive to move to this Pareto-improving area unilaterally.

Pareto-optimality (where one country cannot become better off without another becoming worse off) would be attained anywhere on the contract curve, of which DE is a segment; this traces out points of tangency of the two sets of indifference curves with each other. Moving from N to D, all the benefits of coordination would go to B, and moving to E, all the benefits would go to A. Bargaining would determine the outcome.

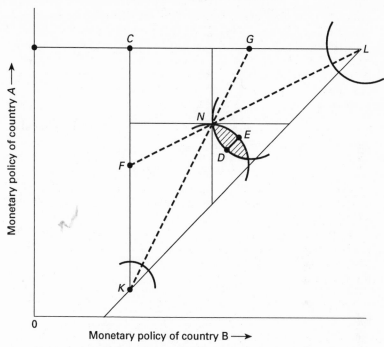

Fig. 13.2. Shaded Area Showing Scope for Pareto Improvement relative to Nash Equilibrium

REFERENCES

Pioneering work on strategic behavior in an international context was done by Hamada in various articles, notably Hamada (1976). Overviews of all the issues of macroeconomic policy coordination can be found in Horne and Masson (1988) and Frenkel *et al.* (1990).

An early survey of policy coordination theory is by Cooper (1985), and there are many relevant contributions in Buiter and Marston (1985). Some of the discussion in this chapter is based on Corden (1985), which contains a fuller exposition (with diagrams) of the two-country co-ordination analysis based on the locomotive theory. Canzoneri and Henderson (1991) provide the fullest exposition of the game theoretical approach, based on the locomotive model. Corden (1986) contains the argument that coordination should be concerned with avoidance of shocks. Recent surveys and expositions are in Currie and Levine (1991) and in Bryant (1994). A critical discussion of theoretical work, in the light of actual realities, is in Kenen (1989).

Dobson (1991), who was a participant in G-7 summits, provides the best description and discussion of actual coordination activities. Dominguez and Frankel (1993) describe concerted exchange rate inter-vention. Feldstein (1988) gives a critical view of coordination, or at least of an excessive emphasis on it. Among other things, he argues that it tends to divert attention from the need for a country (the United States) to deal with its own problems itself.

An account both of synchronized policy episodes and of several short-lived attempts by individual countries to buck the trend (expand more or contract less than other countries) is given in Larsen *et al.* (1983).

Protection and Competitiveness

14

Macroeconomic Policy and Protection

How does protection relate to macroeconomic policies and especially to exchange rate policy? The revival of protectionist sentiment in developed countries, especially the United States, in the 1980s and later makes this topic very relevant. This chapter will also deal with the implications of trade liberalization in developing countries, which has been an outstanding feature of the same period. While protection can take many forms, I shall have in mind here tariffs and quantitative import restrictions.

There are many issues to be discussed. The most important one concerns the integration of trade policy with exchange rate policy. These two kinds of policies are usually—at least in textbooks—treated in separate compartments. This is also true of government policy-making, with the roles of the Ministry of Industry or Trade usually being very distinct from that of the Ministry of Finance. There are other questions. What kind of exchange rate regime is best suited to avoid increases in protection and to encourage trade liberalization? Do floating rates—and especially misalignments—stimulate protectionist pressures? In what circumstances can tariffs or import restrictions improve a country's current account? Finally, do customs unions require—or make desirable—monetary integration?

I. PROTECTION IS A SWITCHING POLICY

Before getting to the main issues, I begin with a simple analytical framework, designed to relate the discussion to the basic analysis of Chapter 2. Protection and devaluation are alternative ways of bringing about switching of spending and of production between tradables and non-tradables or between imports and home-produced goods. This is the most fundamental theoretical concept for the present discussion.

Consider the simple three-product small-country model with

exportables (X), importables (M), and non-tradables (N), and focus on the production effects. Assume that the price of N is given, determined primarily by the nominal wage rate. A devaluation will switch production from N towards both X and M, while protection in the form of tariffs or import restrictions will switch production from N and X towards M. From a macroeconomic point of view, devaluation and import restrictions are alternatives because they both switch production out of N into tradables. In addition, protection switches production from X to M.

Comparing the effects of import restrictions with those of devaluation, the output of M will be higher and of X lower, while the output of N could rise, fall, or stay unchanged, depending on substitution and income effects. Protection reshuffles resources within the tradables sector as a whole. It is this protectionist reshuffling effect, affecting the allocation of resources between X and M, on which trade theory focuses. When the objective of policy is simply to bring about a current account improvement or an increase in demand for non-tradables designed to offset a concurrent reduction in absorption, then the shift of production out of exportables into importables is an unnecessary distortion which normally imposes efficiency costs, these being the classic costs of protection. For this reason, devaluation (or monetary expansion which brings about depreciation) is to be preferred to import restrictions.

I have told this story in terms of production switching, but demand switches in the opposite direction at the same time: a devaluation switches demand from X and M towards N, while a tariff switches it from M towards both X and N. Here protection also creates a distortion. It follows that, for any given increase in protection, there is always—in principle, if not easily measurable in advance—a devaluation that would have the same effect on either the current account or the net demand for non-tradables.

It must also be added that protection may take the form of favoring particular import-competing industries relative both to export industries and to other import-competing industries. This is indeed usual. In that case, the interpretation of the formal analysis given here must be slightly changed. M should represent only those importables which are protected, while X should be defined as including all other tradables, both exportables and importables.

I shall now assume that the distortions in the patterns of tradables output and of tradables demand caused by protection are undesirable. There is no reason to favor production of M relative to X, nor domestic consumption of X relative to M. In other words, none of the popular arguments for protection, such as the infant industry argument, apply. Rather, the standard case for free trade applies. In that case a clear argument against a fixed exchange rate regime emerges. A country may face an adverse shock, for example, a decline in the terms of trade, or a cessation of capital inflow or in the ability of the government to borrow abroad. The pattern of production should be switched towards tradables and the pattern of consumption away from tradables. A fixed exchange rate regime will induce the country to raise tariffs or impose quantitative restrictions. Given the fixed rate, the only alternative would be to rely on a reduction in absorption alone and thus, in the short run at least, to depart from internal balance. The obvious solution is to devalue.

During the Bretton Woods period this was, indeed, the most common argument in favor of exchange rate flexibility: the ability and readiness to devalue reduces the need of deficit countries to impose trade restrictions. Furthermore, the reluctance of developing countries to devalue—at least until the early 1980s—was a major reason for their use of quantitative restrictions. The International Monetary Fund and the World Bank have urged developing countries to devalue primarily to avoid the use of trade restrictions, or to make possible the liberalization of trade.

II. TRADE LIBERALIZATION REQUIRES DEVALUATION

Suppose a country starts in internal and external balance and has a positive degree of protection. It then wishes to liberalize trade by, say, ending or abolishing import restrictions. If the exchange rate were fixed, liberalization would be likely to worsen the trade balance and reduce employment, hence leading to departure from internal and external balance. In the absence of downward flexibility of nominal wages, it would then be necessary to devalue to restore equilibrium. Devaluation would partially restore the profitability of import-competing industries and would make exporting more profitable. Hence, resources would be induced to move out of the previously protected industries into export industries. In addition, import-competing industries that were not previously protected would also gain.

All this is straightforward, and is simply an application of the analysis given above. The message is that—with a fixed-but-adjustable exchange rate regime—trade liberalization needs to be accompanied by devaluation. A policy package is required, and not just trade liberalization on its own. Indeed, it may be best if devaluation preceded liberalization, since the latter will be politically more acceptable if the improved profitability of export industries can be clearly perceived in advance. Of course, a country can liberalize without devaluing if it is intended to increase absorption, perhaps to reduce a current account surplus (the case of Japan and Taiwan in the 1980s). But the historical evidence in developing countries is overwhelming that substantial trade liberalization normally goes with or requires substantial devaluation either beforehand or at the same time.

One can draw a conclusion for exchange rate policy at this point. If a country has extensive trade restrictions, it is unwise to commit itself to a firmly fixed exchange rate regime. Such a regime would make it very difficult to liberalize subsequently. An expectation of liberalization would immediately give rise to speculation and might force a devaluation in crisis conditions. In the absence of devaluation, liberalization would cause unemployment and probably would not be attempted. If some virtue is seen in the nominal anchor approach to exchange rate policy discussed in Chapter 5, this should only be adopted *after* trade liberalization. First, substantial trade liberalization combined with devaluation might be brought about, and then the exchange rate might be fixed as part of the anti-inflation strategy. This is the approach that was followed at one time in Chile, Mexico, and Argentina. Subsequent adverse shocks will have to be ridden out with foreign borrowing or with a temporary recession as current account improvements are obtained purely by cutting absorption and without deliberate switching policies. The danger is that, if the fixed exchange rate regime is maintained, trade restrictions will be reimposed.

A conflict between two long-term objectives can arise. The fixed exchange rate commitment is maintained (always subject to the threat of speculation) for the sake of lowering inflationary expectations, and thus keeping the inflation rate down in the long run. This is the nominal anchor philosophy. Trade liberalization is introduced to improve the long-run efficiency of the economy. But there is a cost of pursuing both policies at the same time: the government no longer has a switching device available. If switching is not possible, an adverse shock may bring about a short-run domestic recession, or demand for home-produced goods may be maintained by an increase in absorption that creates an undesirable current account deficit. To avoid both recession and current account deficit, either the exchange rate or the trade liberalization commitment may have to be given up. Indeed, each commitment increases the possibility that the other one will be given up.

The trade liberalization commitment is in the long run more important for developing countries than the fixed exchange rate commitment, since there are alternatives to the use of the exchange rate as an instrument of anti-inflation policy. Furthermore, developing countries have been very ready in the past to use trade restrictions to an extent much greater than have developed countries, and with great harm to their economies. It would be a tragedy if reluctance to devalue at times of adverse external shocks led them to go back to the old ways. Of course, if real wages are so rigid or an economy is so small that devaluation has very little real effect in any case, this issue does not arise.

One qualification to this argument should be noted. I have assumed here that trade liberalization has a *negative* switching effect, namely, that its net effect is to worsen the trade balance through increasing imports and to reduce demand for home-produced goods. In this case, it needs to be associated with devaluation which brings about *positive* switching. But trade liberalization will also have some positive switching effect on its own, and to that extent the need for devaluation will be moderated, and in some circumstances may disappear altogether. The point is that trade restrictions often discourage exports. This happens when import controls or high tariffs are imposed on imported inputs into exports. The difficulty of obtaining imported supplies may be—and in tight import regimes of many developing countries has been—a crucial limitation to expanding exports, especially of manufactures. When these restrictions or tariffs are reduced, exports may boom. Hence, the need for devaluation is reduced.

III. WILL PROTECTION IMPROVE THE CURRENT ACCOUNT?

I turn now to issues that have arisen in developed countries. Can a country with a floating exchange rate regime and a current account deficit reduce its deficit by increasing protection and without necessarily associating this policy with a deliberate absorption-reduction policy? It has certainly been a popular view in the United States that this is indeed probable. It has seemed obvious—though not to professional economists—that anything that reduces imports must also reduce the trade deficit.

This simple, naïve conclusion ignores the possibility that an increase in US protection would tend to appreciate the dollar. In terms of our earlier discussion, if one switching instrument, namely protection, is activated, the other, namely the exchange rate, will move endogenously in a floating rate regime. The essential issue is whether the combination of increased protection and appreciation of the dollar would reduce the budget deficit, increase private savings, or reduce private investment. The savings-and-investment approach to the current account is relevant here. The basic story is that protection would reduce the demand for foreign currency in the foreign exchange market, and equilibrium would be restored by appreciation of the dollar. If national savings and investment did not change, the offset would be complete. The current account would not change. If savings increased in the process, then—other things being equal—the offset would be incomplete and the current account would indeed improve.

How might savings and investment, public and private, change when import restrictions or tariffs are imposed, and the exchange rate floats? Increased tariff revenue might reduce the budget deficit. On the other hand, import restrictions or voluntary export restraints imposed on foreign suppliers could well have the opposite effect, reducing tariff revenue, and also reducing revenue from income and corporate taxes owing to the reduced real incomes these measures might bring about. Import restrictions might increase savings if the restrictions were believed to be temporary. The industries and persons that gain from protection are likely to save more, at least in the short run, while others, notably export producers, might save less. Investment in the protected industries is likely to go up, as profit expectations improve, while in others it will go down. Income tax revenue from some corporations and persons will rise and from others will fall.

It follows that there is no general presumption that the net effect on savings and investment of an increase in protection combined with appreciation would go one way or the other. The partial equilibrium approach which ignores the indirect effects of protection through the associated exchange rate adjustment will give misleadingly simple and possibly wrong answers.

The exchange rate may not appreciate at the time or shortly after protection has been increased. As noted in Chapter 12, in the short run the fundamentals play only a small role in exchange rate determination. But the main point remains that the effect of a change in the degree of protection on the current account depends on the effects on savings and investment, private and public.

It is conceivable that monetary policy keeps the exchange rate unchanged. One must then consider the effects of protection on their own. If there is initially Keynesian unemployment and excess capacity, protection will raise real incomes, at least in the short run, and this will raise savings (even with a constant propensity to save) and so improve the current account. But there will still be losers as well as gainers. Notably, consumers of imports, including industries using imported inputs, will lose, and hence save less. With both gainers and losers, investment may rise or fall.

It has been a theme of US official policy to pressure Japan to open its domestic market so as to reduce its trade surplus. I have pointed out in earlier chapters that it is most questionable whether a reduction in the Japanese current account surplus is beneficial for the rest of the world. The analysis here suggests that, in any case, further opening of the Japanese domestic market—while no doubt desirable from a standard gains-from-trade point of view—would not necessarily reduce Japan's surplus. It all depends on what happens to Japanese savings and investment, and to Japan's budget deficit. Those Japanese industries that lose from market opening would no doubt invest less, while the export industries might well invest more. In any case, the tendency would be for the yen to depreciate (other things being equal). While Japanese industries would face more competition in their home market, they would actually become more competitive abroad, including in the United States. A paradox indeed! It is quite likely that yen depreciation would lead to increased pressure for protection in the United States. Japan would be accused of unfairly depreciating its currency, protecting its industries indirectly, that is, engaging in exchange rate protection.

Having said all this, a complication remains. It is necessary to think in international general equilibrium terms. Let us suppose that the Japanese current account surplus is not changed by Japanese market opening because the various effects on Japanese savings, investment, and the budget deficit cancel out. Nevertheless, the US bilateral current account balance with Japan could well improve if Japanese market-opening policies are directed specifically to favor imports from the United States. There will be a trade diversion effect that reduces Japanese imports from other countries. Japan will buy more manufactured goods from the United States, and less from Europe. Furthermore, depreciation of the yen will increase exports to other countries. The net effect may be for the Japanese bilateral surplus with the United States to fall—as dearly desired by some US policymakers and Congressmen—while Japan's bilateral surplus with Europe rises. If, at the same time, there is no change in US savings, investment, and the budget deficit, and hence the US current account, the United States will end up with an improved bilateral balance with Japan and a larger deficit or lower surplus with Europe.

IV. DOES A FLOATING RATE REGIME STIMULATE PROTECTION?

When the dollar appreciated so severely in 1983 and 1984, reducing US competitiveness, there were strong protectionist pressures in the United States, clearly manifested in Congress. It became widely accepted that the appreciation needed to be stopped or reversed in order to head off increased protection— quite apart from other reasons. The Plaza Agreement of September 1985, at which the major industrial nations agreed to intervene to bring the dollar down, was motivated by this concern. From this has followed the suggestion that a floating exchange rate regime has the undesirable by-product of leading to increased protection. This experience has provided an additional argument—additional to others discussed in this book—for a commitment to exchange rate stability. It has been argued—for example by Bergsten and Williamson (1983)—that protection tends to increase when currencies appreciate, while depreciations do not lead to reductions in protection to the same extent. An asymmetry is clearly implied. Disturbances in the foreign exchange market—like other disturbances—lead to increased protection, the motive of protection being to protect potential losers.

The empirical evidence is not conclusive on this matter. Protectionist pressures certainly increased in the United States during the dollar appreciation of the early 1980s. And to some extent they were indeed headed off by the subsequent depreciation. But US trade restrictions have increased, mostly through the use of anti-dumping measures and through voluntary export restraints imposed on other countries. By 1993, even after an impressive US export boom from 1987 to 1991 (and especially 1988 and 1989 when annual growth of US exports averaged nearly 16 per cent), pressures for higher protection were still strong, stimulated no doubt by the recession of 1991–2. Furthermore, at the same time that the dollar appreciated, the yen and the DM depreciated. Hence, unless there is extreme asymmetry, there should have been some trade liberalization by Japan and Germany in the early 1980s. This did indeed happen in the case of Japan, though there is no evidence in the case of Germany.

At this point one can perceive a puzzle. What really is the link between the exchange rate regime and the tendency to impose protection? Is a fixed exchange rate regime or a floating one preferable if increased protection is to be avoided? Earlier in this chapter it was argued that a commitment to a fixed exchange rate has in the past led many developing countries, and sometimes others, to impose or intensify quantitative restrictions in order to deal with an adverse balance of payments. This can be called the *traditional link*. It was argued that countries which needed to liberalize trade or wanted to avoid intensifying restrictions should maintain exchange rate flexibility. Now we seem to have an opposite—though empirically much more doubtful—argument: floating rate regimes lead to more protection. That is the *new link*. Can these two arguments be reconciled?

In both cases an asymmetry is assumed. Consider first the

traditional link. A country that suffers an adverse shock which creates a potential or actual balance-of-payments problem must do something about it. Unless it is willing to forgo short-run internal balance, it must either devalue or increase trade restrictions. By contrast, a country that faces a favorable shock is happy to allow its foreign exchange reserves to accumulate and does not feel obliged to appreciate or reduce existing import restrictions. Furthermore, it can restore external equilibrium by allowing domestic prices to rise. Thus, worldwide disturbances which produce both losers and gainers lead to depreciations rather than appreciations in a flexible rate regime and to increases rather than decreases in protection in a fixed rate regime. That is the asymmetry. It is assumed here that the exchange rate adjustments that would take place if exchange rates were flexible (and that would thus avoid the use of import restrictions) would be in an equilibrium direction. Relative to the deficit countries, the surplus countries would find their exchange rates appreciating, but they would not try to counteract the effects by imposing trade restrictions, since they would recognize the need to restore equilibrium.

This kind of story must then be compared with the implicit assumptions of those who argue for the new link, namely, that a floating regime leads to more protection. The exchange rate fluctuations in a free floating rate regime are implicitly assumed by them to be disequilibrium ones. They are misalignments that give rise to the asymmetric protectionist pressures just discussed. The countries whose exchange rates appreciate do not accept appreciation as necessary and are therefore likely to impose restrictions.

The crucial issue, then, is whether one expects exchange rate variations in a flexible rate regime to be equilibrium or disequilibrium ones. In the case of developing countries during the 1970s and 1980s, they have been equilibrium variations. Exchange rates have not been freely floating but have been flexible—fixed or managed, and adjustable. It is harder to generalize about the floating rate experience of the major industrial countries over the whole period since 1973. Did exchange rates move in an equilibrium or disequilibrium direction? There was, of course, one period—from about 1983 to early 1985—when the dollar was seen by some as moving in a disequilibrium direction, and it is this period that gave rise to the argument that a floating rate regime increases protectionist pressures. It was a very special episode which, in its last stage, did justify action through foreign exchange market intervention and through monetary policy to moderate or reverse the appreciation. In general, I would conclude that a flexible exchange rate regime is far more likely to avoid increases in protection than would a fixed rate regime, but that at times severe appreciations may need to be avoided or moderated through monetary policy and exchange rate management to avoid protectionist reactions.

V. DOES A CUSTOMS UNION REQUIRE MONETARY
INTEGRATION?

Finally, is there a connection between trade integration and monetary integration? This question is simply a special aspect of the broader issue discussed here, namely, the relation between trade policy and macroeconomic policy.

It is certainly possible to have free trade between a group of countries without monetary integration or even without a more limited commitment to fixed exchange rates. The European Community has been an area of free trade with a common external trade policy—that is, it has been a customs union—even though intra-European exchange rates have not been fixed. The North American Free Trade Area is not intended to involve monetary integration between the United States, Canada, and Mexico.

It is also possible to have a monetary union, or a long-term fixed exchange rate commitment, without free trade. During the Bretton Woods period many developing countries fixed their exchange rates for long periods to the dollar or to sterling, and yet they all imposed trade restrictions on imports from the United States and Britain. For example, the Mexican peso was fixed to the dollar from 1954 to 1976, and yet Mexico followed highly protectionist policies for the whole of that period. Until 1931 the Australian pound was firmly fixed to the pound sterling, even though Australia had imposed tariffs on imports from Britain since the beginning of the century. Canada has a single money and central bank, and yet the various provinces have imposed a variety of restrictions on imports of goods and services from each other.

It may be possible to have a customs union—and indeed that

more ambitious European animal, a single market—without monetary integration, but it may also be true that in the absence of monetary integration the preservation of an area of free trade will always be under threat. This has been argued by advocates of European monetary integration. If intra-European exchange rates fluctuate, the countries that suffer from real appreciation will face domestic pressures to impose trade restrictions on imports that are believed to be unfairly helped by undervalued exchange rates. The pressure will be to break up the common market. One recognizes here the new-link argument, discussed above and originating in the United States, that disequilibrium exchange rate movements stimulate protection. In this case exchange rate fluctuations would threaten the single market. Even if the customs union were not destroyed by these pressures, the countries that would lose competitiveness would press the union as a whole to increase its tariffs or tighten restrictions against imports from outside the union.

The other side of this coin is that nominal devaluations may be needed by countries that have lost competitiveness or that have encountered adverse shocks. If they cannot devalue, they may end up imposing trade restrictions on imports from fellow members of the customs union. They would, of course, be breaking the rules of the customs union in doing so. This traditional-link argument in favor of exchange rate flexibility within a customs union implies that exchange rate adjustments would be of an equilibrium nature.

Under the European Monetary System exchange rate adjustments have been of an equilibrium nature. They generally restored real exchange rates that had moved out of line. The adjustments were mutually agreed, and there was no tendency for Germany to impose trade restrictions against imports from other countries which devalued against the DM. Hence, if the choice were between a restored EMS and complete monetary integration, a concern with the revival of protection seems to lead to a vote for the EMS. But the restoration of a fixed-but-adjustable system like the EMS is improbable because of high capital mobility, itself resulting in part from the Single-Market Program. Thus, as discussed in Chapter 7, the choice is really between what is effectively a managed floating regime and complete monetary integration. And since intra-European bilateral exchange rates have started floating, short-term misalignments, and thus real appreciations that have not been mutually agreed upon, are certainly possible.

Conceivably a prolonged period of floating could endanger the single market. It would certainly endanger the Common Agricultural Policy, which is not just a single market but which actually involves fixing common prices. On the other hand, even in a floating rate regime, exchange rate movements could be in an equilibrating direction—especially if influenced by sensible, stabilizing monetary policies. In that case the single market would be more endangered by moving from floating to monetary integration, than the other way around. Probably the single market—and especially the less ambitious customs union—was by 1993 so well established that these considerations would not endanger it. It seems to follow that the choice of exchange rate regime within the European Union should be determined by the matters discussed in Chapters 7 and 8 and—because of the opposing forces at work—not by a concern with the preservation of the common market.

REFERENCES

The theoretical relationship between exchange rate adjustment and tariff protection in a model with non-tradables is laid out in Corden (1971) and Dornbusch (1974). On the interaction of trade liberalization with devaluation in developing countries, see Krueger (1978), Michaely *et al.* (1991), and Little *et al.* (1993).

There are many empirical studies on the relationship between exchange rate volatility and trade, some supporting and some rejecting the hypothesis that volatility since 1973 has reduced trade. The literature is surveyed in Aschheim *et al.* (1993). These authors, from their own work, reject the hypothesis. Of course, many factors other than changes in trade restrictions (which are hard to measure) affect changes in the ratios of trade to gross domestic product.

15

What Is the Competitiveness Problem?

Has the United States been losing competitiveness relative to Japan and is this a problem that calls for government action—perhaps in the form of protection or subsidization? More generally, is the rise of East Asia, and especially the fast growth of the People's Republic of China, a threat to the United States and to Europe through reducing the latter's competitiveness? Can the high unemployment rates in Europe be attributed to a loss of international competitiveness? There is a great deal of muddled thinking in this area, and some sorting-out is needed. Above all, the term *competitiveness*, which is so popular, must be defined precisely, as far as this is possible. Clearly, it refers to *international* competitiveness. It needs to be given a meaning which makes economic sense and at the same time is not far removed from the rather imprecise ideas that are popularly implied in the term. This requires making use of various concepts discussed earlier in this book as well as drawing on standard international trade theory.

I. A FRAMEWORK

Speaking loosely, one might say that an industry is internationally competitive if it produces tradables and is profitable. A reduction in competitiveness is then a reduction in profitability in some or all tradables industries. The lower is profitability, the lower will be output and probably employment in an industry. It is hard to define absolute profitability or competitiveness, and it makes sense to interpret the popular discussion to refer to changes in profitability, which have given rise to—or threaten to bring about—declines in output and employment. An alternative definition is that competitiveness has declined if an industry has lost international market shares, whether at home or abroad. For reasons to be discussed below, this definition is not helpful.

I have in mind a specific factors model here. Profitability must refer to the returns to the factors of production that are specific to an industry. With a given stock of capital in an industry and a given production function, the rate of return on capital (i.e. profitability) depends on the product prices and the nominal wages it faces. If wages rise faster than the prices of the products it sells, profitability will fall and the industry's output and employment is likely to fall. Productivity improvement will raise profitability for given prices and wages. Of course, gradually capital will move between industries in response to different rates of return, so that reduced relative profitability will lead not only to less employment with a given capital stock but also to lower output as investment in the industry falls off, or there is disinvestment. Input prices also enter the story. A rise in input prices will reduce profitability, given final goods' prices, wages, and productivity.

A distinction will be made here between three cases, which have quite different policy implications. Popular discussion tends to mix up these three cases. In Case I, sectoral profitability has declined within the tradables sector, but the average profitability of tradables has not necessarily declined. There are losers and gainers. I shall label this a sectoral competitiveness problem. In Case II, average profitability of tradables has declined, but not the average for the economy as a whole. I shall call this a real appreciation problem. In Case III, profitability in the economy as a whole—national profitability—has declined. In this case there is a productivity problem. Consider our familiar model with X (exportables), M (importables), and N (non-tradables). There are no produced inputs. In Case I, profitability of X (or, alternatively, of M) declines, and this is offset by increased profitability of M (or, alternatively, of X). In Case II, profitability of both X and M declines, but this is offset by increased profitability of N. In the third case, the profitability of X, M, and N all decline, and thus output of all three falls. All three cases are expounded diagrammatically in the Appendix. I begin with Case I.

II. GAINERS AND LOSERS: SECTORAL COMPETITIVENESS

In the post-war period Japan developed a comparative advantage in high-quality mass production products, notably automobiles. Thus, the fast growth of Japan has, among other things, reduced the relative international prices and raised the quality of automobiles. Similarly, the fast growth of the People's Republic of China is likely to reduce the relative international prices of various labor-intensive products, notably clothing, textiles, and footwear, and no doubt many other products. Seen from the point of view of the United States and the European Community, growth in other countries, such as the countries of East Asia, affects international relative prices and thus the world pattern of comparative advantage. The automobile industries of the United States and Europe have lost competitiveness—i.e. profitability—as have labor-intensive industries. Many more changes are in prospect, as Chinese growth impacts on world trade, and as large developing countries, notably Brazil and India, raise growth rates and become more outward-oriented.

Yet a focus on the adverse effects of foreign growth on some industries, like automobiles and clothing and textiles, is only half the story. The other half is that the fast-growing economies become growing markets for the exports of the United States and Europe. Reduced profitability for some industries will go with increased profitability of others. The loss of competitiveness is only sectoral. There has been a redistribution of competitiveness, not an overall national decline. Much of the popular preoccupation about loss of competitiveness has concerned only sectoral competitiveness.

The role of exchange rate adjustment is crucial. The export growth of a particular country, say China, may adversely affect some import-competing or export industries of another country, say Thailand, without a direct offsetting favorable effect through increased demand. China's increased imports may come principally from the United States while her increased exports may compete with those of Thailand. Thus, Thailand may not benefit directly from the growing market of China. One must then allow for the appropriate exchange rate adjustment by Thailand. Making here the standard short-term Keynesian assumption that nominal wages are inflexible downwards and real wages are flexible, Thailand must devalue. This will partly restore the profitability of its adversely affected tradables industries, and will increase the profitability of other tradables. Thus, it remains true that there will be gainers in Thailand as well as losers. Once appropriate exchange rate adjustment is allowed for, some Thai industries will become more competitive even though the direct effect on Thailand was wholly adverse.

III. A CURRENT ACCOUNT DEFICIT AND REAL APPRECIATION

I come now to Case II, where the profitability of the tradable sector as a whole deteriorates rather than one part of it losing and another gaining. The case is familiar from earlier discussion in this book of real appreciation, and especially the model of Chapter 2. Hence, I can be brief.

For one reason or another, the country goes into current account deficit, or a previous deficit increases. This is normally associated with real appreciation, the domestic prices of tradables falling relative to those of non-tradables. Profitability in tradables falls and in non-tradables rises. Resources move out of tradables into non-tradables. As before, there are gainers and losers, and there is no general presumption that overall profitability declines. But one can legitimately say that the country has become internationally less competitive. There has been a general loss of competitiveness of the country's tradables sector. This was the experience of the United States in the early 1980s. From the point of view of tradables producers, there is a real appreciation problem, one that I discussed in Chapter 4 and elsewhere. Whether this is undesirable raises all the issues also discussed earlier, namely the desirability or otherwise of a higher current account deficit. A decline in competitiveness may be the inevitable by-product of an international borrowing policy that is optimal. On the other hand, it may itself create problems for the future through the eventual need to reverse real appreciation, so that the full consequences of a borrowing policy become non-optimal.

It must be added that the relationship between real appreciation and the current account is not strict. It assumes (as in Chapter 2) that internal balance is maintained, that there are no lags, and no structural or relative productivity changes which affect the real exchange rate for a given current account balance. In the case of the United States, various measures of the real exchange rate (or competitiveness) all show real depreciation from early 1985 (because of nominal depreciation), but the current account only began improving in 1988. The fiscal deficit began to fall in 1987.

IV. RELATIVE PRODUCTIVITY GROWTH AND THE EXCHANGE RATE

So far I have dealt with two cases, Case I, where changing international conditions, reflected in prices and qualities of products, affect some domestic tradable industries adversely even though others gain, and Case II, where an increase in a current account deficit affects adversely all tradable industries, while at the same time benefiting producers of non-tradables. I now come to the third case, where there is an economy-wide problem of low or declining productivity growth, both tradables and non-tradables being adversely affected. In the discussion of this third case, the crucial distinction must be made between the sub-case where real wages (or their rate of growth) are flexible, and the other sub-case, where they are rigid. I shall discuss the real wage rigidity case in Section VI.

The main point is that, if real wages are flexible and the exchange is adjusted appropriately, low productivity growth, whether absolute or relative to other countries, does not mean declining competitiveness. With given nominal wages, or their rate of growth, appropriate depreciation of the exchange rate can always offset low or declining productivity growth and so maintain the competitiveness of the tradables sector. This conclusion flows from our basic model of Chapters 2 and 3, and is perfectly general. At any point in time, with given nominal wages, domestic production functions, and demand patterns, there is always some nominal exchange rate that can (together with appropriate absorption policy) maintain internal and external balance, however defined. This conclusion can readily be translated into rates of growth terms.

It is useful to employ an extremely simple Ricardian two-country model here, simpler than other models in this chapter. It is not a small-country model; each country determines the price of its own product on the basis of its own labor costs. This model can be used to show clearly that—when the exchange rate is flexible—the relation between national and foreign productivity growth is *not* relevant for competitiveness. I refer here to overall national, and not sectoral, productivity. It follows that an increase in foreign productivity growth does not reduce the home country's competitiveness. The conclusion applies in more general models of the kind used earlier in this and other chapters.

This time I assume that each country produces only one good, which is its exportable, and consumes this good, as well as the export of the other. This means that no non-tradable is produced, each country only producing an exportable. The price of this good depends on the nominal wage rate and labor productivity. Nominal wage growth is $\hat{w}$, labor productivity growth is $\hat{q}$, and the inflation rate of the domestic good is $\hat{p}$, so that $\hat{p} = \hat{w} - \hat{q}$. Similarly, for the foreign good, $\hat{p}^\star = \hat{w}^\star - \hat{q}^\star$. The rate of depreciation of the domestic currency is $\hat{e}$, and competitiveness will be maintained if $\hat{e} = \hat{p} - \hat{p}^\star$. If nominal wage growth at home and abroad stayed unchanged but foreign productivity growth rose while that at home stayed unchanged, e would increase to maintain competitiveness. Hence, high productivity growth abroad would create no problem at all. There would be a problem only if the exchange rate did not depreciate, i.e. if $\hat{e} = 0$. In that case, continuous real appreciation of the home currency would result, with the usual adverse effect on the tradables sector, which, in this example, is the whole economy.

It follows that a decline in productivity at home, for whatever reason, or a rise in nominal wages, can always be offset by an appropriate depreciation of the exchange rate. Similarly, a rise in productivity abroad can be offset. The general point is that the competitiveness of tradable goods industries can always be maintained if the exchange rate is flexible and given the fundamental assumption at this stage of real wage flexibility. The argument is thus applicable to the United States, which does indeed have a flexible exchange rate and flexible real wages. The relation between the rate of productivity growth abroad and productivity growth at home—i.e. $\hat{q}^\star - \hat{q}$—is relevant only for the rate of depreciation required (with given nominal wage growth abroad and at home). The rate of growth of real wages (and real incomes) at home, $\hat{w} - \hat{p}$, does not depend at all on *relative* productivity growth. It may be influenced by productivity growth abroad through terms-of-trade effects (and other complications) discussed below, but such effects may well be positive. Primarily, the rates of growth of domestic real wages and real incomes depend on the rate of growth of productivity at home—i.e. on $\hat{q}$. "The fault, dear Brutus, is not in our stars but in ourselves."

In many of the countries of the European Union there are very high taxes on employers which pay for social security and unemployment benefits. Such taxes raise labor costs to employers and hence the product wage for a given income wage. It is the product nominal wage, and not just the income wage, that is relevant here. The point here is that the apparently adverse effects on competitiveness of such taxes can be offset by appropriate exchange rate depreciation. The same argument applies to the competitiveness effects of increased charges for health insurance that may be imposed on employers in the United States. Similarly, various regulations in the United States and Europe may well have reduced the productivity of industries, and for a given exchange rate would have reduced their competitiveness. But, again, this can be offset by appropriate depreciation.

It would be wrong to conclude that low productivity growth, and government policies that reduce productivity, are nothing to worry about. There can certainly be a productivity problem. The conclusion is only that industries can still be internationally competitive even when productivity is low. Indeed, this explains why low-productivity developing countries have internationally competitive industries. The cost of low productivity is borne in the form of lower real wages.

V. IS FOREIGN GROWTH HARMFUL?

Coming back to the United States as the example, some industries have gained from foreign growth and some have lost. But can one say anything about the overall gain or loss? This means looking at two significant aspects, namely the adjustment costs and the terms of trade.

All changes, whether resulting from foreign growth, from technological progress, or from changes in international tastes, create the need for adjustment, and hence adjustment costs. This is obvious. It raises large issues going beyond the scope of this book. Labor must move between industries, usually gradually. Changes in patterns of real wages, involving some declines in real wages, must be accepted. The pattern of investment, especially in human capital, needs to adjust to changes, and, ideally, to anticipate them. If a country cut itself off from international trade, it could avoid some of these costs, but would also forgo the gains from trade. Furthermore, the ability to adjust to changes originating domestically would be reduced.

Leaving aside adjustment costs, and assuming appropriate exchange rate and real wage adjustment, the overall effects of foreign growth on the United States are transmitted through effects on the terms of trade. I must stress at this stage the assumptions of exchange rate and real wage adjustment, designed to maintain the overall level of employment and a constant current account balance.

The question, then, is: would foreign growth improve or worsen the US terms of trade? The analysis of the effect of foreign growth on the terms of trade derives from standard trade theory and leads to an important conclusion, namely, that there is some presumption that foreign growth is, on balance, likely to be beneficial. But it must be said right at the beginning that for the United States, where exports of goods and services account for only about 10 per cent of GDP, such terms-of-trade effects, whether favorable or otherwise, are likely to have a small effect on per capita real incomes relative to the effect of domestic labor productivity growth. Furthermore, foreign growth may not actually bring about any significant terms-of-trade effects at all. World relative prices will change, with prices (quality adjusted) for some US exports falling and for others rising. But there may be no general fall of US export prices relative to US import prices, or the reverse. The more diverse is the pattern of a country's trade—and the US trade pattern is certainly diverse—the more likely is such an outcome.

The presumption that foreign growth is beneficial by improving the home country's terms of trade follows from a simple trade theory model that originated with Harry Johnson. I shall assume now that there are no particular biases in the pattern of foreign growth, which is the most neutral, or agnostic, assumption. Consider an example. There are just two countries, the United States and China. The United States is growing at 4 per cent and China at 8 per cent. There are two goods, both of which are produced and consumed in both countries. The United States is a net exporter of A and China of B. There is only one price ratio, namely that of A to B. If the relative price of A rises, the US terms of trade have improved. Assume that growth in both countries is neutral or unbiased. This means that in China, at a constant price ratio, the demands for A and for B, and the supplies of A and of B, all rise at 8 per cent. Hence, desired net exports of B

(and net imports of A) also rise at 8 per cent. In the United States, where growth is only 4 per cent, demands and supplies all rise by 4 per cent so that, at constant prices, desired net exports of A (and hence net imports of B) also rise at 4 per cent. This is a disequilibrium situation, with excess supply of B and excess demand for A in the world market. Equilibrium will be restored by a rise in the relative price of A, that is, by an improvement in the US terms of trade.

The terms of trade of the slower-growing country have thus improved. The general conclusion is that, in the absence of biases in growth on the side of either production or consumption, a country benefits from the growth of other countries. Sufficient anti-trade bias—i.e. a tendency to import substitution—in the faster growing country can alter this result. But, when many diverse foreign countries are growing faster, the likelihood of a general bias in world growth is reduced. If we think of the prospective growth of developing countries, it is more likely to be pro-trade biased (biased to increasing exports rather than import replacement) and hence more likely to improve the terms of trade of the developed countries. This, of course, would be no comfort to particular industries in the developed countries, especially labor-intensive ones, that would lose.

It is often believed that the growth of Japan has been heavily biased towards the kinds of products in which the United States has also specialized—automobiles being the main example—in which case the net effect of high Japanese growth would have been a deterioration in the US terms of trade. In this view Japan is competitive rather than complementary with the United States. On the other hand, the terms of trade of exporters of food and raw materials have undoubtedly improved as a result of Japanese growth, and the United States has been such an exporter. In fact, the United States is the most diverse of traders, and it is unlikely that, once Japanese growth passed through its labor-intensive phase, the net effect of Japanese growth on the US terms of trade went one way or another. During the phase of Japan's labor-intensive growth (i.e. when Japan exported low-skill labor-intensive products), the net effect on the US terms of trade would have been favorable.

Long-term biases in the pattern of foreign growth affecting the United States are certainly possible. The growth of China is very likely to improve the terms of trade both of the United States and of the developed countries of the European Union, and to worsen the terms of trade of countries that specialize in labor-intensive exports. On the other hand, there is the technology-diffusion effect. Some people believe this to be important. The international diffusion of technology originating in the United States has tended to improve the productivity of foreign industries producing the kinds of products in which the United States has a lead, and hence a comparative advantage. It has thus reduced the foreign demand for these US exports, giving foreign growth an anti-trade bias relative to the United States. A technological leader derives quasi-monopoly gains from its temporary monopoly in new products and prices. Foreign growth in the form of technological catching-up will erode such monopoly positions. Hence, the diffusion process has tended to worsen the US terms of trade. This, at least, has been a common argument, though the empirical significance of this effect, if any, is (in my view) unclear.

The locomotive theory discussed in Chapter 11 may be recalled at this point. The basic argument was that country B benefits from the faster short-term growth of country A. The more country A stimulates its economy through demand-expansionary policies, the more country B will benefit. The argument assumes that there are short-term Keynesian effects on output and real spending in both countries. It was shown that the spillover effect works through the terms of trade. Country A's expansion allows country B to expand without the latter's exchange rate having to depreciate. On the basis of this kind of logic, the United States Administration has regularly pressed Japan to expand demand more. The concern has always been short term, but surely this analysis is also relevant for long-term growth. If the United States benefits from a short-term acceleration of Japanese growth brought about by fiscal and monetary demand stimulus, would it not also have benefited—again through a terms-of-trade effect—from Japan's remarkable long-term growth brought about by high investment and total productivity growth?

The market-share approach to competitiveness should also be noted. Sometimes a decline in competitiveness is meant to refer to a decline in international market share. The United States has certainly been losing market shares in the world. In 1960, US exports of goods and services were valued at 16 per cent of world exports, and by 1989 the share was down to 12 per cent. The same applies to Britain. In the nineteenth century it dominated world trade and by 1989 the British share was down to 5 per cent. And in the same period that the US share fell, the Japanese share rose—i.e. from 3 per cent of world trade in 1960 to 9 per cent in 1989. But all the time that the United States and Britain were losing market shares, they were themselves growing and becoming richer. They lost market shares because other countries were catching up. This did not necessarily damage these leading countries—which were also the slower growing ones—and, indeed, as just noted, they may have benefited through improved terms of trade.

A simple example, using a two-country model, can make the point. Again, suppose China is growing at 8 per cent and the United States at 4 per cent. Suppose that the US terms of trade do not need to change to maintain international equilibrium. The share of trade in US GDP stays unchanged. Hence, US exports and imports to China grow at 4 per cent. The United States will then steadily lose market shares in China, since demands and supplies there are growing at 8 per cent. In that sense the United States has lost competitiveness, but the effect has not been adverse. The profitability of US industries has not declined. Indeed, it is quite likely that, for the reasons just given (i.e. an absence of biases in growth), the US terms of trade improve, so that a steady decline in market share would go with a terms-of-trade improvement, and thus a net gain. At the same time, of course, owing to the relative price change implicit in the terms-of-trade improvement, US import-competing industries would indeed have lost competitiveness.

If foreign growth did cause the US terms of trade to deteriorate, the effect would certainly be adverse for the United States as a whole, though not for each sector, since import-competing industries would tend to gain. There would still be gainers and losers. But the overall competitiveness of tradable industries would not need to decline, provided the exchange rate were adjusted appropriately and real wages were flexible. Nevertheless, one can give a particular interpretation to the competitiveness problem, which is different from the one I gave at the beginning of this chapter. It can be interpreted as referring to international competition which worsens the country's terms of trade.

I mentioned above that Japan might (in some people's view) be competitive rather than complementary with the United States, in which case Japanese growth might worsen, rather than improve, the US terms of trade. I want to come back to this idea, asking whether this possible biases effect could be interpreted as a competitiveness' problem for the United States even when the assumptions of a flexible exchange rate and flexible real wages are maintained.

For this purpose we need a three-country model, but it is sufficient to assume that each country produces just one product. The United States and Japan both produce only product A, and the Rest of the World (ROW) produces only product B. All three consume both A and B. Thus the United States and Japan are competitive, but are both complementary with ROW. The higher is Japanese productivity growth, the more the price of A will fall in the world market, and hence the greater the terms-of-trade deterioration for the United States. In that special sense, the United States has a competitiveness problem resulting from Japanese growth even though the sole export product of the United States continues to be profitable, and there is no reason for US output or employment to fall.

Faster ROW growth, of course, would improve the terms of trade of both the United States and Japan. In this model, the problem only arises if Japan grows faster than ROW. In that case there is a foreign growth bias against the United States of the kind discussed earlier. More important, faster US productivity growth would also lower the price of A and worsen the US terms of trade. Except in the extreme case of immiserizing growth, the United States still benefits from its own productivity growth irrespective of Japanese growth. I have presented this model as a stripped-down rigorous version of a popular argument, but it is unlikely to give a correct picture of what has happened. It is unlikely that total growth of Japan and other countries has, on balance, had the kind of bias that would have clearly worsened the US terms of trade. The adverse effect in the United States has, indeed, only been sectoral.

Once one goes beyond the simple model just presented, many other considerations can be added. Faster growth by a large manufacturing country is likely to increase the variety of products on offer in the world market, as well as their quality. It is exactly this benefit that Japan has offered to the rest of the world. This improvement in variety and quality could be described as a terms-of-trade gain to a country's foreign customers since the effective price of services provided by its exports will have declined even when the price of physically defined goods has not. In this sense Japan is certainly complementary with other countries, including the United States, and its growth has benefited them. Exactly the same remarks could be made about the international benefits that US growth has bestowed.

VI. PRODUCTIVITY GROWTH AND REAL-WAGE RIGIDITY

I now come to the interaction between real-wage rigidity and an economy-wide problem of low productivity growth. The concern is thus with Case III, where the productivity problem is not sectoral but economy wide, affecting both tradables and nontradables. The issue of the relationship between productivity growth and international competitiveness only becomes really interesting once real-wage rigidity, or at least some tendency to such rigidity, is introduced. The following argument is important for understanding the European unemployment problem, though it is not really relevant for the United States, where there appears to be little tendency to real-wage rigidity.

As discussed earlier in this book, with real-wage rigidity, nominal depreciation cannot bring about real depreciation. Hence the process described in Section IV above, where relatively low productivity growth can be offset by exchange rate depreciation, cannot operate. In fact, the central argument is quite elementary and applies as much in the closed as in the open economy. If the rate of growth of real wages (including taxes on employment) exceeds the rate of growth of labor productivity, profitability and employment will steadily fall. In a model with tradables and nontradables, employment will normally fall in both sectors, though not necessarily in the same proportion. If a decline in competitiveness means, as I have suggested, a decline in profitability and employment in tradables, then competitiveness has indeed declined. Yet a focus on international competitiveness avoids the central issue, since there has also been a decline in profitability and employment in non-tradables. If the economy were closed, so that all goods and services were non-tradables, the problem would still remain. The problem does not derive from the openness of the economy, and thus is not essentially a problem of international competitiveness. The problem is one of the interaction of the desired real wage (including services that are financed by taxes on labor and on employers) and productivity. In the open economy the problem just *manifests* itself partly as a decline in international competitiveness.

In 1991 the US President established a Competitiveness Policy Council which was meant to "develop and deliver a comprehensive competitiveness strategy for the United States". The Council devoted itself to proposing various ways in which US productivity could be improved, no doubt a valuable activity.

In its second annual report to the President and Congress, the Council provided a definition: "Competitiveness is defined as our ability to produce goods and services that meet the test of international markets while our citizens earn a standard of living that is both rising and sustainable in the long-run." This definition might be interpreted as saying that—*given* a desirable rate of growth of real wages or real incomes—competitiveness results from a rate of growth of productivity that is adequate to maintain full (or adequate) employment. Thus it did not assert that real wages were rigid downward in the United States, which would indeed be false. Rather, it set implicitly a target rate of growth of real wages and then interpreted the competitiveness problem to be a productivity problem—a problem of getting the rate of productivity to be sufficient to sustain the target rate of growth of real wages at full (or high) employment. But, as I have said, there could be a productivity problem even if international trade did not enter the story. The popular link between international competitiveness and adequate productivity growth is really rather misleading.

VII. DOES FOREIGN GROWTH INCREASE DOMESTIC UNEMPLOYMENT?

Finally, one might ask whether foreign growth is likely to reduce or to worsen the unemployment problem when there is real-wage rigidity. To be specific, is the European unemployment problem intensified by the growth of East Asia? This was certainly a topical question in 1993 when Europeans were searching for the causes of high unemployment. Here, there are two aspects.

First, one can ask how foreign growth affects the country's terms of trade. Various possibilities were discussed earlier. A terms-of-trade improvement can be described as representing an improvement in the productivity of international trade: for given resources used to produce exports, more imports can be obtained. A terms-of-trade improvement means that, relative to the price of domestic products, the price of imports declines, so that, for a given income real wage, the product real wage can fall, and so employment can increase. (This was analyzed in Chapter 11.) Furthermore, some of the gains from a terms-of-trade improvement will go to the government in increased revenue, so that taxes on employment (which have increased unemployment) can be reduced. It follows that the presumption (but not certainty) that a terms-of-trade improvement would result from foreign growth—as discussed earlier in this chapter—also suggests a presumption that with given real wages, foreign growth would actually *raise* employment and thus also competitiveness of tradables. Europe should thus welcome the growth of East Asia. Of course, if foreign growth worsened the terms of trade, it would have an adverse effect on employment and competitiveness.

The second aspect is currently much discussed. Foreign growth may increase unemployment of low-skilled workers. If foreign growth takes primarily the form of growth by developing countries that export low-skilled labor-intensive products, it will adversely affect those industries in developed countries that produce such products. If real wages of low-skilled workers are indeed rigid downwards, foreign growth will tend to increase unemployment of this kind of labor. The simple Stolper and Samuelson (1941) model of trade theory, when combined with the assumption of a rigid real wage, brings out this point. But here it has to be borne in mind that this model is really too simple, and a favorable terms-of-trade movement can have an offsetting effect. An improvement in the terms of trade makes the nation as a whole richer, which increases the demand for labor-intensive non-tradables. It also boosts the tax base, hence reducing the need for taxes on employers. Bearing in mind that labor is differentiated both regionally and by skills, so that there are many kinds of labor, it is likely that the net effect of foreign growth would be to increase employment of some kinds of labor and reduce that of others.

VIII. POLICY IMPLICATIONS: IS THERE A CASE FOR
INTERVENTION?

The main message of this chapter is that there are three very distinct competitiveness cases, and they have different policy implications.

In Case I, it is clear that, over a long period, some industries in the United States and in Europe have lost competitiveness, the principal reason having been the growth of Japan. The outstanding example is the automobile industry. Of course, if their own productivity growth had been higher, these adversely affected industries could have avoided the problem, but, realistically, there will always be sectoral competitiveness problems. Surely the continuous or even accelerating growth of developing countries that one hopes for, and that is in prospect because of highly desirable policy changes in China, India, and Latin America, will bring about more sectoral competitiveness problems in the United States and Europe. It is well to be prepared for these, and, above all, to realize that they will not represent a *national* loss of competitiveness, and that they may actually be associated with an improvement in the terms of trade for the developed countries.

The policy implication is to resist the usual pressures for sectoral protection, and to favor policies that raise national productivity (such as improvements in education and training), which will moderate adverse sectoral effects. Sectoral protection only benefits one industry at the expense of another, with a net national loss through forgoing the gains from trade. Assistance for adjustment, and the removal of policies and laws that inhibit the flexibility of the economy, will be justified.

Coming to Case II, a loss of national competitiveness, owing to a movement into current account deficit, is simply a by-product of a set of policies and private decisions that have produced the deficit. It must be analyzed as suggested in Chapter 6, and may justify some exchange rate protection that is directly motivated by a concern with the consequences, both short term and long term, of real appreciation. Above all, it requires an increase in national savings or a decline in investment. The analysis of this case applies directly to the situation of the United States in the early and mid-1980s. I noted the reshuffling effect of protection in

Chapter 14. Sectoral protection would simply reshuffle the effects of real appreciation between different tradables industries—with the usual national cost owing to gains from trade being lost—but it would not affect the decline of *national* competitiveness.

In Case III—conceivably the European problem—the policy implication is that the rigidity of real wages should be reduced and national productivity raised. In this case, sectoral policies to aid adjustment could help in reducing adverse employment effects. In the second-best situation of real-wage rigidity, sectoral interventionist policies focused on particularly adversely affected industries or particular kinds of labor could conceivably yield a net national gain, but there is also the danger that they simply discourage the longer-term adjustment of the economy—including adjustment of real wages. If the fundamental problem underlying the high unemployment rate is not sectoral, but is a general national discrepancy between the desired rate of growth of real wages and productivity growth, sectorally biased policies (including protection) have primarily again a reshuffling effect and impose an additional cost through distorting the pattern of output and employment.

Finally, it cannot be presumed that high growth abroad is harmful to an economy. This is the principal conclusion of this chapter. Foreign growth may present adjustment problems, and one can certainly produce models with growth biases and some arguments suggesting that such growth would worsen the terms of trade. I have presented a three-country model where Japanese growth adversely affects the US terms of trade, but this is really too simple. If anything, there is a presumption that the terms-of-trade effects of foreign growth would actually be favorable.

APPENDIX 15.1

Loss of Competitiveness in the Specific Factors Model

Fig. 15.1 illustrates the three competitiveness cases in terms of the specific factors model. We begin with Case I (sectoral competitiveness problem), and assume that there are two tradable industries, A and B, and (to begin with) no non-tradable industry. The vertical axes show the

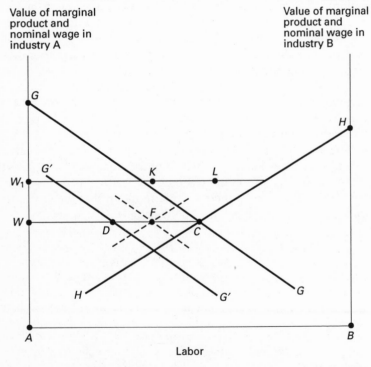

FIG. 15.1. Allocation of Labor between Two Industries and Possibility of Unemployment

values of marginal product of labor and the nominal wages in the two industries (curves *GG* and *HH*), and the horizontal axis the total stock of labor in the (small) country. The curves *GG* and *HH* show how the marginal products decline as employment increases.

GG and *HH* are drawn for given production functions and given domestic prices of *A* and *B*, the latter depending on their foreign prices and the exchange rate. Initial equilibrium showing the allocation of labor between *A* and *B* is at *C*, and the initial nominal wage (equal to the value of the marginal products) is *W*. Each industry has one or more factors of production specific to it (i.e. not movable in the short run into the other industry), while labor is mobile. The return to the specific factor (profitability) is the area under the marginal product curve minus the wages bill.

Assume the nominal wage stays constant. A fall in the world price of *A* shifts *GG* downwards to *G'G'*. This lowers profitability in *A* with given employment. Employment will fall until *D* is attained. Industry *A* has become less competitive. The world price of *B* could also change, possibly rising, so raising employment there. But assume that the world price of *B* remains unchanged, and hence employment in *B* stays at *C*. If the nominal wage does not fall, there must then be a depreciation, which raises the domestic prices of *A* and *B*, shifting both curves upwards. An appropriate depreciation will restore the initial level of total employment, bringing equilibrium to *F*. Hence, finally, employment and output in *B* is higher and in *A* is lower than before the decline in the world price of *A*.

For Case II (the real appreciation problem), we reinterpret *A* and *B* as representing tradables and non-tradables. With a given nominal wage, a rise in the price of *B* (non-tradables) associated with a decline in the price of *A* (tradables) leads to a movement from *C* to *F*. This is the equivalent of a movement along the transformation curve towards non-tradables in Fig. 2.1. Again, total employment is maintained, but owing to the real appreciation, industry *A* has lost competitiveness.

For Case III (real-wage rigidity problem), we again interpret *A* as representing tradables and *B* non-tradables. This is a more complicated case. Again we start at *C*, and suppose that the desired income real wage rises while the production functions stay unchanged. The real wage in terms of both products would rise, in which case output and employment of both would fall. Suppose that the nominal wage rises from *W* to W_1. Employment finally falls to *K* and *L* (these points being arbitrarily selected), yielding unemployment of *KL* caused by the higher real wage. In this case there must be some depreciation to raise the domestic price of *A* until *GG* passes through *K*, and some rise in the price of *N* until *HH* passes through *L*. Given the rise in the nominal wage, the solution might have required appreciation and/or a fall in the price of N, or indeed no change in the domestic prices of A and B. Improvements in productivity (upward shifts of GG and HH) could, of course, reduce or avoid the decline in employment in the two industries.

REFERENCES

On the specific factors trade theory model, see Neary (1978). The Harry Johnson model, showing how growth in two countries affects their terms of trade with various biases in production and consumption, is in Johnson (1958b, 1962).

At the time of writing, a substantial literature on competitiveness was developing. In the text I referred to the report of the Competitiveness Policy Council (1993). Sometimes the competitiveness problem in the United States is interpreted as referring only to the manufacturing sector, the implication being that deindustrialization caused by foreign competition is taking place. Lawrence (1984) already examined this carefully earlier and showed it was not so. More recently, Krugman and Lawrence (1993) have shown that while employment in US manufacturing declined over the past decade, the share of manufacturing in total output remained unchanged, owing to faster productivity growth compared with services.

Usually an improvement in competitiveness is interpreted to mean a depreciation in the real effective (i.e. trade weighted) exchange rate. A measure of the relative price of tradables to non-tradables is usually not available (one problem being that the two categories are difficult to separate empirically), but several competitiveness indices for industrial countries are regularly given in the International Monetary Fund's *International Financial Statistics*, including ones based on relative unit labor costs, on relative value-added deflators, on relative wholesale prices, and on relative consumer prices. The OECD also publishes indices of competitiveness, and the conceptual issues involving various measures are explained in Durand and Giorno (1987).

The Future

16

The Exchange Rate Regime: Choices and Plans

WHAT kinds of exchange rate regimes are feasible and what kind is desirable? In particular, bearing in mind the disadvantages of the current non-system, would it be desirable to move to some kind of fixed exchange rate regime? In this chapter I shall discuss these issues systematically, drawing on earlier chapters, and taking into account, above all, the implications of high and growing international capital mobility.

I. A CLASSIFICATION

I described the current non-system of managed floating in Chapters 10 and 12. In such a system countries have monetary independence, there is no commitment to particular exchange rates and, inevitably, exchange rates fluctuate, move about, or are misaligned for reasons that may be explained by fundamentals or that may appear irrational. Intermittent cooperation and coordination to a limited extent modify the anarchic or decentralized nature of the system.

The alternative is some kind of fixed rate regime applying to varying numbers of countries. Fixed rate regimes can be classified by two criteria, the combinations yielding four possible cases.

First, the regime may be either hegemonic or symmetric. In a hegemonic system, the hegemonic country pursues an independent monetary policy, with no exchange rate commitment, while the other countries pursue monetary and exchange rate intervention policies that bring about the exchange rate objective. Both Bretton Woods and the EMS turned out to be hegemonic systems, although this was not embodied in the formal arrangements. Drawing on these two experiences, it appears to be a natural tendency for a fixed exchange rate system to develop in this way. A symmetric system is one where the participants mutually agree on monetary policy, forming it cooperatively. There is no special privilege or obligation on any one country. If a European Monetary Union were ever established, it would be a symmetric system.

Second, the regime may be loose or solid. If it is loose, each country retains its control over monetary policy, and the possibility of exchange rate realignment remains, even though a fixed exchange rate commitment may be made either for a limited period or with no limit specified. Hence, this is a fixed-but-adjustable system. Adjustments may be frequent, as in the first act of the EMS, or infrequent, as in the Bretton Woods system and the second act of the EMS. Indeed, the proclaimed intention may be to make no adjustments at all. But as long as independent control over monetary policy is retained, it must be described as a loose system, since the potentiality of adjustment exists. The regime is solid if the fixed exchange rate is embodied in an institutional arrangement that is difficult to change and that represents a genuine or irrevocable long-term commitment. The EMU would be such a regime, fixing the bilateral exchange rates of the members irrevocably.

We have, then, four cases. By far the most common is the loose-and-hegemonic system, and I shall discuss this at length shortly. The loose-and-symmetric system has been proposed by McKinnon (1984) and was proposed in various plans for reform of the hegemonic Bretton Woods system. But it has never existed. I shall discuss (and dismiss) it briefly.

The solid-and-hegemonic system is one where the non-hegemon has an institutional arrangement, such as a currency board, and a legal or constitutional commitment to keep the value of its currency fixed to that of a hegemon. There are many historical examples, especially from the British colonies, and the recent examples that come fairly close can be found in the West African franc zone (as it was until 1994) and in Argentina. Such a system is very unlikely to be adopted by any major country unless it has had recent traumatic experience of very high inflation and thus is ready to give up any influence over its monetary policy at all. Finally, the solid-and-symmetric system is a monetary union, with a single central bank which has sole control over the monetary policy of the whole area, and is, in turn, owned and controlled (perhaps very indirectly) by its members.

For the time being I shall put aside the McKinnon (loose-and-symmetric) case and the currency board (solid-and-hegemonic) case, but I shall come back to them later when discussing various reform proposals in more detail. That leaves the fixed-but-adjustable (loose-and-hegemonic) system and monetary union (solid-and-symmetric) as the two alternatives to the present managed floating non-system. By 1983, monetary union had doubtful prospects in the European Union, and was unlikely to come about soon. Furthermore, it seems inconceivable for an area embracing all the G-7. But I shall also return to these visions below. Hence, the current choice is really between the present system and a loose-and-hegemonic (fixed-but-adjustable) system, and perhaps various hybrids of these two. The central question is to what extent a fixed-but-adjustable system is feasible in a world of high capital mobility.

II. CAPITAL MOBILITY AND FIXED-BUT-ADJUSTABLE EXCHANGE RATES

A country may fix the value of its currency to the dollar or the DM because it wants an anchor against inflation or just wants to stabilize the real exchange rate. But it still wants to allow for the possibility of shocks, and thus wants to be able to switch from the nominal anchor to the real targets approach. Hence, it chooses a loose rather than a solid regime. If international capital mobility were low, the exchange rate could be effectively fixed with sterilized intervention. Of course, there could still be problems. The exchange rate commitment may not be credible in the labor market, so that real wages rise and the real exchange rate appreciates. Discipline in monetary policy (probably responding to fiscal deficits) may not be attained, so that the foreign exchange reserves may run down.

High capital mobility makes the task of maintaining a fixed exchange rate with sterilized intervention much more difficult. As soon as expectations of devaluation develop, capital outflow will lead to a loss of reserves that will force a devaluation. All this is familiar, for example from the 1992 and 1993 crises of the EMS. The central bank will make large losses with its unsuccessful attempt to maintain the rate, selling dollars or DM when these are cheap in terms of its own currency, and buying them back when they are dear. As I have noted in Chapter 12, because of the size of international capital movements relative to the funds available to central banks, sterilized intervention may be unable to hold the rate even in the short run. Sometimes there is a short-run signaling effect, but this channel will not work (as it did not work in the case of Britain and Italy in September 1992) if the fundamentals seem to signal that a devaluation is inevitable.

The only method left to maintain a fixed-but-adjustable regime is then monetary policy. This could be conducted either through open market operations in domestic bonds, through variations in reserve requirements of commercial banks, or through non-sterilized intervention in the foreign exchange market—which affects the money supply and interest rates, and is thus a form of monetary policy. In principle there is always some monetary policy—some very high domestic interest rate—that can maintain a fixed exchange rate to which the country's monetary authorities have committed themselves.

It is through monetary policy that countries can manage, or at least greatly influence, exchange rates. The problem is that extremely high short-term interest rates may be required to support the exchange rate when expectations of a devaluation develop. These high interest rates may need to be sustained for a long time, until the determination of the authorities to support the exchange rate becomes evident and the credibility of the existing exchange rate thus becomes established. There must be no doubt about the fundamentals, including the political commitment to the required tight monetary policy.

The more the market expects a looser monetary policy in the future, and hence a devaluation, the tighter monetary policy must be to hold the rate. This is the paradox of expectations which I illustrated in Appendix 7.1. Once credibility is established, monetary policy will no longer need to be so tight. The problem is that a very high interest rate sustained for any significant length of time will conflict with domestic objectives, having adverse effects on banks, on private borrowers, and on aggregate demand. It will also increase fiscal deficits owing to the higher cost of refinancing debt. It is this conflict with domestic objectives that limits the use of monetary policy for maintaining a firm exchange rate commitment when there is a credibility problem.

It must be added that, even when there is no short-term credibility problem and hence no foreign exchange crisis, a potential conflict between the exchange rate and the internal objective may exist. Monetary policy can be targeted on maintaining a fixed nominal exchange rate or it can be targeted on an internal balance objective. If the fixed exchange rate is a nominal anchor that would yield low inflation, and low inflation were the only internal balance objective, there would be no conflict. The conflict arises when internal balance involves a trade-off between an inflation and a short-term employment objective.

The maintenance of a fixed-but-adjustable exchange rate regime by means of sterilized intervention supported strongly by monetary policy is not impossible when credibility exists. Such credibility would be based on a long period during which monetary policy was directed to maintaining the exchange rate target. The narrow margins regime of the Dutch guilder relative to the DM was maintained throughout the EMS crises even though capital mobility was certainly high, because complete credibility existed. In 1993 the French authorities believed that a firm monetary policy could establish the necessary credibility. Some developing countries have maintained fixed-but-adjustable regimes based on limited capital mobility and considerable credibility. Low capital mobility usually resulted from effective exchange controls.

Nevertheless, with increasing international capital mobility affecting more and more countries, and the degree of mobility between the major world currencies steadily increasing, the sustainability of fixed-but-adjustable regimes, or of hybrids that contain elements of such regimes, is doubtful. It is this thought that dominates the discussion below of various reform plans.

III. SHOULD CAPITAL MOVEMENTS BE RESTRICTED?

If capital movements were severely and effectively restricted, it would certainly be possible to have a fixed-but-adjustable exchange rate regime, as was prevalent during the Bretton Woods period. Extreme movements of real exchange rates brought about by speculative bubbles would be avoided. The exchange rate could provide a nominal anchor, provided the appropriate monetary discipline and credibility in the labor market were attained. At the same time the exchange rate could be altered in response to shocks: policy could switch from nominal anchor to real target, as desired.

It all sounds too good to be true. The system would work best if the parity adjustments were not delayed, but were made, if necessary, frequently, as in the EMS during its early (Act I) stage. When adjustments are delayed, real exchange rate movements become jerky: periods of rigid nominal exchange rates and gradual real appreciation (owing to high inflation relative to trading partners) are interspersed with large nominal and real devaluations. This was the story of many developing countries up to the early 1980s.

Here I must give a warning against conventional wisdom. Speculative capital movements in a fixed-but-adjustable regime can be *apparently* destabilizing but *actually* stabilizing. They appear destabilizing because they force a devaluation at a time when the authorities would otherwise have continued to maintain the existing rate, either with the help of trade restrictions or by running down foreign exchange reserves and use of official foreign credits. But speculation is actually stabilizing because it brings about earlier a devaluation that was, in any case, inevitable, and would eventually have been larger. The discipline of capital mobility will ensure that real exchange rates depreciate (or appreciate) more gradually, instead of following the jerky path normal in a fixed-but-adjustable regime where exchange rate adjustment is usually postponed as long as possible. This view assumes that the markets have a correct view of the fundamentals. They do not force a devaluation that, in the absence of speculation, would have been unnecessary.

The issue can be put in another way. If the central bank is trying to sustain a rate that is fundamentally unsustainable and the markets see this, then central bank intervention is destabilizing and speculation in the markets is stabilizing. The effects of capital movements may be undesirable from the short-term perspective of the official sector (and hence are conventionally thought of as destabilizing) but are basically favorable. On the other hand, if the central bank is trying to maintain a rate that is really a fundamental equilibrium rate, and that could be sustained in the absence of speculation, while speculators in the markets still attack it, then central bank intervention is stabilizing and the markets are destabilizing.

The same issue arises when the concern is not to make possible a fixed-but-adjustable regime but rather to reduce volatility of exchange rates in a floating rate regime. In an oft-cited article, Tobin (1982) proposed a small tax on all transactions that involve converting one currency into another. This would be a significant discouragement to short-term capital movements and would be designed to reduce short-term volatility in exchange markets. The assumption is that such capital movements are destabilizing. But they are at least as likely to be stabilizing—and more likely to be profitable when they are. Volatility of exchange rates could well be increased when not only bubble speculation but also market-making is discouraged.

Even if restrictions on international capital movements could be enforced, and even if, on balance, the result would allow fixed-but-adjustable exchange rate regimes to be sustained longer, and this were desirable, there are some strong arguments on the other side. The essential point is that there are gains from international trade in assets—notably in portfolio diversification—and from trade in assets for goods and services as reflected in current account imbalances.

It is widely accepted that long-term capital movements are likely to be beneficial, while short-term capital movements are said to create unnecessary volatility of exchange rates. But, if short-term capital movements were restricted, long-term movements would also be reduced. For example, a pension fund is less likely to diversify its portfolio internationally if it will be difficult to move out of a foreign asset quickly when a new risk of some kind is perceived. More generally, capital that cannot readily leave a country is less likely to want to settle there in the first place.

One can think of many occasions when a country or a government borrowed unwisely, and restrictions on capital outflow from lending countries might, in retrospect, have been beneficial. Surely this was true of much borrowing by those developing countries in the period 1975–82 that subsequently faced debt crises. But others, at that time or other times, borrowed wisely. Furthermore, the surplus funds of oil exporters that were recycled to developing countries in the 1970s through the intermediation of a small number of international banks had to be lent somewhere, and general restrictions on international lending would not necessarily have led to better results. Would Texans have made better use of extra funds than Koreans? At this point one should recall the argument advanced in Chapter 10: the presumption is that freedom of international capital flows and the associated current account imbalances yield the familiar gains from trade, even though particular borrowing and lending decisions may in retrospect (and sometimes also on the basis of information available at the time) have been unwise.

The advantage of a free international capital market is not only that it allows current account imbalances to be financed through the market, and not just through changes in official foreign exchange reserves or official loans, but also that it allows individual savers and institutions to hold internationally diversified portfolios and thus makes them less vulnerable to domestic shocks. Net international capital flows may be very small for a country, and yet these portfolio effects, reflected in gross flows, can be large. In addition, there are benefits from increased international specialization of financial services and from increased competition for domestic financial sectors. These are all versions of the standard gains from trade, applied in this case to trade in assets and financial services. All these benefits have become very evident in recent years.

Even if restrictions on international capital flows were desirable, they would be difficult and costly to enforce. Partially effective enforcement can make a difference, as the interest differentials between controlled (domestic) and uncontrolled (offshore) markets showed in the case of the French franc and the Italian lira before the removal of controls in 1990. But controls are getting more and more difficult to enforce owing to improvements in communications, the computer revolution, the continuing importance of multinationals, and the liberalization and increased competitiveness of domestic financial markets.

The scope for avoidance and evasion is vast. The more integrated are countries through trade in goods and services (including tourism), through foreign direct investment, and through flows of remittances from migrant workers, the more can controls be avoided or evaded. The scope is particularly great when cross-border inter-company transactions of multinationals are involved. It should be recalled that until 1979 Britain had well enforced exchange controls on explicit capital movements, and yet it suffered regular sterling crises resulting from indirect capital movements by means of so-called leads and lags. When a sterling devaluation was expected, foreign suppliers of imports into Britain would be paid their dollars in advance or quickly (leads), while foreign buyers of British exports would delay their payments (lags), hence delaying the conversion of dollars into sterling. Through this mechanism an expectation of sterling devaluation could quickly deplete Britain's foreign exchange reserves.

A common way of evading capital controls is through the under- and over-invoicing of trade contracts. For example, an exporter who wishes to shift funds abroad will under-invoice the foreign supplier, and then invest the surplus funds abroad. Trade financing also provides scope for hidden capital exports. The general point is that it is difficult to enforce exchange controls on capital account transactions when the controls do not also apply to current account transactions. But the latter controls interfere with trade. It was the introduction of convertibility for current account transactions and for trade-related capital flows in the late 1950s and the 1960s by most developed countries that provided many opportunities for evasion of controls on capital account transactions.

Controls that are truly effective could be reimposed. But enforcement in many countries would have to be severe, would be costly to administer, would create scope for rent-seeking and corruption, and would have adverse effects on trade, as well as depriving countries of the various gains described above from opening to the international capital market.

IV. A SKEPTICAL REVIEW OF VARIOUS PLANS

I shall now briefly review various proposals—most of which I have already discussed earlier in this book—which involve some degree of fixing of exchange rates, or at least the use of intervention and monetary policies to influence exchange rates according to predetermined criteria.

(1) *Monetary Union: Solid and Symmetrical*

If any group of independent nations will ever form a monetary union, it will certainly be the members of the European Union, or, more likely, a core group within it consisting of Germany, France, Belgium, the Netherlands, and Austria. I have already discussed the EMU proposal at great length, and the trade-offs involved. Hence, no more need be said. Coming to an even more ambitious proposal, Cooper (1984) has suggested a monetary union with a single currency for a larger group, namely the industrialized democracies, that is, the G-7 and some others. The issues here are the same as in the case of EMU, but surely the likelihood or desirability of this coming about is much less, to put it mildly.

Cooper proposed that a single central bank, modeled on the Federal Reserve System, be established. Perhaps, if EMU actually eventuated and turned out to be a success, a radical extension of it to embrace the United States, Japan, and Canada might enter the discussion. Cooper himself, being a realist, did not expect such a grand monetary union to come about soon. But the world has changed drastically in the past, and in many unexpected ways, so perhaps one should not be so skeptical!

(2) *McKinnon's Proposal: Loose and Symmetrical*

McKinnon (1984) proposed something approximating a fixed exchange rate arrangement that included only the United States, Germany, and Japan (the G-3). But each country would maintain its own central bank and monetary policy, and some element of flexibility would be left. The three monetary policies would be so managed as to maintain (more or less) fixed exchange rates between them, and also a rate of growth of the aggregate money stock designed to stabilize an index of traded goods prices. This would truly be a symmetrical arrangement. The two aims of exchange rate stability and low inflation would thus be attained.

This proposal is much less radical than Cooper's and appears to go just a step or two beyond the kind of coordination that has at times been pursued or attempted. Hence, the McKinnon scheme could be approached gradually, which seems to make it more feasible. But there are three powerful objections.

First, monetary policy would be allocated wholly to the fixed exchange rate and low-inflation objectives. It would not be available for short-term demand management (other than for the G-3 region as a whole), nor for altering nominal exchange rates so as to change real rates in response to shocks. In other words, there would be a permanent commitment to the nominal anchor approach with no possibility of a switch to the real targets approach. This objection is the same as that to a monetary union, an objection that is surely more serious in the case of an arrangement embracing the G-3 than one embracing the more integrated and politically closer European Union countries.

Second, agreement would have to be reached on a common rate of growth of the money stock designed to stabilize an agreed price index. This requires a degree of coordination that would go far beyond anything that has been attained so far, and that is at present conceivable.

Third—and surely this objection is overwhelming—since this would be a loose arrangement with national control over monetary policies remaining, it would be a system without full commitments, and thus subject to speculative crises. Recessions, fiscal policy shocks, differential terms-of-trade effects, ideological shifts in the political arena (as the United States incurred when the Reagan administration took over), can all create incentives for governments to break from or cheat on the system, and market expectations which anticipate such motives would break the system just as the EMS was damaged or broken in 1992 and 1993.

(3) *Target Zones: Very Loose, Symmetrical, and Hybrid*

I discussed the elaborate Williamson and Miller (1987) target zone scheme in Chapter 13. A somewhat similar proposal has also been made by Kenen (1988). It must first be noted that the proposal is really a hybrid with a strong floating exchange rate component. The reason is that there would be very wide target zones (they suggest 10 per cent) around the agreed central rates so that it would be closer to the current (early 1994) ERM situation with its 15-per-cent margins. The exchange rates would be maintained within the margins by a combination of intervention and monetary policy. Other than in extreme cases, the rates would just float. The other main feature is that the central rates would be adjusted in line with inflation, the aim being to maintain real exchange rates rather than nominal rates.

The scheme is thus quite similar to the way the ERM worked during its first act (from 1979 to 1987), except that the margins would be much wider than they were in the ERM then. Calculations of fundamental equilibrium real exchange rates would be made to determine central rates on a long-term basis. Thus the central real rates would not be permanently fixed.

This scheme is a product of ideas that developed during the big up-and-down of the dollar from 1983 to 1987, and was designed to avoid such extreme movements in real exchange rates which the authors clearly thought either irrational or undesirable. It is also the product of euphoria from 1985 to 1987 about the willingness of the G-7 to engage in ambitious coordination arrangements.

The scheme reflects neither a nominal anchor nor a real targets approach to exchange rate policy. It is not a real targets approach, even at the margins of the zones, because it does not allow real exchange rates to change outside the zones even when real factors, such as external shocks or divergent fiscal policies, require such changes (unless the fundamental rates have been altered appropriately). Within the zones monetary policy could be directed at a domestic internal balance target, but at the limits it would be committed solely to the fixed real exchange rate objective.

At the limits, but only at or near the limits, the same coordination and speculation problems would arise as I have already discussed in connection with the McKinnon proposal. Could G-3 finance ministers and central bankers agree on fundamental equilibrium real exchange rates any more than they could agree on a desirable target for the world money stock? With regard to speculation, a commitment not to allow real exchange rates to move beyond some rather extreme values is a very moderate commitment, and thus might carry credibility and so avoid speculative pressures. Thus the Williamson–Miller target zone proposal is, because of its softness, not as unrealistic as the others I have discussed.

(4) *The Maastricht Program: Loose and Hegemonic*

For completeness only, I recall here the program laid out in the Maastricht Treaty for gradual movement towards EMU, and the discussion of the transition process in Chapter 9. The program involved a stage when exchange rates would be essentially fixed, but still adjustable. Monetary policies would still be nationally determined. Thus, exchange rates would be subject to speculative pressures since commitments would not yet be solid. Act 2 of the EMS had been thought of as the first stage of this program, anticipating the formal requirements of the Treaty before it was generally ratified. The crises of 1992 and 1993 bear out the objections to a transition which requires countries to maintain essentially fixed rates to the DM for a period when there may well be incentives to engage in a final devaluation. All the objections discussed above to a loose regime apply to the Maastricht transition program.

(5) *A Currency Board: Solid and Hegemonic*

If an economy is very small, a nominal devaluation may not succeed in bringing about real devaluation. Exchange rate adjustment would not achieve any real target. In that case the country is not an optimum currency area, and it should fix its exchange rate to a stable currency. This currency would provide the nominal anchor. One can then go on to argue that—if the exchange rate is to be fixed—it should be fixed credibly, to avoid the nominal anchor problems I discussed in Chapter 5. Various institutional arrangements to give credibility both in the labor market and the foreign exchange market can then be envisaged, some arrangements providing more assurance that the rate is permanently fixed than others.

The domestic money supply will have to adjust automatically to changes in the monetary authority's foreign exchange reserves. The most automatic system giving the maximum degree of credibility is a currency board system of the kind that has operated quite effectively in the past in British colonies and elsewhere. The board would have a monopoly on creating domestic money, but this would have to be backed 100 per cent by foreign exchange or gold to give full credibility. The board would not be permitted to create credit. Hence, the authority could not be a lender of last resort for the government, nor for the commercial banks or any kind of public or private agency. The fixed exchange rate commitment would be embodied in the constitution of the authority or of the country. A current account deficit that was not financed by capital inflow would lead to a decline in foreign exchange reserves and thus automatically to a decline in the money supply.

This kind of system could be appropriate not only for very small economies, but also for a few larger economies that have a history of high inflation and where the independence of a central bank from political pressure to finance budget deficits cannot be assured. It has been suggested by Hanke *et al.* (1993) for Russia. In these cases the need for a fully credible nominal anchor may outweigh the occasional need for the exchange rate to fulfil a real-targets role. The more flexible downwards are nominal wages, the less is the need to retain a real-targets role for the exchange rate—this being the same point that I made when discussing the argument for a monetary union. But for the larger economies, the absence of such flexibility is a powerful argument against a currency board system.

The monetary arrangements of both the CFA (franc) zone of Africa and that of Argentina (the latter instituted in 1991) come close to this kind of currency board scheme. But in both cases the possibility of a change in the exchange rate is not fully ruled out, so that credibility is not complete, as manifested in interest rate differentials. In the case of Argentina, the convertibility law fixes the exchange rate, but the rate can be altered by the legislature.

Until the early 1980s, most developing countries had fixed-but-adjustable exchange rate regimes, some (like Thailand) having hardly any adjustments, others (like Argentina) very many, and two (Brazil and Colombia) having crawling pegs, that is, rates that were almost continuously adjusted to compensate for the high inflation of these countries. During the 1980s most developing countries moved either to managed floating regimes or to regimes where the exchange rate was indeed pegged (either to the dollar or to a currency basket) but was very frequently adjusted, so that they could be described as flexible peg regimes. It is likely that managed floating—with varying degrees of intervention and attempts to maintain stability of exchange rates—will become the norm.

But there could be exceptions. For very small economies, and possibly also for larger countries that have a recurrence of high inflation, a currency board system, or something like it, may well be best. The alternative is to make the central bank independent (as was legislated since 1990 in Argentina, Chile, Colombia, and Mexico). This should provide some assurance of the central bank's ability to resist political pressures to inflate, while still allowing exchange rate adjustment in response to real shocks. Naturally, such a regime will not give the same credibility to a fixed rate commitment as a currency board system would, because the possibility of exchange rate adjustment would not be ruled out. The primary aim would be to avoid inflationary financing of budget deficits.

V. THE WAY AHEAD: MANAGED FLOATING IS HERE TO STAY

A simple conclusion follows. Leaving aside a few remaining countries that are able and choose to impose and enforce effective exchange controls, loose fixed-rate regimes, or hybrids incorporating a loose fixed rate commitment, are not feasible any more. The choice is between the regime that now prevails for almost all the developed and many developing countries, namely managed floating, and a solid regime in the form of monetary union or a currency board. Countries that choose a solid regime are forgoing permanently the use of the exchange rate instrument as indicated in the real targets approach. They must either hand over control over monetary policy to a hegemonic country (the currency board case) or establish a monetary union with a common central bank. Leaving aside those countries (if any) that choose a currency board, and those that eventually join EMU—if it ever comes to pass—it seems that managed floating is here to stay.

Exchange rate management will be through a combination of sterilized intervention and monetary policy, with the latter playing the main role. Inevitably, in its monetary policy management, each country faces a trade-off between internal objectives and an exchange rate objective.

I shall conclude on an optimistic note. Managed floating is not incompatible with considerable exchange rate stability. If the principal internal objective of the monetary authorities of a country is to maintain low inflation, if the aim is also to maintain the exchange rate stable relative to the currency of a hegemonic country which also has low inflation, and if shocks that require the real exchange rate to change are rare, then there will be little conflict between the internal and the exchange rate objective. If this happy situation prevails for some time, the market is likely to recognize it. In that case, it will be possible to maintain something close to a fixed rate regime, with the adjustment option still open. A (more or less) fixed rate objective will be credible, though commitment would be too strong a word for this objective. There will be no need for big interest rate changes designed to preserve a stable exchange rate. A managed floating regime could then lead to some degree of exchange rate stability.

Of course, there can be shocks and expectations of shocks. Exchange rate adjustment then has a role. There can be recessions that are likely to lead to different monetary policy responses in various countries. In these cases, it is necessary either for the exchange rate to be allowed to float down or up, or for realignments to be quick and preferably small, as they were in the early EMS. Furthermore, there is some scope for coordination of policies among the major countries. But I shall not repeat the content of Chapter 13. Such coordination is likely to be *ad hoc* and apply to monetary rather than fiscal policy, with coordination of sterilized intervention becoming less important.

REFERENCES

Eichengreen (1994) thoroughly reviews historical and recent experience and, looking to the twenty-first century, concludes that "countries that have traditionally pegged their exchange rate will be forced to choose between independent floating on the one hand and monetary unification on the other. . . . [Increasing capital mobility] will undermine the viability of intermediate exchange rate arrangements in which governments commit to preventing exchange rate movements from exceeding explicit limits." This is also the conclusion of this chapter.

Reform proposals mentioned in the text are by Tobin (1982), McKinnon (1984), Cooper (1984), Williamson and Miller (1987), and Kenen (1988). Hanke *et al.* (1993) deal with all aspects of currency boards.

De Grauwe (1989) reviews reform proposals and also the costs of exchange rate instability, concluding that these have been considerable. Other discussions of reform proposals are in Frenkel (1987) and in contributions by various authors (especially Shinkai, Swoboda, and Cooper) in Suzuki *et al.* (1990).

On capital mobility and exchange controls, see Mathieson and Rojas-Suarez (1993), Group of Ten (1993), and Goldstein and Mussa (1994).

BIBLIOGRAPHY

AGHEVLI, B. B. *et al.* (1990) *The Role of National Saving in the World Economy: Recent Trends and Prospects*, Occasional Paper 67, Washington, DC: International Monetary Fund.

—— (1991) *Exchange Rate Policy in Developing Countries: Some Analytical Issues*, Occasional Paper 78, Washington, DC: International Monetary Fund.

ALLEN, P. R., and KENEN, P. B. (1980) *Asset Markets, Exchange Rates, and Economic Integration: A Synthesis*, Cambridge: Cambridge University Press.

ARGY, V. (1994) *International Macroeconomics: Theory and Policy*, London: Routledge.

—— and SALOP, J. (1979) 'Price and Output Effects of Monetary and Fiscal Policy under Flexible Exchange Rates', *IMF Staff Papers*, 26, 2: 224–56.

ARTUS, J. R. (1984) 'Effects of United States Monetary Restraint on the DM/$ Exchange Rate and the German Economy', in J. F. O. Bilson and R. C. Marston (eds.), *Exchange Rate Theory and Practice*, Chicago: University of Chicago Press.

ASCHHEIM, J., TAVLAS, G. S., and ULAN, M. (1993) 'The Relationship between Exchange-Rate Variability and Protection', in D. Salvatore (ed.), *Protectionism and World Welfare*, Cambridge: Cambridge University Press.

BARRO, R. (1974) 'Are Government Bonds Net Wealth?', *Journal of Political Economy*, 82: 1095–118.

—— (1989) 'The Ricardian Approach to Budget Deficits', *Journal of Economic Perspectives*, 3: 37–54.

—— and GORDON, D. (1983*a*) 'Rules, Discretion and Reputation in a Model of Monetary Policy', *Journal of Monetary Economics*, 12: 101–21.

—— and —— (1983*b*) 'A Positive Theory of Monetary Policy in a Natural Rate Model', *Journal of Political Economy*, 91: 589–610.

BAYOUMI, T., and EICHENGREEN, B. (1993) 'Shocking Aspects of European Monetary Unification', in F. Giavazzi and F. Torres (eds.), *The Transition to Economic and Monetary Union in Europe*, Cambridge: Cambridge University Press.

BERGSTEN, C. F., and WILLIAMSON, J. (1983) 'Exchange Rates and Trade Policy', in W. R. Cline (ed.), *Trade Policy in the 1980s*, Washington, DC: Institute for International Economics.

BERNHEIM, B. D. (1987) 'Ricardian Equivalence: An Evaluation of Theory and Evidence', in S. Fischer (ed.), *NBER Macroeconomics Annual 1987*, New York: National Bureau of Economic Research.

BLACK, S. W. (1985) 'International Money and Monetary Arrangements', in R. W. Jones and P. B. Kenen (eds.), *Handbook of International Economics*, *ii*, Amsterdam: North-Holland.

—— (1990) 'The International Use of Currencies', in Y. Suzuki, J. Miyake, and M. Okabe (eds.), *The Evolution of the International Monetary System*, Tokyo: University of Tokyo Press.

BRANSON, W. H. (1979) 'Exchange Rate Dynamics and Monetary Policy', in A. Lindbeck (ed.), *Inflation and Employment in Open Economies*, Amsterdam: North-Holland.

—— (1984) 'Exchange Rate Policy after a Decade of "Floating"', in J. F. O. Bilson and R. C. Marston (eds.), *Exchange Rate Theory and Practice*, Chicago: University of Chicago Press.

—— and BUITER, W. H. (1983) 'Monetary and Fiscal Policy with Flexible Exchange Rates', in J. S. Bhandari and B. H. Putnam (eds.), *Economic Interdependence and Flexible Exchange Rates*, Cambridge, Mass.: MIT Press.

BRUCE, N., and PURVIS, D. D. (1985) 'The Specification of Goods and Factor Markets in Open Economy Macroeconomics Models', in R. W. Jones and P. B. Kenen (eds.), *Handbook of International Economics*, *ii*, Amsterdam: North-Holland.

BRUNO, M. (1991) *High Inflation and the Nominal Anchors of an Open Economy*, Essays in International Finance No. 183, Princeton, NJ: International Finance Section, Princeton University.

BRYANT, R. C. (1994) 'Coordination of National Macroeconomic Policies in an Integrated World Economy' (Project on Integration in the World Economy), Washington, DC: The Brookings Institution.

—— et al. (eds.) (1988) *Empirical Macroeconomics for Interdependent Economies*, Washington, DC: The Brookings Institution.

BUITER, W. H., and MARSTON, R. C. (eds.) (1985) *International Economic Policy Coordination*, Cambridge: Cambridge University Press.

CALVO, G. A., LEIDERMAN, L., and REINHART, C. M. (1993) 'Capital Inflows and Real Exchange Rate Appreciation in Latin America', *IMF Staff Papers*, 40: 108–51.

CANZONERI, M. B., and HENDERSON, D. W. (1991) *Monetary Policy in Interdependent Economies: A Game-Theoretic Approach*, Cambridge, Mass.: MIT Press.

CATTE, P., GALLI, G., and REBECCINI, S. (1992) 'Exchange Rates Can Be Managed', *International Economic Insights*, 3: 17–21.

Commission of the European Communities (1990) 'One Market, One

Money', *European Economy*, No. 44, Brussels: Commission of the European Communities.

Competitiveness Policy Council (1993), *A Competitiveness Strategy for America. Second Report to the President and Congress*, Washington, DC: US Government Printing Office.

COOPER, R. N. (1984) 'A Monetary System for the Future', *Foreign Affairs*, Fall, reprinted in R. N. Cooper (1987) *The International Monetary System*, Cambridge, Mass.: MIT Press.

—— (1985) 'Economic Interdependence and Coordination of Economic Policies', in R. W. Jones and P. B. Kenen (eds.), *Handbook of International Economics*, *ii*, Amsterdam: North-Holland.

CORDEN, W. M. (1971) *The Theory of Protection*, Oxford: Clarendon Press.

—— (1972) *Monetary Integration*, Essays in International Finance No. 93, Princeton, NJ: International Finance Section, Princeton University. Reprinted in *International Trade Theory and Policy: Selected Essays of W. Max Corden* (1992) Aldershot: Edward Elgar Publishing Limited.

—— (1977) *Inflation, Exchange Rates and the World Economy*, Oxford: Clarendon Press, and Chicago: University of Chicago Press.

—— (1981) 'Exchange Rate Protection', in R. N. Cooper *et al.* (eds.), *The International Monetary System under Flexible Exchange Rates: Global, Regional and National. Essays in Honor of Robert Triffin*, Cambridge, Mass.: Ballinger Publishing Company. Reprinted in *International Trade Theory and Policy: Selected Essays of W. Max Corden*.

—— (1983) 'The Logic of the International Monetary Non-System', in F. Machlup *et al.* (eds.), *Reflections on a Troubled World Economy: Essays in Honor of Herbert Giersch*, London: Macmillan.

—— (1984) 'The Normative Theory of International Trade', in R. W. Jones and P. B. Kenen (eds.), *Handbook of International Economics*, *i*, Amsterdam: North-Holland.

—— (1985) 'Macroeconomic Policy Interaction under Flexible Exchange Rates: A Two-Country Model', *Economica*, 52: 9–23.

—— (1986) 'Fiscal Policies, Current Accounts and Real Exchange Rates: In Search of a Logic of International Policy Coordination' (Bernhard Harms Lecture), *Weltwirtschaftliches Archiv*, 122: 3–18.

—— (1991*a*) 'Does the Current Account Matter? The Old View and the New', in J. A. Frenkel and M. Goldstein (eds.), *International Financial Policy. Essays in Honor of Jacques J. Polak*, Washington, DC: International Monetary Fund.

—— (1991*b*) 'Exchange Rate Policy in Developing Countries', in J. de Melo and A. Sapir (eds.), *Trade Theory and Economic Reform: North, South and East: Essays in Honor of Bela Balassa*, Oxford: Basil Blackwell.

—— (1993) 'Absorption, the Budget, and Debt: The Wonderland of Possibilities', in H. Herberg and N. V. Long (eds.), *Trade, Welfare, and Economic Policies: Essays in Honor of Murray C. Kemp*, Ann Arbor, Mich.: University of Michigan Press.

—— and TURNOVSKY, S. J. (1983) 'Negative Transmission of Economic Expansion', *European Economic Review*, 20: 289–310.

CURRIE, D., and LEVINE, P. (1991) 'The International Co-ordination of Macroeconomic Policy', in D. Greenaway, M. Bleaney, and I. Stewart (eds.), *Companion to Contemporary Economic Thought*, London: Routledge.

DE GRAUWE, P. (1989) *International Money: Post-war Trends and Theories*, Oxford: Oxford University Press.

—— (1992) *The Economics of Monetary Integration*, Oxford: Oxford University Press.

Delors Report (1989) *Report on Economic and Monetary Union in the European Community*, Brussels: Commission of the European Communities.

DOBSON, W. (1991) *Economic Policy Coordination: Requiem or Prologue?*, Policy Analyses in International Economics 30, Washington, DC: Institute for International Economics.

DOMINGUEZ, K. M., and FRANKEL, J. A. (1993) *Does Foreign Exchange Intervention Work?*, Washington, DC: Institute for International Economics.

DORNBUSCH, R. (1974) 'Tariffs and Non-Traded Goods', *Journal of International Economics*, 4: 177–85.

—— (1975) 'Alternative Price Stabilization Rules and the Effects of Exchange Rate Changes', *Manchester School*, 43: 275–97.

—— (1976) 'Expectations and Exchange Rate Dynamics', *Journal of Political Economy*, 84: 1161–76.

—— (1983) 'Flexible Exchange Rates and Interdependence', *IMF Staff Papers*, 30: 3–38.

—— and DE PABLO, J. C. (1990) 'Debt and Macroeconomic Instability in Argentina', in J. D. Sachs (ed.), *Developing Country Debt and Economic Performance*, *ii*, Chicago: University of Chicago Press.

DURAND, M., and GIORNO, C. (1987) 'Indicators of International Competitiveness: Conceptual Aspects and Evaluation', *OECD Economic Studies*, 9: 147–82.

EDISON, H. J. (1993) *The Effectiveness of Central-Bank Intervention: A Survey of the Literature after 1982*, Special Papers in International Economics No. 18, Princeton, NJ: International Finance Section, Princeton University.

EDWARDS, S. (1989*a*) *Real Exchange Rates, Devaluation, and Adjustment: Exchange Rate Policy in Developing Countries*, Cambridge, Mass.: MIT Press.

EDWARDS, S. (1989*b*) 'Economic Liberalization and the Equilibrium Real Exchange Rate in Developing Countries', in G. Calvo *et al.* (eds.), *Debt, Stabilization and Development: Essays in Memory of Carlos Diaz-Alejandro*, Oxford: Basil Blackwell.

—— and EDWARDS, A. C. (1991) *Monetarism and Liberalization: The Chilean Experiment*, 2nd edn., Cambridge, Mass.: Ballinger.

EICHENGREEN, B. (1992*a*) *Should the Maastricht Treaty Be Saved?*, Princeton Studies in International Finance No. 74, Princeton, NJ: International Finance Section, Princeton University.

—— (1992*b*) 'Is Europe an Optimum Currency Area?', in S. Borner and H. Grubel (eds.), *The European Community after 1992: The View from Outside*, London: Macmillan.

—— (1994) *International Monetary Arrangements for the 21st Century*, Washington, DC: The Brookings Institution.

FELDSTEIN, M. (1988) 'Distinguished Lecture on Economics in Government: Thinking about International Economic Coordination', *The Journal of Economic Perspectives*, 2: 3–13.

—— and HORIOKA, C. (1980) 'Domestic Saving and International Capital Flows', *Economic Journal*, 90: 314–29.

FLEMING, J. M. (1962) 'Domestic Financial Policies under Fixed and under Flexible Exchange Rates', *IMF Staff Papers*, 9/3: 369–80.

FRANKEL, J. A. (1993) *On Exchange Rates*, Cambridge, Mass.: MIT Press.

—— and FROOT, K. (1986) 'Understanding the US Dollar in the Eighties: The Expectations of Chartists and Fundamentalists', *Economic Record, Supplement*, 62: 24–8. Reprinted in J. A. Frankel (1993). *On Exchange Rates*, Cambridge, Mass.: MIT Press.

—— and —— (1987) 'Using Survey Data to Test Standard Propositions regarding Exchange Rate Expectations', *American Economic Review*, 77: 133–53.

—— and —— (1990) 'Chartists, Fundamentalists, and Trading in the Foreign Exchange Market', *American Economic Review*, 80: 181–5. Reprinted in J. A. Frankel (1993). *On Exchange Rates*, Cambridge, Mass.: MIT Press.

—— and MEESE, R. (1987) 'Are Exchange Rates Excessively Variable?', in S. Fischer (ed.), *NBER Macroeconomics Annual 1987*, Cambridge, Mass.: MIT Press.

FRENKEL, J. A. (1987) 'The International Monetary System: Should It Be Reformed?', *American Economic Review: Papers and Proceedings*, 77: 205–10.

—— GOLDSTEIN, M., and MASSON, P. R. (1990) 'The Rationale for, and Effects of, International Economic Policy Coordination', in W. H. Branson, J. A. Frenkel, and M. Goldstein (eds.), *International Policy*

Coordination and Exchange Rate Fluctuations, Chicago: University of Chicago Press.

—— and JOHNSON, H. G. (eds.) (1976) *The Monetary Approach to the Balance of Payments*, London: Allen & Unwin.

—— and MUSSA, M. L. (1985) 'Asset Markets, Exchange Rates, and the Balance of Payments', in R. W. Jones and P. B. Kenen (eds.), *Handbook of International Economics*, *ii*, Amsterdam: North-Holland.

—— and RAZIN, A. (1987) *Fiscal Policies and the World Economy*, Cambridge, Mass.: MIT Press.

GIAVAZZI, F. (1990) 'The EMS Experience', in Y. Suzuki, J. Miyake, and M. Okabe (eds.), *The Evolution of the International Monetary System*, Tokyo: University of Tokyo Press.

—— and GIOVANNINI, A. (1989) *Limited Exchange Rate Flexibility*: *The European Monetary System*, Cambridge, Mass.: MIT Press.

—— and —— (1990) 'Can the European Monetary System Be Copied outside Europe? Lessons from Ten Years of Monetary Policy Coordination in Europe', in W. H. Branson, J. A. Frenkel, and M. Goldstein (eds.), *International Policy Coordination and Exchange Rate Fluctuations*, Chicago: University of Chicago Press.

—— and PAGANO, M. (1988) 'The Advantage of Tying One's Hands: EMS Discipline and Central Bank Credibility', *European Economic Review*, 32: 1055–82.

GOLDSTEIN, M., FOLKERTS-LANDAU, D., GARBER, P., ROJAS-SUAREZ, L., and SPENCER, M. (1993) *International Capital Markets. Part I: Exchange Rate Management and Capital Flows*, Washington, DC: International Monetary Fund.

—— and MUSSA, M. (1994) 'The Integration of World Capital Markets', in *Changing Capital Markets—Implications for Monetary Policy*, Kansas City, Kan.: Federal Reserve Bank of Kansas.

GRAMLICH, E. M. (1989) 'Budget Deficits and National Saving: Are Politicians Exogenous?', *Journal of Economic Perspectives*, 3: 23–35.

GROS, D., and THYGESEN, N. (1992) *European Monetary Integration*: *From the European Monetary System to European Monetary Union*, London: Longmans.

Group of Ten (1993) *International Capital Movements and Foreign Exchange Markets* (A Report to the Ministers and Governors by the Group of Deputies), Rome: Banca d'Italia.

HAMADA, K. (1976) 'A Strategic Analysis of Monetary Interdependence', *Journal of Political Economy*, 84: 677–700.

—— and SAKURAI, M. (1978) 'International Transmission of Stagflation under Fixed and Flexible Exchange Rates', *Journal of Political Economy*, 89: 877–95.

HANKE, S. H., JONUNG, L., and SCHULER, K. (1993) *Russian Currency and Finance: A Currency Board Approach to Reform*, London: Routledge.

HAYASHI, F. (1986) 'Why Is Japan's Saving Rate so Apparently High?', in S. Fischer (ed.), *NBER Macroeconomics Annual 1986*, Cambridge, Mass.: MIT Press.

HORNE, J., and MASSON, P. R. (1988) 'Scope and Limits of International Economic Cooperation and Policy Coordination', *IMF Staff Papers*, 35: 259–96.

INGRAM, J. C. (1973) *The Case for European Monetary Integration*, Essays in International Finance No. 98, Princeton, NJ: International Finance Section, Princeton University.

International Monetary Fund (1987a) *Final Report of the Working Party on the Statistical Discrepancy in World Current Account Balances*, Washington, DC: IMF.

—— (1987b) *World Economic Outlook, April 1987*, Washington, DC: IMF.

—— (1992) *World Economic Outlook, May 1992*, Washington, DC: IMF.

—— (1993) *World Economic Outlook, October 1993*, Washington, DC: IMF.

ISHIYAMA, Y. (1975) 'The Theory of Optimum Currency Areas: A Survey', *IMF Staff Papers*, 22: 344–83.

JOHNSON, H. G. (1958a) 'Towards a General Theory of the Balance of Payments', in H. G. Johnson, *International Trade and Economic Growth: Studies in Pure Theory*, London: Allen & Unwin.

—— (1958b) 'Economic Expansion and International Trade', in H. G. Johnson, *International Trade and Economic Growth: Studies in Pure Theory*, London: Allen & Unwin.

—— (1962) *Money, Trade and Economic Growth*, London: Allen & Unwin.

JONES, R. W., and CORDEN, W. M. (1976) 'Devaluation, Non-Flexible Prices, and the Trade Balance for a Small Country', *Canadian Journal of Economics*, 9: 150–61.

KENEN, P. B. (1969) 'The Theory of Optimum Currency Areas: An Eclectic View', in R. Mundell and A. Swoboda (eds.), *Monetary Problems of the International Economy*, Chicago: University of Chicago Press.

—— (1983) *The Role of the Dollar as International Currency*, Occasional Paper 13, New York: Group of Thirty.

—— (1988) *Managing Exchange Rates*, London: Routledge.

—— (1989) *Exchange Rates and Policy Coordination*, Ann Arbor, Mich.: University of Michigan Press.

—— (1992) *EMU after Maastricht*, Washington, DC: Group of Thirty.

KREININ, M. E., and OFFICER, L. H. (1978) *The Monetary Approach to the Balance of Payments: A Survey*, Studies in International Finance No. 43, Princeton, NJ: International Finance Section, Princeton University.

KRUEGER, A. (1978) *Foreign Trade Regimes and Economic Development: Liberalization Attempts and Consequences*, Cambridge, Mass.: Ballinger.

KRUGMAN, P. R., and LAWRENCE, R. Z. (1993) 'Trade, Jobs and Wages', *Working Paper*, No. 478, Cambridge, Mass.: National Bureau of Economic Research.

—— and OBSTFELD, M. (1991) *International Economics: Theory and Policy*, 2nd edn., New York: HarperCollins.

—— and TAYLOR, L. (1978) 'Contractionary Effects of Devaluation', *Journal of International Economics*, 8: 445–56.

LARSEN, F., LLEWELLYN, J., and POTTER, S. (1983) 'International Economic Linkages', *OECD Economic Studies*, 1: 43–91.

LAWRENCE, R. Z. (1984) *Can America Compete?*, Washington, DC: The Brookings Institution.

LAWSON, N. (1992) *The View from No. 11: Memoirs of a Tory Radical*, London: Bantam.

LEVICH, R. M. (1985) 'Empirical Studies of Exchange Rates: Price Behavior, Rate Determination and Market Efficiency', in R. W. Jones and P. B. Kenen (eds.), *Handbook of International Economics*, ii, Amsterdam: North-Holland.

LITTLE, I. M. D., COOPER, R. N., CORDEN, W. M., and RAJAPATIRANA, S. (1993) *Boom, Crisis and Adjustment: The Macroeconomic Experience of Developing Countries*, New York: Oxford University Press, for the World Bank.

LIZONDO, J. S., and MONTIEL, P. (1989) 'Contractionary Devaluation in Developing Countries: An Analytical Overview', *IMF Staff Papers*, 36: 182–227.

MACDONALD, R. (1988) *Floating Exchange Rates: Theories and Evidence*, London: Unwin Hyman.

MCKINNON, R. I. (1963) 'Optimum Currency Areas', *American Economic Review*, 53: 717–25.

—— (1982) 'Currency Substitution and Instability in the World Dollar Standard', *American Economic Review*, 72: 320–33.

—— (1984) *An International Standard for Monetary Stabilization*, Policy Analyses in International Economics 8, Washington, DC: Institute for International Economics.

—— (1993) 'International Money in Historical Perspective', *Journal of Economic Literature*, 31: 1–44.

MARSTON, R. C. (1985) 'Stabilization Policies in Open Economies', in R. W. Jones and P. B. Kenen (eds.), *Handbook of International Economics*, ii, Amsterdam: North-Holland.

MATHIESON, D. J., and ROJAS-SUAREZ, L. (1993) *Liberalization of the Capital Account: Experiences and Issues*, Occasional Paper 103, Washington, DC: International Monetary Fund.

MEADE, J. E. (1951) *The Balance of Payments*, London: Oxford University Press.

MICHAELY, M., *et al.* (1991) *Liberalizing Foreign Trade 7: Lessons of Experience in the Developing World*, Oxford: Basil Blackwell.

MUNDELL, R. A. (1961) 'A Theory of Optimum Currency Areas', *American Economic Review*, 51: 657–65.

—— (1963) 'Capital Mobility and Stabilization Policy under Fixed and Flexible Exchange Rates', *Canadian Journal of Economics and Political Science*, 29: 475–85.

—— (1964) 'A Reply: Capital Mobility and Size', *Canadian Journal of Economics and Political Science*, 30: 421–31.

MUSSA, M. (1979) 'Macroeconomic Interdependence and the Exchange Rate Regime', in R. Dornbusch and J. A. Frenkel (eds.), *International Economic Policy: Theory and Evidence*, Baltimore: Johns Hopkins University Press.

—— (1984) 'The Theory of Exchange Rate Determina T. F. O. Bilson and R. C. Marston (eds.), *Exchange Rate Theory and Practice*, Chicago: University of Chicago Press.

NEARY, J. P. (1978) 'Short-Run Capital Specificity and the Pure Theory of International Trade', *Economic Journal*, 88: 488–510.

OBSTFELD, M. (1994) 'International Capital Mobility', in P. B. Kenen (ed.), *Understanding Interdependence: The Macroeconomics of the Open Economy*, Princeton, NJ: Princeton University Press.

PITCHFORD, J. D. (1989) 'Optimum Borrowing and the Current Account When There Are Fluctuations in Income', *Journal of International Economics*, 26: 345–58.

—— (1990) *Australia's Foreign Debt: Myths and Realities*, Sydney: Allen & Unwin.

POLAK, J. J. (1957) 'Monetary Analysis of Income Formation and Payments Problems', *IMF Staff Papers*, 6: 1–50.

ROGOFF, K. (1985) 'Can International Monetary Cooperation Be Counterproductive?', *Journal of International Economics*, 18: 199–217.

SALOP, J., and SPITTALLER, E. (1980) 'Why Does the Current Account Matter',? *IMF Staff Papers*, 27: 101–34.

SALTER, W. E. G. (1959) 'Internal and External Balance: The Role of Price and Expenditure Effects', *Economic Record*, 35: 226–38.

STOCKMAN, A. C. (1988) 'On the Roles of International Financial Markets and Their Relevance for Economic Policy', *Journal of Money, Credit and Banking* 20: 531–49.

STOLPER, W., and SAMUELSON, P. A. (1941) 'Protection and Real Wages', *Review of Economic Studies*, 9: 58–73.

SUZUKI, Y., MIYAKE, J., and OKABE, M. (eds.) (1990) *The Evolution of the International Monetary System*, Tokyo: University of Tokyo Press.

TAVLAS, G. S. (1991) *On the International Use of Currencies: The Case of the Deutsche Mark*, Essays in International Finance No. 181, Princeton, NJ: International Finance Section, Princeton University.

TAYLOR, M. P. (1994) 'Exchange-Rate Behavior under Alternative Exchange-Rate Arrangements', in P. B. Kenen (ed.), *Understanding Interdependence: The Macroeconomics of the Open Economy*, Princeton, NJ: Princeton University Press.

TOBIN, J. (1982) 'A Proposal for International Monetary Reform', in J. Tobin, *Essays in Economics*, Cambridge, Mass.: MIT Press.

TOWER, E., and WILLETT, T. (1976) *The Theory of Optimum Currency Areas and Exchange Rate Flexibility*, Special Papers in International Economics No. 11, Princeton, NJ: International Finance Section, Princeton University.

WERNER, P., *et al.* (1970) *Report to the Council and the Commission on the Realization by Stages of Economic and Monetary Union in the European Communities* (Werner Report), Brussels: Commission of the European Communities.

WILLIAMSON, J. (1983) 'The Exchange Rate System', *Policy Analyses in International Economics* 5, Washington, DC: Institute for International Economics.

—— and MILLER, M. H. (1987) 'Targets and Indicators: A Blueprint for the International Coordination of Economic Policy', *Policy Analyses in International Economics*, 22, Washington, DC: Institute for International Economics.

INDEX OF NAMES

INDEX OF SUBJECTS